Mo & Ann:

Happy Cooking!

Christine Liu

營養食譜　黃雪燦著

About the Author

Christine Liu was born in Shanghai and raised in Mainland China where she studied and learned Chinese culture and experienced traditional Chinese cuisine. She studied biology in college and received her first university degree from the National Taiwan University.

After a short stay in Minnesota Christine and her husband Stephen, together with their first son, Ted, moved to Sao Paulo, Brazil where they resided for several years. The Chinese community in that city was sizeable and known for its affluence and Chinese cuisine. This afforded a great opportunity for Christine to learn the different styles and methods of diversified Chinese cooking. Accordingly, she acquired a great deal of skill and expertise. This extensive exposure and experience kindled her latent talent and interest in culinary arts which ultimately led her to pursue graduate studies, writing, and a teaching career.

The Lius returned to the United States in 1965 and settled in Ann Arbor, Michigan. Christine undertook her graduate work in nutrition at the School of Public Health and received the M.P.H. degree in nutrition from the University of Michigan in 1971. She later did further graduate work at the Massachusetts Institute of Technology.

For more than 20 years, Christine Liu has taught subjects such a "Creative Chinese Cooking," "Nutrition and Diet with Chinese Foods," and has coordinated classes in "International Gourmet Cooking" at the Continuing Education Department of the Ann Arbor Public Schools. She has also taught and lectured on "Traveling and Eating in China" through the University Extension of the University of Michigan.

Her first book, **Nutrition and Diet with Chinese Cooking**, which was launched in 1976, has been very popular and is in its seventh printing. Her third book, **Nutritional Cooking with Tofu**, is unique and has been well received by the public. Christine has been invited and has appeared on numerous occasions on TV programs and has given many lectures and demonstrations concerning the method of preparation and the nutritional qualities of Chinese cooking. From time to time, she has been invited to participate in college symposia and educational conferences around the country. Christine is also food-fair advisor for, and board member of, the Chinese American Educational and Cultural Center of Michigan; Consultant for the Chinese American Restaurant Council of Michigan; and nutritional consultant for local restaurants. Christine is currently active in developing nutritious vegetarian dishes for student dormitories at the

University of Michigan. Her expertise and enthusiasm have invariably won her admiration and endorsement from the public. For many years she has enjoyed the reputation for popularizing nutrition and diet through Chinese cooking.

Since normalization of diplomatic relations between the United States and China, Christine has returned to her homeland almost every year. She taught at universities and spoke to various groups about American food and culture. While in China, Christine traveled extensively in the northern, northwestern, northeastern, southern, southwestern, and eastern parts of the country and gained first-hand experience concerning many varieties of Chinese cuisine. Consequently, she was able to bring back a great deal of new knowledge about regional Chinese cooking to share with her American readers in this beloved and chosen country of hers. She is the only one who has written Chinese recipes in English for the *China Daily*, China's only English language newspaper.

The author at the Great Wall in China. Built in the 5th century BC, the Great Wall is 6,350 kilometers from east to west. It is one of the man-made objects astronauts can see from space.

Other books by Christine Liu:

Nutrition and Diet with Chinese Cooking
Nutritional Cooking with Tofu

To my friends, students, and family:
Stephen, Ted, Paul, Becky, Peter,
Christopher, Talitha, and Anna

Calligraphy by Jiang Min Quan

Book design by Jacqueline Sharp
Paper-cut illustrations by Hu Zen Rong

Library of Congress Number: 81-90263
Printed in the United States of America
ISBN: 0-9610566-5-7
Third Edition

More Nutritional

CHINESE COOKING

with Christine Y.C. Liu, M.P.H.

Graphique Publishing
Ann Arbor, Michigan

Acknowledgment

With pleasure I wish to thank the students (participants in classes taught in Ann Arbor) and friends who used my first book. Their suggestions and feedback have enabled me to share more effectively my knowledge of the art of Chinese cuisine. My thanks to colleagues and friends, who in one way or another, expressed their endorsement of my efforts and encouraged me to write this second volume. Their friendship and confidence are a source of sustenance.

My special appreciation goes to Jacqueline (Jaye) Sharp who is responsible for the book design and descriptive illustrations. No word could adequately convey my sincere appreciation and gratitude. To both Mrs. Anna Chapekis and Mrs. Patti Stock, I acknowledge their generous assistance in editing. I greatly appreciate the professional courtesy and assistance of Professor Ninfa Springer and her colleagues at the School of Public Health of the University of Michigan, who made their computer facilities available for my use. With this modern equipment, I was able to be more accurate in the calculation of the nutritional value of each of the recipes.

My special thanks also to Mr. Hu Zen Rong of Shanghai Arts and Crafts Bureau for all the beautiful paper cuttings which he did especially for me. They add a unique beauty and dimension to this book.

To Jiang Min Quan (Mrs. Sha Ju Ren) for her exquisite Chinese calligraphy—my appreciation and thanks.

Last but not least, I want to thank my dear husband, Stephen, and our lovely children. As always and without asking, they gave me unconditional support and affection whenever needed.

Forward

If you are interested in learning how to cook authentic Chinese dishes that are not only delicious but also easy to prepare, are inexpensive and highly nutritious, then this is probably the best cookbook you could own. That's a pretty big statement. Please allow us to prove ourselves.

As physicians, we had long been aware of the nutritional soundness of Chinese cooking. We truly loved its taste. But like many other American couples, our exposure to Chinese cooking was limited to dining in a few of the better Chinese restaurants during our travels. To us good Chinese cooking was something you could only experience in fancy restaurants blessed with a master chef skilled in the mysterious ways of an ancient art. Whatever else it was, *real* Chinese cooking was something we were convinced we could never do.

This attitude began to change when one of us developed a high blood cholesterol problem. We knew the time had come to make a major change in our family diet. After considerable research we decided that a major part of our diet would have to come from Chinese-style food preparation. This led us to Christine Liu's first cookbook. As luck would have it, we later had the opportunity to enroll in Mrs. Liu's cooking class. What we learned and now experience for ourselves, contributed so much to our pleasure and well-being that we welcomed this opportunity to share why we find her newest cookbook so rewarding. We think you will feel the same way.

To begin with, if there is another Chinese cookbook that provides a computer-based analysis of the nutritional content of every dish, we don't know about it. Mrs. Liu's book provides the exact information necessary to make nutritionally intelligent meal planning a snap. In our calorie conscious nation, the awareness of the importance of various dietary fats is growing. Statistics prove that this awareness has made us a healthier nation. Mrs. Liu's section "Facts about Fats" will prove to be valuable reading for health conscious Americans.

You will find that most of the recipes in Mrs. Liu's book are tailor-made for low-fat, low-cholesterol diets. At the same time, you don't give up great taste for healthful eating. In this book you can learn why modern science says most of Chinese cooking is nutritionally sound. You will also learn time-honored traditional techniques which maximize your nutritional benefit. The dishes in this book range from quick preparation meals to banquets and they can all be prepared by the average person. We know this from personal experience.

If you were like us before discovering the joys of Mrs. Liu's book, you have serious misgivings about Chinese food. You may feel that Chinese cooking means hours or even days of hard work and the special skills of an artisan. Well, some Chinese dishes do require all that but they're not in this book. Christine Liu made a choice. She decided to write a cookbook for the average American cook while accounting for the special needs of time economy and the limitations of food, spices, and equipment. The results of her work are delightful!

From her long experience of teaching Chinese cooking, Christine knew of the common misgivings and problems of people encountering Chinese cooking for the first time. That's why her "How to" section will help to get you started. You will learn what to do, why it's done, and the principles behind the technique. This not only helps you to remember, it actually encourages you to be more adventuresome.

Through her book Christine Liu takes advantage of all the technology in the average American kitchen. If you have the Chinese utensils, all the better. Whatever the case may be, Mrs. Liu has found a workable integration of Chinese cooking to the American kitchen. There's even a section on Chinese dishes which can be prepared in a microwave oven. You will find that good nutrition is not sacrificed, nor the character of Chinese cuisine. It takes a special talent to walk that fine line.

Of course the ultimate criterion of a good cookbook is the taste of the dishes. Well, the following short story is quite telling. Recently Mrs. Liu received a special invitation to travel to her native land and experience the results of recent developments in Chinese cuisine. While in Peking a group of journalists from the *China Daily* gave her the supreme test. After her culinary tour of the country, she was granted special permission to enter the kitchen of the journalist's favorite restaurants. There the master chefs permitted her to observe their cooking methods for certain dishes. While she watched, Mrs. Liu translated their lightning quick pinches, handfuls, and scoops, into American teaspoons, cups, and quarts. She then followed her recipes and cooked the dishes herself. The journalists then tasted, compared, and voted. They selected Mrs. Liu as weekly columnist on cooking and nutrition for *China Daily*, China's first English-language newspaper. All the new recipes from her recent tour are included in this book.

When you taste her fabulous recipe for Peking Duck, remember the *China Daily* story and enjoy.

Oh, and one other thing. That high blood cholesterol problem—it's now normal. Thank you, Christine.

Paul Y Ertel, MD and Inta J. Ertel, MD
University of Michigan, Ann Arbor

Merry Christmas 1996!
from Inta & Paul

Preface

This is not just another Chinese cookbook. It is a book designed to explain the merit of good nutrition in relation to Chinese food with a concern for convenience for Americans. Ninety percent of the ingredients used in the recipes can be easily obtained in any regular supermarket.

The book is a result of years of study and research in the nutrition field and of teaching and lecturing on the subject of Chinese cooking. The recipes are a new collection resulting from my two recent trips to China.

Despite many claims that *all* Chinese food contributes to good health and is low in calories, it is not. Deep-fried, thick batter-covered foods, so often associated with Chinese food, are *not* considered nutritionally sound. The popular use of lard and other animal fats, so often found in Chinese cooking is not good nutritional practice; it has been completely eliminated in this book. The recipes found here are suitable for heart patients (low cholesterol), as well as diabetics (carbohydrate contents calculated) and others on special diets. In addition, the dishes described are tasty, authentic, economical, and simple to prepare. To my knowledge, there is no other Chinese cookbook on the market that provides the complete nutritional information as this one does.

Because cooking good food and teaching nutrition are my professional work, I welcome your comments and suggestions concerning the material in this book.

May you enjoy good food and good health.

Christine Liu
Ann Arbor, Michigan

List of Photographs

Contents

Introduction

There can be little doubt that Chinese cuisine is unique among the world's great culinary arts. Not only are Chinese food and cooking favorite subjects of discussion and writing in many culinary circles, but one can even find Chinese restaurants in some of the most remote corners of the globe.

What makes Chinese food so universally popular? Chinese food is delicious and satisfying and endlessly varied. The combination of ingredients and presentation of dishes is so intricate, that cooking and eating Chinese food can never be monotonous. Chinese people have an incredible talent for combining ingredients in just the proper proportions, tastefully seasoned, so as to maximize the unique flavor of each ingredient and thus enhance the taste of the total dish.

The food in China, like all national cooking, reflects her long history, economic development, geographic environment, prosperity of the society, refinement of culture, and creativity of the Chinese people. In times past, the availability of food rather than its taste was the principle factor in creating a menu. Chinese people had to learn to cook with food stuffs that were available or could be produced in their surroundings. Geography shaped the four regional styles of Chinese cooking: Eastern, Western, Northern, and Southern. With the exception of the northern region, the staple food of China is rice. In northern China, wheat, millet, and corn are the daily staples.

Eastern cooking is famous for slow-cooked meat and poultry dishes with plenty of soy sauce, the so called "red-cooked" dishes. It is also well known for seafood dishes since the entire area lies on the Pacific seacoast. The seafood is prepared in a variety of ways depending upon the seasonal availability of fish or other sea products. This style of cooking is prevalent in Shanghai, Hongchow, Youngchow, and their vicinities.

Western cooking is hot, spicy, and oily because the warm and humid climate in that region permits spices of all kinds to grow profusely. Hot chili and Sichuan peppercorns are the most popular spices and are used in many dishes. Hot chili as well as flavored and preserved bean sauces of various kinds are served with meals as side dishes or dips. They are also cooked with foods as seasonings. Using these basic ingredients is a smart way of increasing the nutritional value of a meal because of the rich vitamin A content of the chili and high-quality protein of the beans. This style of cooking is prevalant in the Sichuan and Hunan provices and the neighboring regions.

Northern cooking is found in the provinces of Honan, Hopei, and Shantung. The taste of food in this area tends to be bland and light. Influenced by the nomads of the north, people used more preserved food and mutton. Garlic and onions (or scallions) are favorite seasonings while the staple foods are steamed breads and buns, unleavened cakes (*Bing*), and noodles made of wheat and millet flours. Noodles are collectively known as *Mian*. Dumplings made of flour dough stuffed with various kinds of minced meat and vegetables are northern Chinese favorites. These dumplings can be cooked in different ways and served as a complete meal. Peking (Beijing), the capitol city, where the Imperial Court was located for centuries, contributed many delicious dishes to northern fare, the more famous being Peking duck.

Southern cooking is well known for its stir-fried dishes with many varieties of fresh vegetables and fruits. Because of the sub-tropical climate and abundant rainfall, fresh produce and fruits of all kinds grow abundantly in the south where Canton province and its surrounding areas are located. The Cantonese Chinese are creative and adventurous, constantly inventing epicurean delights. Roasted milk-pig is one of the many famous dishes of the south. Snake and monkey's brain are among the foods included in Cantonese menus.

There are always some people who cannot tolerate foods of the other regions, however, most Chinese people are open-minded and adventure-some. They are generally willing to experiment with new dishes and new ingredients. Extreme prejudice against foods of other regions is certainly not a serious problem in China. In fact, most of the famous local dishes become nationally popular dishes. For example, Peking duck from the north and Lion's head from the east are served in every part of China.

In this book you will find dishes of the four regions. Some of them were newly collected from my two recent trips in China. For the con-venience of cooking and easy achievement of each dish I tried to use the ingredients and method of cooking which are most suitable to the American taste and kitchen, but without sacrificing the authentic flavor.

Since the turn of the century, China has undergone great changes, most dramatically since World War II. Today many people live in cities and they are increasingly mobile as jobs move them from one place to another to live, often in urban communities. Naturally, people exchange their cooking talents and share the distinctive recipes for dishes of their province or hometown with one another. Consequently, most famous regional dishes have become nationally popular dishes. Since special ingredients are canned or dried, they can be transported easily everywhere; thus, the cooking of regional foods can be done in any place and at any time. People of the younger generation in China have the opportunity to taste and learn about all the good dishes, although they seldom are aware of the origins of those dishes.

Although the flavor and seasoning spices are different from one region to another, the principle of cooking is much the same throughout China. Many dishes are cooked with meat and vegetables together; as a result, the food contains fewer calories and is not so rich as some American foods. Vegetables stay bright and crisp since they are cooked for only a short time over high heat, either in their own juice or in a small amount of water. This method of cooking retains most of the vitamins and minerals. It also saves fuel. The energy crisis is not new to China. The conservation of fuel continues to be important and necessary. Stir-fried dishes which take only ten minutes to cook on one burner save fuel. And as if the fuel savings were not enough, food cooked in this manner is more nutritious, an added blessing to us even though the ancient Chinese were not aware of this value of their cooking method.

Today, we in the United States are very conscious of our nutrition and diet. We want to be sure that eating is not only for enjoyment, but also for good health. We strive to find a way of eating that satisfies our appetite, nourishes our bodies, maintains good health, yet does not cause weight gain. Some of us have come to realize that most Chinese dishes meet these prerequisites. A word of professional advice here is that we cannot indulge ourselves in Chinese food without any restrictions. There are many delicious, well-known Chinese dishes that are high in calories and cholesterol and are nutritionally unbalanced.

In order to provide my readers with the opportunity to choose the right dishes for balanced meals, I have undertaken the task of compiling and evaluating nutritional information for every recipe in this book. With this information, you will find the quantities of eleven important nutrients, as well as fiber, in most of the dishes. You will know what you are serving in nutritional as well as culinary terms. On special or rare occasions you may wish to indulge yourself with some very rich dishes. But don't forget to select some nutritious, low calorie dishes to serve on the days following your splurge in order to balance your calorie intake. The chapter "Nutrition and Suggested Menus" will help you to plan your overall diet.

All the recipes in this book have been tested repeatedly not only to my satisfaction but also to that of my many students. The recipes are easy to follow, nutritious, economical, and authentic. The ingredients can be found in most American supermarkets.

Good food does something more than fill our stomachs. Good food makes us feel like whole persons. It can bring to life our keen enjoyment of the present and the future. It can change our attitudes toward our daily work. Its preparation can be seen as an act of love, self-fulfillment, and creativity. Enjoying good food with loved ones gives us a sense of communion. But above all, let us not neglect the spiritual aspect of life. For the Bible says, "Man shall not live by bread alone, but by every word that proceeds from the mouth of God." (*Matt.* 4:4). While we enjoy good food, let us remind ourselves that out of His bountifulness and His presence we derive every bit of our enjoyment.

I hope that you will enjoy visiting the historical sites of China through the photographs, enjoy a sampling of China's culinary art through the recipes and most importantly, enjoy good health.

Customs, Rice, Chopsticks, Tea and Dinner

CUSTOMS

China is an ancient nation with 5000 years of rich cultural development. The art of Chinese cooking reflects that rich heritage. Among the ancient civilized people of the world, the Chinese have shown the greatest creativity in the preparation of food. Few other cultures are as food-oriented as the Chinese.

In China, eating has always been a very serious business. The joy of eating good food was recorded in earliest history and was appreciated by all levels of society. Confucius stated, "Appetite for good food is one of the basic natures of the human being." For the Chinese, a delicious and fulfilling meal creates happiness, harmony, and mental and physical well being. It is important to remember that when you cook Chinese food, you are recreating the millennial experience of experimentation, taste, culture, and art.

Meal times are important events in the day of a Chinese family. They are a time of relaxed family reunion when each person has the oppurtunity to report his or her activities, exchange views, express love, and show concern for the others. The Chinese people eat three meals a day, with the evening meal the most substantial and elaborate one. In between meals, snacks (*Dim Sum*) are served on certain occasions.

Most Chinese are very hospitable. They love to entertain guests and share good food with their friends. In fact, food and friendships are inseparable in China. Opportunities to dine together are used for a variety of social functions, for example, transacting business, making new friends, showing one's appreciation, settling disputes, and so on. Any gathering that does not include food of one kind or another is considered incomplete and improper.

RICE

Rice is the staple food of most Chinese except for that of the northern region. In speaking of rice in China, one fundamental clarification must be made. Rice before being cooked (or raw rice) is called *Mi*. Rice cooked to a fluffy consistency, the form with which all Americans are familiar is called *Fan*.

The term *Fan* in China has even a broader meaning. The Chinese call all the cooked grains (rice, wheat, millet, sorgum, or corn) used as staple food, *Fan*. The Fan made from cooked, polished white rice is called *Bai Mi Fan*, 白米飯 . The *Fan* made from steamed wheat flour is called *Man Tou Fan*, 饅頭飯; the *Fan* made from sorgum is called *Kaolian Fan*, 高粱飯; the *Fan* made from corn is called *Yu Mi Fan*, 玉米飯 and so on.

The cooked grain, *Fan*, is served in a separate bowl at dinner, then eaten with the delicious dishes made from vegetables and meats. The Chinese call these vegetable and meat dishes *Cai*. Cai dishes are placed in the center of the table for all the diners to share. The dinner tables are usually square or round and seat 8-12 people.

In the ordinary family meal, *Fan* is considered the primary food and the *Cai* dishes are secondary. In the past, the forefathers of China believed that *Fan* was the most important substance, the sustainer of life. All the delicious *Cai* dishes were invented to help the people eat more *Fan*. This order is generally reversed between the well-to-do and poor and on special occasions, such as the New Year celebration as opposed to the everyday meal. For the well-to-do and for all on special occasions, most attention is devoted to the quality and quantity of the *Cai* dishes and not to that of *Fan*, even though the cooking style is the same.

The staple food, *Fan*, plays such an important role in Chinese life, that the word *Fan* is used in many everyday idioms. For example; "No *Fan* bowl," in Chinese, translates as "No job." "Only for a bowl of *Fan*" means "only to earn a living." "Eat *Fan*" means "Time to eat!" or "Meal time!" "We would like invite you to eat *Fan* with us" means "We would like to invite you to have a meal with us." People even use the term *Fan* as a greeting word. For instance, "Have you had your *Fan*?" means "How are you?"

CHOPSTICKS

Food is served with chopsticks and spoons. Fingers are not considered proper in picking up foods. The Chinese consider using fingers as bad manners and barbarous. Chopsticks are made of bamboo, wood, plastic, ivory, silver or gold; they are usually square at the top and tappered slightly at the end for picking up food, and are often used as an all-purpose cooking utensil in the Chinese kitchen. They can be used to stir, turn, beat, sort, or pick up food from deep-frying oil or boiling water. To be able to use a pair of chopsticks is a part of Chinese life. Children learn to use them by watching and practicing. Americans can learn the same way. Although we might feel it is difficult to use chopsticks at first, with a little practice we can manage very well.

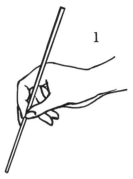

To use chopsticks:

(1) Hold one of the chopsticks like a pencil, between the tips of the thumb, index and middle fingers.

(2) Rest the upper part of the other stick at the base of your thumb and index fingers. The lower part of this stick rests on the tips of the ring and small fingers.

(3) Move the stick that is being held like a pencil in an up-and-down motion to meet the tip of the other stick. Food will be picked up and held between the tips of the two chopsticks.

Experiment and have fun.

TEA

Tea plays an important role in Chinese society. No one who visits China can avoid drinking at least a little tea. It is the people's favorite drink and the beverage of the nation. It is a long-standing custom and courtesy to offer a cup of tea to visitors or guests as soon as they arrive in the house, regardless of what time of the day it is. People can relax with a cup of tea or use it as a thirst quencher. Hot tea is served at most of the meals or at the end of meals. It is always available in the home, in business offices, at ceremonial occasions, and at social gatherings. It is somewhat like coffee in the United States.

Tea houses exist in every city, town, and village in China. Most parks supply tea, which is served in pavilions so people can relax with a cup of tea and enjoy the beauty of nature.

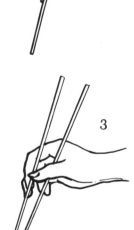

Tea is an ancient beverage in China; a legend explaining the beginning of tea drinking dates back to 2000 BC when Shen Nong tasted tea during his reign and realized the medical properties of the drink as compared to other herbs. Even today, Chinese people believe that tea drinking is beneficial to health.

There are hundreds of varieties of tea in China; each has its own distinctive flavor. The quality of the tea depends upon the soil in which it grows, the time of the day and the season of the year in which the tea leaves are picked, and the way they are processed. The black teas are made by fermenting the leaves. The resulting oxidation gives the beverage its reddish color. Green tea is not fermented. Semi-fermented tea and scented tea are prepared by adding flower petals, usually jasmine, rose, or magnolia to the tea leaves.

Tea is best brewed in porcelain pots or cups, although pottery or glass is also suitable. Place the tea leaves in the pot, then pour the boiling water over the tea leaves. Cover the pot promptly and let the tea leaves steep for 5-8 minutes. It is then ready to be served in cups.

The Chinese drink tea plain without adding cream and sugar. Drinking it this way, the delicate flavor of the tea is not disturbed. It is also a healthier way to drink tea. Imagine if tea drinkers like the Chinese were to put cream and sugar in every cup of tea they drank, the calories and cholesterol they would get each day would be unhealthy.

DINNER

Chinese do not drink water with their meals. On special festive occasions or when having company, warm wine is sometimes served in small porcelain cups. The wine is for adults only; children are not allowed to sample. Most Chinese are not very fond of wine; drinking alcoholic beverages is not very common in China.

At a Chinese feast, the guests are seated at the table shortly after they arrive. The guest of honor sits facing the door while the host and hostess sit opposite him. Traditional Chinese feasts are very elaborate. *Cai* dishes are served in abundance. They usually start with four to six cold *Cai* dishes. These dishes are served one or two at a time. Somehow, in between the main courses, two sweet dishes are served. Rice and soup are usually served at the end of the main courses, except in Canton, where soup is served as the first course. The host or hostess will serve the guests portion after portion of *Cai*. One of the duties of the host is to make sure the guests enjoy the food to its maximum.

A simple family meal for six people would include one soup placed at the center of the table and surrounded by four main *Cai* diahes. Two of the main dishes would be heavy meat dishes which contained more meat than vegetables. The other two would be light meat dishes, in which the proportions would be reversed. Rice (*Fan*) is always available to eat with the *Cai* dishes. Each person serves himself. The Chinese seldom count how many helpings they consume at a meal. Mothers always encourage their children to take extra portions in order to make sure they are well fed.

In China, people do not serve heavy appetizers before a meal. Instead, a cup of plain tea accompanied by roasted watermelon or pumpkin seeds in the shell, or a few kinds of delicate fruit preserves may be served. These delicacies tend to create an atmosphere of relaxation but do not ruin the appetite like heavy appetizers do. The cold dishes served at the beginning of the meal are the Chinese equivalent of the appetizers of the western world. In China, nowadays, some of the more elaborate restaurants have developed many fancy cold dishes. They arrange the cold food in different designs such as butterflies, the

Phoenix bird, dragons and flower baskets. These cold dishes also serve as a center piece and accent the whole dinner.

The busy American lifestyle makes it impossible to cook and serve as the Chinese might. However, a meal of only a few nutritionally balanced dishes made with careful planning, creatively arranged, and artistically presented can be both successful and enjoyable.

Cold dishes in butterfly and peacock designs from a cooking competition near Shanghai, China.

Nutrition and Suggested Diet Menus

Chinese cooking can be fun, interesting, creative, inexpensive and nutritious. By using a variety of everyday food items in your kitchen and adopting a few basic Chinese cooking techniques, you can easily prepare Chinese meals. The only major difference between Chinese cooking and American cooking is the quantity of meat use. Unlike most people in America who eat whole pieces of meat, untreated, the Chinese eat small amounts of meat and larger quantities of vegetables. They make the meat complementary to other ingredients; sometimes meat is used as a flavoring agent or a seasoning for the vegetable.

Since the Chinese use a reduced amount of meat in their cooking, many people question the nutritional quality of Chinese food. The widespread belief that meat is essential to our diet is deeply rooted in our minds. Some people might be shocked to know that meat itself is not essential to good nutrition. It is the protein which meat contains that is essential.

Protein of both animal and plant origin are digested by the body into amino acids; these are the building blocks of proteins. The body picks up the necessary amino acids to build up numerous proteins for growth, repair, and proper functioning. There are some twenty amino acids. Eight of these are essential and the body cannot manufacture them. These essential amino acids must be supplied by the protein from the food we eat.

Why do people put so much emphasis on meat? Simply because meat is a food rich in high-quality protein. Meat contains favorable proportions of essential amino acids. In general, all animal protein is high in quality while some plant protein is low in certain essential amino acids. When looking for foods rich in high-quality protein we should not overlook the fact that meat is also a high-calorie food. Almost one-half to two-thirds of the calories in meat is found in meat fat. This fat is high in cholesterol and saturated fatty acids, and these do not add substantially to our bodies' good health. For this reason, the use of small amounts of meat in Chinese cooking can keep our calorie intake low, keep us healthier, and save us money. It is also significant that the large quantity of vegetables used in Chinese cooking adds to the richness of vitamins, minerals, and fiber (bulk) in our diet.

When we use animal and plant protein together, they complement each other so that more proteins are available to our bodies than when we eat them separately. The essential amino acids lacking in one kind of food are made up for by those present in another food. The usability of the protein by the body depends upon the presence of the correct proportions of these essential amino acids. It makes no difference whether protein comes from an animal source or plant source. We can erase the idea that animal protein is basically different and therefore cannot be equated with plant protein.

9

The essential amino acids from the small amount of meat in Chinese cooking extends its highest effectiveness nutritionally. It is the most economical and healthiest way to utilize animal proteins.

According to a USDA estimate, the average American consumes from 10-12% more protein than his body needs. The recommended dietary allowances for adults is from 46-56 grams daily. Meat consumption in the U.S. in the last decade has risen about fifty percent in spite of the fact that, to be well fed, all that is necessary is a protein mixture yielding sufficient amino acids in the right proportion. There is no need to worry that the body will not function well if the present excessive meat-eating pattern is reversed.

As soaring food prices continue, more than ever before, nutritional knowledge is needed for wise food buying and intelligent menu planning. In planning menus, we must look for foods that provide all the necessary nutrients to meet the nutritional requirements of the body. Protein foods are among our first priorities. We also have to make sure that enough vitamins and minerals are obtained from our food. We should try to choose the foods that contain multiple nutrients. For example, meat supplies high quality protein and is rich in B vitamins. Broccoli is not only rich in vitamin C but also in vitamin A, iron, and calcium. In contrast lard, butter or oil provide only fat; sugar supplies only carbohydrates. Again, we should always consider the advantage of the protein complement when choosing foods. For instance, rice and soybean products (or beans) are complementary to each other. The essential amino acids, low in rice, are complemented by high amino acids in soybeans. As we remember protein balance in meal planning, we must also be sure that the calories in a balanced and nutritious meal do not exceed our bodies' need.

For each recipe, I have endeavored to obtain as complete and accurate nutrition information as possible. However, certain foods such as wood ears, lily buds, bean threads, curry powder, Winter melon, canned sweet red-bean paste, and sea cucumber etc. have never been analyzed for their nutritional value. Rather than not give nutritional information for recipes containing these ingredients, I have calculated the information for these recipes with the awareness that they cannot be completely accurate.

When you want to lose weight, all you have to do is to cut down on calories. For an average adult to lose one pound of body fat, it requires a loss of an approximate total of 3,500 calories. If you eat 500 calories less each day, within one week you would lose one pound of body weight. If you try to cut 500 calories each day and at the same time eat good and balanced food you will not feel too depressed. The same goal can be accomplished by doing a lot of exercises while maintaining normal caloric intake.

To avoid cholesterol, I use vegetable oil in all the recipes. Also the visible fat is removed from the meat before cooking in order to reduce the calorie content of the food as well as to minimize cholesterol.

If you are interested in more nutritional information, please read the section "Is Chinese Food Nutritious?" in Christine Liu's first book *Nutrition and Diet with Chinese Cooking*, pages 4-6.

NOTE: The nutrition information following each recipe is the calculation for the entire recipe, not for individual servings.

When an optional measurement or ingredient is used, the nutrition calculation is based on the first measurement or ingredient.

The following suggested menus are delicious and nutritionally balanced. They are designed to help you obtain the most proteins, vitamins, and minerals with the least calories. They are suitable not only for company and family meals, but also for dieters who wish to lose weight and remain healthy while enjoying good food.

SUGGESTED DIET MENUS

The following menus have been chosen as samples for a dinner for eight men, four persons, eight vegetarians, and banquet menus for thirty people or more.

Five menus for a dinnner for eight men (ages 23-50). Calories and protein for each person are evaluated.

I. Sour and Hot Soup*
    Beef with Green Onions
    Steamed Pork with Spicy-rice Powder*
    Almond Chicken
    Deep-fried String Beans*
    Rice
    16 Sesame Cookies*
        Calories: 950
        Protein: 46 gm

II. Fresh Cucumber Soup
    Oyster-sauce Beef with Fresh Mushrooms
    Stir-fry Curried Chicken
    Miniature Lion's Head*
    Stir-fry Asparagus or Stir-fry Fresh Bean Sprouts
    Rice
    ¼ recipe of Red bean Steamed Cake (rich-type)*
        Calories: 900
        Protein: 67 gm

III.   Fish Soup
       Sweet and Sour Pork*
       Zucchini with Beef
       Fermented Black Bean Chicken with Nuts
       Fresh Spinach Salad, Chinese Style
       Rice
       ½ recipe of Three-colored Bean Gelatin

              Calories: 1000
              Protein: 53 gm

IV.   Meat Ball Soup*
       Chicken in Lemon Sauce
       Sa Cha Beef
       Spicy Quick Fry Shrimp
       Fresh Mushrooms with Vegetable
       Rice
       ½ recipe of Sa Gi Ma*

              Calories: 925
              Protein: 45

V.   Egg Drop Soup
       Oyster Sauce Beef with Broccoli
       Chicken with Snow Pea Pods
       Shrimp Balls with Cashew Nuts
       Bean Threads with Ham and Leeks
       Rice
       Coconut and Walnut Sweet Soup*

              Calories: 848
              Protein: 37 gm

       *Dishes that can be made in advance

The menus given above are low in calories. The protein as the most important nutrient is adequately supplied both from vegetables and meats. The vitamins and minerals are sufficiently provided because the ingredients used in the recipes are from large varieties. The cholesterol level is low because a small amount of meat and only vegetable oil is used in cooking. The meals themselves are not only delicious but healthy, nutritious, and well balanced.

Two menus for a dinner for four persons. The recipes are low in calories and carbohydrates. Nutritional calculations are for each person.

I.   ½ recipe of Miniature Lion's Head*
        Shrimp with broccoli
        ¼ recipe of Fried Rice
        Fresh fruit (2 C grapes, American type, slip skin)
            Calories: 789
            Protein: 55 gm
            Carbohydrate: 49 gm

II.   Oyster Sauce Beef with Broccoli
        Chicken with Snow Pea Pods
        ½ recipe of Fried Rice
        4 fresh peaches
            Calories: 722
            Protein: 50 gm
            Carbohydrate: 49 gm

*Dishes that can be made in advance.

Two menus for a dinner for eight vegetarians. The recipes are low in calories and adequate in protein. Nutritional calculations are for each person.

I.   Fried Bean Curd Balls
      Meatless Bean Curd
      Bean Pasted Nuts*
      Stir-fry Vegetables with Egg Hat
      Eggplant with Curry
      Rice
      ¼ recipe of Red Bean Steamed Cake
           Calories: 960
           Protein: 38 gm

II.   Braised Fried Bean Curd*
      Pot Sticker Bean Curd
      Braised Steamed Gluten*
      Golden Coined Eggs
      Fresh Spinach Salad, Chinese Style
      Rice
      Laughing Balls*
           Calories: 951
           Protein: 34 gm

*Dishes that can be made in advance.

Two banquet menus for thirty people or more. Most of the dishes are chosen for advance preparation.

I.   Sour and Hot Soup*
     Salted Duck*
     Crisp Skinned Chicken*
     Lotus Leaf Wrapped Steamed Pork*
     Chicken in Lemon Sauce
     Braised Beef Shank*
     Miniature Lion's Head*
     Steamed Meat in Noodle Case
     Dry Cooked Shrimp, Sichuan Style
     Fried Rice*
     Fried Noodles*
     Fresh Spinach, Chinese Style
     Steamed Bread*
     Red Bean Steamed Cake (rich type)*

II. Meat Ball Soup*
     Steamed Duck or Peking Duck
     Drumsticks, Sichuan Style*
     Oyster Sauce Chicken Wings*
     Almond Chicken
     Sweet and Sour Pork*
     Pork Fresh Ham, Sichuan Style*
     Braised Beef with Tomato Sauce*
     Squrrel Fish or Meat Stuffed Fish
     Shrimp Balls with Cashew Nuts
     Braised Mushroom Balls*
     Fried Noodles
     Fresh Spinach, Chinese Style or Cucumber with Sesame Paste
     Steamed Bread*
     Three-colored Bean Gelatin*

     *Dishes that can be made in advance.

14

Facts About Fat

Because this Chinese cookbook emphasizes nutrition, we cannot avoid the subject and importance of *fat*. Present day American society seems obsessed with fat and its effects on health. Hopefully this section will contribute to your understanding of this important subject.

DO WE NEED FATS?

Fats are vital, necessary, and important components in one's diet. They furnish our body with a concentrated source of fuel necessary to carry on life processes. They carry fatty acids and fat-soluble vitamins that are essential for health. A moderate amount of fats stored in the body provides an energy reserve, an insulation against temperature extremes, and a padding for joints and vital organs. Fats also give flavor to the food that we eat. They add satiety value to a meal and make people feel "full" longer. A lack of fats can cause abnormalities just as a deficiency of other nutrients can.

COMMON QUESTIONS ABOUT FATS

What is the best kind of fat to use in cooking? Does peanut oil give more flavor in Chinese cooking? Is it more nutritious than other oils? What about lard? Which *fat* has the greatest nutritional advantages? What are the differences between animal and vegetable fats in cooking and in nutrition? These are some of the questions people frequently ask nutritionists.

The fat problem, it seems, is an important one to question; but it is confusing, in more ways than one might initially anticipate. Therefore, let us examine the subject of fat in the diet in a methodical way by answering some specific questions with nutritional implications.

(1) *What are the types of fats?*

First we ought to know that fat and lipids are the same thing and are often used interchangeably in science books. Triglyceride is the chemical name for fat.

Now let's clarify some of the confusion about fats by classifying the types of fat we use most often in Chinese cooking. Generally speaking, there are two types of fat. The one that is liquid at room temperature is called oil. Oils are exclusively of vegetable origin such as safflower, sunflower, canola, corn, soybean oil, etc. They contain a large amount of "polyunsaturated" and "monounsaturated" fatty acids. The one that is solid at room temperature is generally spoken of as fat. Fats are mostly of animal origin such as lard, chicken fat, and butter, etc. (not used very often in Chinese cooking). Fats have a large amount of "saturated" fatty acids.

There is another type of fat called "hydrogenated fat." This type of fat is made from liquid oils. A process called "hydrogenation" is used to change the liquid vegetable oils to solid fats, such as those found in margarine or shortening.

The hydrogenation process produces trans-fatty acids. Recent studies found that a diet moderately high (10 grams per day) or higher in trans-fatty acids raised the blood cholesterol and increased LDL cholesterol when compared to diets low in trans-fatty acids. However, fats containing a high level of saturated fatty acids raised total cholesterol levels more than fats containing a high level of trans-fatty acids. But only a diet high in trans-fatty acids lowers the protective HDL level. Fortunately, this type of fat is seldom used in Chinese cooking, therefore, we will not discuss it here.

(2) *What are cholesterol and fatty acids?*

Cholesterol is a fat soluble, waxy substance found only in animal fats. It is used by the body to manufacture certain hormones and to produce bile acids. It is also an essential part of cell membranes.

Total blood cholesterol is made up of several components. Two of the major components are high-density lipoprotein (HDL) and low density lipoprotein (LDL). LDL forms plaques inside your coronary arteries, which can lead to heart attacks. HDL is what the body uses to remove excess LDL from the blood stream.

Every molecule of fat is formed by a union of three fatty acids with a molecule of glycerol.

```
              ⎧  G ▪▪▪▪▪▪ Fatty acid
              ⎪  l
              ⎪  y
              ⎪  c
     Fat   ⎨  e ▪▪▪▪▪▪ Fatty acid
              ⎪  r
              ⎪  o
              ⎩  l ▪▪▪▪▪▪ Fatty acid
```

Fat is liquid or solid at room temperature, depending on the types and amounts of fatty acids in their composition.

There are three kinds of fatty acids: (1) saturated fatty acids—fatty acids which are saturated with hydrogen and have no room on their chemical chain to take up more hydrogen; (2) monounsaturated fatty acids—fatty acids which have one place on their chemical chain to take up more hydrogen; and (3) polyunsaturated fatty acids—fatty acids which have two to four places on their chemical chain to take up more hydrogen.

16

Any one kind of fat never contains only one type of fatty acid exclusively but a combination of three types in varying amounts and proportions. The fats that are predominate in saturated fats usually solidify at room temperature and are usually of animal origin. When these fats are eaten, they tend to raise blood cholesterol. The fats that are predominate in polyunsaturated fatty acids are usually in a liquid state at room temperature, and are usually of vegetable origin. They have the capacity to lower both HDL and LDL cholesterol. Monounsaturated fat lowers LDL cholesterol without lowering the protective HDL cholesterol. From the nutritional point of view, lowering cholesterol and substituting monounsaturated fats for saturated fats, avoiding trans fats, in the diet is a sensible contribution to good health. See page 19 about canola oil.

(3) What are essential fatty acids?

Polyunsaturated fatty acids, in general, are believed to have the capacity of lowering the cholesterol level of the blood. Linoleic acid (a polyunsaturated fatty acid), in particular, is believed by many researchers to be the most helpful substance to reduce fatty deposits in blood vessels. Linoleic acid is also an essential fatty acid. It must be furnished by the food we eat and cannot be synthesized by the human body. Linoleic acid exists plentifully in vegetable oils, but a small portion can also be found in animal fats. The table shows the approximate percentage of linoleic acid in a variety of fats of animal and plant origin that we use in common household cooking. The list suggests the comparative importance of the different kinds of fats and oils as sources of linoleic acid.

Linoleic Acid Content in Some Commonly Used Fats [*]

	Total saturated fatty acids %	Total unsaturated fatty acids %	Linoleic acid %
Butter	55	39	3
Lard	38	57	10
Corn	10	84	53
Soybean	15	80	52
Peanut[**]	18	76	29
Cottonseed	25	71	50
Olive	11	84	7
Sesame	14	80	42
Sunflower	12	83	63
Safflower	8	87	72

[*] "Fatty Acids in Food Fats," Home Economics Research Reports No. 7, United States Department of Agriculture, 1958.

[**] Using linoleic acid as a criterion, peanut oil is not polyunsaturated to the same degree as other oils.

(4) What is the calorie content of fats?

Fats, whether they are of animal or vegetable origin, do not differ in the number of calories per gram. They all have nine calories per gram. On the other hand, both protein and carbohydrate furnishes four calories per gram. Fat provides not only more than double the calories per unit than protein and carbohydrate, but also exists mostly in concentrated forms; consequently, a small amount of fat contributes a large number of calories to the diet.

In our daily intake of foods, the differences in the number of calories present in fats (such as oil or butter) and in carbohydrate food) are very impressive. For example, an apple (a carbohydrate food) of 150 grams, provides 70 calories. This same number of calories is provided by two little teaspoons of oil or butter (roughly 8 grams). The reason for such differences is that fats provide more calories per gram and are more concentrated. This is so because butter contains water in a very low percentage. Oil contains no water at all while carbohydrate foods, such as apples, contain a large amount of water (85%). In some cases the water content is even higher, resulting in a low calorie count per unit of weight.

When someone eats an apple, he can satisfy his appetite a bit. However, two teaspoons of butter which provide almost the same number of calories, are not even enough to spread on a piece of toast. Therefore, one wants to eat more and as a result adds greater calorie intake to his diet. When the body gets more calories than it needs, the overloaded calories are converted to fat and stored in the body. Eventually this leads to overweight or obesity.

(5) What are visible and invisible fats?

The oil and butter we use in cooking and eating are the visible fats. They are readily seen and their quantity can be easily controlled. There are many kinds of foods on the market that contain fats which are not visible, especially the foods of animal origin; these contain a large proportion of hidden fat. For example, three ounces of regular hamburger (ground beef, broiled) provide 235 calories; 153 of these calories are derived from fat. A cup of whole milk provides 160 calories and of those, 81 calories are derived from milk fat. On the other hand, one cup of skimmed milk provides 86 fat-free calories. Cookies, cakes, and pies are also high in invisible fat content. Most of the fats in these foods are saturated and high in cholesterol. Therefore, if one wants to watch calories and the quality of the fat in his diet, he must beware of the hidden fats.

(6) What does fat contribute to flavor?

The most popular animal fat in Chinese cooking is lard (hog fat). It gives a meaty flavor to both the vegetable dishes and the dishes that use little meat. In making Chinese pastries and desserts, lard is used.

Soybean, peanut, canola, and cottonseed oils are four common vegetable oils used for cooking in China. In the old days, peanut oil was considered the best oil because it is mild in taste and least disturbing to the flavor of foods. The oils extracted from seed components retain its own particular smell and taste. Somehow, the taste and smell of soybean, canola, and cottonseed oils are stronger than peanut oil. Today, however, all vegetable oils are deodorized after extraction. People can hardly tell the oil's origin by smell or differences in flavor.

(7) Which fat is best and how much should one use?

Which fat to use and how much to use is a personal choice. One should make his own decision on the basis of scientific information available as well as one's own needs and taste.

It is well known that in the American diet, about 40-50% of energy may come from fat and fat-rich food and almost 60% of the fat is of animal origin. In comparison, only 10% of energy is furnished by fat in Asian people's diet, while 25% of energy is furnished by fat in most European countries. The American diet is too high in fat. Personally, I feel that cutting down on total fat consumption and the use of more monounsaturated and polyunsaturated fats (vegetable oils) will lead to reduced weight and better health for most people. For example, recent research indicates that **canola oil** (the oil extracted from rape seeds) **is the lowest of all oils in saturated fat.** And after olive oil, it is the second highest in monounsaturated fat.

In this book, vegetable oil is used for all cooking; this is for the sake of our health. Lard is avoided because it is high in saturates and cholesterol. The recipes still have excellent flavor and are nutritionally sound at the same time. Not only will we eat delicious food but we will also be healthier in the long run.

Method of Preparation and Cooking

PREPARATION:

In general, Chinese cooking needs more preparation time than cooking time. Most Chinese dishes are a variety of ingredients combined together for fast cooking over high heat. The possible combinations of the ingredients are infinite. The ingredients are properly cut and seasoned beforehand. Once a dish is cooked and brought to the table, it is ready to be eaten with a pair of chopsticks. Knives are unnecessary at the dinner table.

Cutting is very important in Chinese cooking, especially for the quick stir-fried dishes. The ingredients used in a given dish should be sliced, shredded, diced or chopped beforehand into uniform small sizes and shapes so that they can be picked up with a pair of chopsticks, are easy to stir, and will all be done at the same time. Cutting also exposes larger amounts of the food's surface area to heat and seasonings, thus shortening the cooking time as well as improving the flavor. In determining how to cut a given ingredient it depends on the texture and composition of the ingredient, how it is to be cooked, and with what it is to be combined. In stir-fried dishes, the dominant ingredient in a dish determines the cutting of the other ingredients that go into the dish. For example, if sliced meat is the dominant ingredient, then all the vegetables to be cooked with the meat will be sliced. If the dominant ingredient is bean sprouts, then the meat and other vegetables cooked with it will be shredded. All the cuttings are done in the kitchen.

Here are some of the cutting methods often used in Chinese cooking:

Slicing: To cut into straight, vertical 1½" long, 1" wide and ⅛" thick, flat pieces. Slicing is used mostly in cutting tender meat and vegetables.

Slant Slicing: Cutting diagonally to increase the surface area. Put the material at an angle of 45 degrees to the cleaver, then slice it into thin pieces. Slant slicing is used mostly in cutting tough meats, and long, narrow vegetables such as asparagus, carrots, celery stalks, etc.

Shredding: Slice the material first, then pile a few pieces together and cut into fine strips.

Rolling-cutting: Slant slice first, then roll the cutting surface upward and slant slice again at the end of the first cutting surface.

Chopping: To cut the ingredients into irregular dices, then pile them together and cut them into the consistency that meets your recipe's needs.

Mincing: To cut the ingredients into very fine pieces. It is used mainly in steamed dishes and the fillings for buns, dumplings, etc. Machine-ground meat, or vegetables minced by food processors are acceptable.

Dicing: To cut the ingredients into small cubes ranging from ¼"-½". First cut the ingredients into strips, then cut them into cubes.

Cubing: To cut the ingredients into large-sized cubes ranging from 1"-2". Used mostly for the meats that are to be fried or stewed. Cubing is also used for thick vegetables such as potatoes or eggplants, etc.

Crushing: To increase surface area by pounding the ingredient with the broad side of a cleaver or a knife. This is for vegetables such as radishes or baby cucumbers to be used in a salad. The surface area speeds up the absorption of seasonings or dressings into the ingredients. Crushing garlic, green onioin, or ginger root releases their full flavor during cooking.

Scoring: To cut some incisions either straight (on large pieces of meat, ham or on squid and kidneys) or diagonally (on whole fish). The depth of the incisions depends on how thick the ingredient is. Scoring is used to shorten the cooking time as well as to allow the seasoning to penetrate the food faster and easier. Some scoring improves the appearance. For instance, light scoring done on squid and kidneys makes the food unique and interesting looking.

Marinating: To soak the ingredients (meat, poultry, seafood and some vegetables) in a seasoned sauce or to mix the ingredients with seasonings before cooking. Marinating improves the flavor of the food or makes the flavor of the food more outstanding. It plays an important role in Chinese cooking. This explains why so many dishes that only take a few minutes of cooking time turn out to be so delicious.

How long an ingredient needs to be marinated depends on the size of the cut. Thinly sliced or shredded meat only needs a short period to marinate. Ten to twenty minutes is long enough. Whole poultry or a large cut of meat needs a few hours or sometimes a day or two so that the marinade can penetrate into the ingredient. Marinating can be hastened by high temperature. If the marination period is one hour or more, for safety's sake, refrigerate the ingredient in its marinade. On some occasions, the marinade sauce is also cooked with the ingredient to improve the flavor of the whole dish. So do not discard the marinade before you decide whether you need to use it or not.

Soda should never be added to food while marinating. The alkalinity of the soda, even to a slight degree, is distinctly destructive to vitamin C. Since Chinese use large portions of vegetables which are rich in vitamin C, soda will destroy one of the important nutrients of the vegetables.

Some people suggest mixing soda with meat in order to tenderize it. This is not necessary in the United States because the meats sold in the market here are generally tenderized through a process called ageing or ripening.

The ageing or ripening is done by hanging the animal carcass in a cold room for a short period of time. During that time the natural proteolytic enzymes in the meat slowly break down the connective tissue between the muscle fibers as well as the muscle fibers themselves. Consequently, the meat in general, is tender enough; adding soda is not needed.

Washing: The Chinese wash all ingredients that are going to be cooked, carefully and thoroughly. It is a good practice. Years ago in China, improper packaging and storage of food, along with the application of manure on the plants made careful washing essential and helped reduce contanimation from any germs, thus helping to avoid diseases.

For instance, the Chinese would advise you to thoroughly wash rice by rubbing and rinsing under running water until all the excess powder on the rice is removed. They would recommend washing vegetables in a large amount of water before and after cutting·

Nutritionally, over-washing is not recommended in certain instances. For example, with most rice, the vitamins and minerals, and much of the proteins are removed in milling. The very little original vitamins and minerals that are left on the grain will be washed away by rubbing and rinsing.

In the United States, programs of enrichment have restored the important micronutrients back to the rice. You should not wash the rice at all before cooking. The instructions on the packages of the enriched rice clearly indicate that "to retain vitamins do not rinse before or drain after cooking." Some researchers found that washing rice before cooking lost 25% of the vitamin B1.

By the same token, vegetables are good sources of vitamins and minerals. Some of them are very easily lost during processing. For instance, we need a fair quantity of vitamin C for our health and well being, but it is the most easily destroyed of all vitamins. It is highly water soluble and easily oxidized. The best way to preserve this vitamin is to wash the vegetables just prior to cooking. Wash the vegetables when its leaves are whole. Cutting enlarges the surface area to the air, hastening the destruction of the vitamin. When vegetables are soaking in water, water soluble vitamins are lost by leaking out into the water. All food has its full nutritional potential, but some of the nutritive value of the food is lost before it ever reaches the table. Proper washing, storing and cooking will help get the full nutritional potential of foods.

COOKING METHODS:

Many different cooking methods have developed in China throughout a thousand years. Each dish has its own appropriate cooking method and always with justified reasons. For the tender, fresh vegetables, the quick, stir-fried method is used to preserve their natural fresh flavor. For a large piece of meat or whole poultry, the red-cooked stewing or simmering method is used. The long hours of slow cooking over low heat allows the seasonings to penetrate to the innermost part of the meat. The meat will become extremely tender but will remain intact. The heat of the simmering or stewing methods is very gentle. It will not break up the meat while it is cooking.

No matter which method is chosen, Chinese cooking saves fuel. The fuel crisis is not a new issue, but an age old one in China. The cooking methods developed are done on top of the stove. The food either is cooked in a few minutes over high heat or cooked for a long time using the lowest heat setting. Thus it saves fuel. The need to conserve fuel not only influences the method of preparation and cooking but even the kind of crops planted. For instance, to cook a pot of rice takes much less fuel than to bake or steam a loaf of bread. That might explain why rice became the staple in the diet of most parts of China. For the same reason, baking or roasting are rare in Chinese cooking. Foods which need baking or roasting are prepared in a special bakery, roasting house, or restaurant. Ordinary Chinese homes do not own ovens.

Nowadays, the government and people here are striving together to save fuel and are trying to devise all the possible ways to conserve fuel. Why don't we try to save fuel by cooking the Chinese way? Besides, Chinese food is healthy, nutritious and delicious.

Here are some principle cooking methods which are used in Chinese cooking.

Stir-frying or quick stirring: This is the most popular method of Chinese cooking. Meats and vegetables are cut into small, uniform sizes. They are quickly stirred and constantly turned in a small amount of oil over high heat. The whole dish is completely cooked within 5-10 minutes. Most of the dishes are cooked in their natural juices. Very small amounts of broth or water will be added during cooking in some dishes. The quick cooking preserves all the vitamins and minerals of the ingredients. From the nutritional point of view, it is the healthiest way of cooking food. Because of the short cooking time, all the ingredients should be completely prepared in advance. In order to preserve the vitamins, color and crunchiness of the vegetables, the food should be served and eaten immediately after cooking.

Sautéing: The cooking is done in an open pan. The process is rapid. The food is usually cut into small pieces and is cooked in a small quantity. The heat must be kept up and the food is stirred constantly while sauteing until it is done. The stir-frying method is very much the same as sautéing except the food is cooked in larger amounts.

Pan-frying: Using a small amount of oil to cover the bottom of a frying pan or a skillet (a depth of 1/10" to 1/2" oil), ingredients are added to the heated oil and fried over medium heat until they are done. Turn the ingredients once or twice during cooking. The pan should be covered or open depending upon the kind of food being cooked. Pan-fried stuffed buns, meat dumplings or meat patties etc. are cooked by this method.

Deep-frying: Using a large amount of oil (a depth of 2"-4" of oil). Ingredients are immersed in the hot oil and fried over medium or high heat until they are done. The ingredients should be cut into 1/2"-2 ½" pieces depending on the recipe. They should be coated with cornstarch or batter before frying to prevent splattering as well as to seal in the flavor and juice. Smaller cuts of the ingredients can be cooked at once by deep-frying. Larger cuts of the ingredients should be fried in two to three intervals in order to insure doneness inside and out. To do this, first fry the food in hot oil until light brown, then remove and drain. Return the food to hot oil after a few minutes and fry until golden brown and crispy. Food cooked in this way is called double fried or triple fried food. The first stage of this multiple frying method is called pre-frying. Sometimes, you can pre-fry the food first and refrigerate or freeze it, then re-fry it again before serving.

Foods should not be added to the oil in a large quantity. Add a few pieces at a time, so that there will be enough room for the food to cook. Also it is easier to maintain the oil temperature.

The oil used for deep-frying can be reused if it is clean. When the oil is used for deep-frying fish or fatty meat, it might be too fishy to use again, or the oil might contain too much animal fat which has melted from the meat. In this case, reusing the oil is not advisable.

Simmering: Used to make stocks or soups or slow cooked dishes. Ingredients (poultry, meats with bones, fresh or dried fish etc.) are put in a tightly covered large pan with plenty of water. First bring the water to a boil, then turn the burner to the lowest heat and cook for a few hours. It needs no attention during cooking.

Simmering can also be used for cooking food that is relatively dry. The low heat will keep it cooking, but will not burn. For example, after the water has been boiled away from the rice, cover the pan tightly and simmer.The rice will be thoroughly expanded and cooked without burning.

Stewing: There are two variations of stewing:
1. Red stewing or red cooking: The ingredients are put in a deep sauce pan and covered with water. Add soy sauce, spices and seasonings. Cover pan and bring to a boil, then turn to low heat and cook until the ingredients become tender and the cooking liquid is reduced to a small amount. The cooking liquid, as expected, should turn to a thick, dark brown or reddish-colored natural gravy (the name "red cooking" comes from this dark color). Turn the ingredients several times during cooking for an even flavor. This is one of the most famous cooking methods in Chinese cooking.
2. White stewing or white cooking: The ingredients are cooked in the same manner as red cooking, but without using soy sauce. White stewing is used to cook whole poultry or large pieces of meat, etc. The food will be eaten with dips.

Braising: First brown or saute the ingredients. Then cook the ingredients over low heat for a long period of time, usually with a small quantity of water in a tightly covered pan until done.

Boiling: The ingredients are put in the boiling water and cooked until they are done. Boiling is seldom used alone. It is usually combined with other cooking methods to cook food (noodles are the exception). Many dishes call for boiling first, then simmering or stewing to complete the cooking.

Parboiling: Cooking the ingredients in boiling water until they are partially done. The water will be discarded after cooking. The ingredients are chilled and then served with dressing or dips.

The parboiled ingredients are also used in stir-fried dishes when combined with other materials. Parboiling is used for certain tough vegetables or some ingredients that have a strong or bitter tast. Parboiling takes this taste away. From the nutritional point of view, parboiling is a poor practice, because nutrients will leak out into the boiling water, thus reducing the nutritional potential of a food.

Blanching: Pour boiling water over the ingredients and drain after a few minutes. This method is used to loosen the skin of dried nuts, vegetables (such as fresh tomatoes) and fresh fruits. The skin can be easily peeled off after blanching.

Roasting: To barbecue a large piece of meat or whole poultry over a fire until it is done. In China the roasting is done in a mud or brick oven in a special roasting house owned by a restaurant or bakery. The meat is hung high over the fire. The temperature is adjusted by moving the piece farther or closer to the fire. Ordinarily families do not own an oven, therefore, they seldom roast at home. Besides, it takes too much fuel.

In the United States, we can use the oven, electric rotisseries or charcoal grills to make roasted dishes. When roasting food the Chinese way, first marinate the food, or rub it with a layer of fat, then hang or rest the food on a rack. Cook the food on high heat for a few minutes in order to form a crust on the skin, then turn to low heat and roast until it is done. This explains why Chinese roasted food is crispy outside and juicy inside.

Smoking: Smoking adds flavor to the food with a thick, strong, aromatic smoke. Home smoking is done in an enclosed large pan. First, cook the food in a seasoning sauce and then drain. put a layer of foil in the bottom of the pan. Spread a mixture of spices, (camphor, pine and tea etc.) sugar, and flour on the foil. Set a rack in the pan over the spice and flour mixture. Put the food on the rack. Cover the pan and turn to medium heat and cook. The heat burns the spice and flour mixture and produces the smoke. The smoke penetrates the food and flavors it. Sometimes, smoking helps to preserve food also. For larger quantities of food, the Chinese smoke it in a special smoking house.

Steaming: Cook ingredients by direct wet steam over boiling water. Water is boiled in a large pot or pan. The ingredients are put in a bowl, or on a plate. Insert the ingredients on a tier of a perforated pan (which is a part of a steamer) or set it on a rack which should be raised 2"-3" above the boiling water (for a home made steamer, see illustration. Cover and keep the water boiling until the ingredients are cooked.

One can steam several dishes at the same time if the steamer has more than one tier. Put each dish on an individual tier and set one tier on top of the other and steam. To get the best results, the ingredients in each dish should require almost the same cooking time, so opening the lid during cooking time is not necessary. Opening the steamer during steaming will cause heat loss. If you do so, readjusting the cooking time will be necessary. When steaming Chinese bread or stuffed buns, opening the steamer during steaming is not advisable.

The quantity of water to be boiled in the pan before steaming depends on how long a dish is required to be steamed. When a dish needs only 5-10 minutes steaming time, a 2" depth of water is enough. Some dishes require half an hour or several hours steaming time. Enough water should be added in the beginning and the water level checked at intervals. If the water boils away before cooking is completed, refill the pot or pan with boiling water. Open the lid (or tier) slightly and pour the boiling water down the edges of the pan when refilling the water to prevent the loss of steam. Also you should be extremely careful so that you will not be burned by the hot steam. As a rule, the water added to the pan should be 2"-3" below the dish that is to be steamed, so that the water will not boil up to the food or tip the bowl or plate.

Steaming preserves nutrients and the flavor of the food. When steaming in the serving dish, the dish can go directly to the table when the food is done, saving another dish. Food needs very little attention while steaming. Steaming saves fuel especially when steaming several dishes at the same time. It is a most convenient cooking method, and worth trying.

Cooking Utensils

The years of teaching, giving demonstrations, and speaking in different places after my first book was published gave me a great opportunity to meet a large number of people. The majority of people think that without proper Chinese cooking utensils and ingredients from China they are not equipped to make Chinese dishes. This is partially true; the proper utensils and ingredients add efficiency in Chinese cooking, but more important, are the preparation and cooking techniques. If one throws all the ingredients into the wok without properly cutting, marinating and using the right cooking method, the food will not be Chinese. The cooking utensils perform no magic. By the same token, you don't have to use the rice raised in China to make Chinese fried rice.

Chinese cooking utensils are not absolutely necessary when you start to explore Chinese cooking. The skillets, pots and pans available in the American kitchen can do the job well. However, a few authentic Chinese utensils add a more enthusiastic spirit and fun when you are cooking. Besides, exotic utensils in the kitchen make your kitchen more interesting and more cosmopolitan. Then with a creative and imaginative mind, you can even use the Chinese cooking utensils to cook American or other kinds of your favorite foods.

Here are some suggested cooking utensils that you need in order to cook Chinese food efficiently. Among them, the wok, cleaver, large cutting board and a pair of chopsticks (longer than the regular ones) are most important in the Chinese kitchen. With these, one can make practically any dish desired. Others are nice to have.

Wok: This is an all-purpose, bowl-shaped cooking pan designed especially for the Chinese fuel-saving stove. The wok sets half way down into an opening on top of the stove. With the fire directly underneath the wok, ingredients can be cooked in just a few minutes as they are being stirred.

It is an ancient cooking utensil which the Chinese invented a thousand years ago. The shape of the wok has never been changed because it is perfectly designed. It is a most versatile cooking utensil. Almost all the cooking methods can be performed by using the wok, be it stir-frying, deep-frying, stewing, steaming, etc. (except roasting). The round bottom and sloping sides of the wok provide a funnel effect, so very little oil is needed and it is easy to stir and turn the food. The sloping sides, which force the food down to the bottom, allows the food to be coated with oil and to come in contact with the hot sides of the wok.

Woks come in different sizes, ranging from 10" to 22" in diameter. For the American home, a 10", 12" or 14" wok is considered the right size. In the Chinese kitchen in China, families own one to several sets of different sized woks, depending upon how large the kitchen and stove are. The woks are set in openings on the surface of their stove. The openings are tailored to the sizes of the wok. After the wok has been used, it is rinsed and dried and put back on the stove with its lid on. It is ready to be used again.

The ring stand is designed for modern American flat stoves to stabilize the wok and prevent its tipping. (The vents or holes are to release heat). It is absolutely unnecessary for the Chinese stove. When using the ring stand, be sure it is large enough to allow the wok to come in contact with the heat and does not raise the wok too high. If the wok is raised too high, it prolongs the cooking time. Very often, I prefer using the wok without the ring stand. It makes it easier for me to manipulate the wok, but that is only my opinion. In the United States, it is not proper to store our cooking utensils on top of the stove when we have finished cooking. The ring stand can be used to stabilize the wok while it is stored in the cabinet.

Woks are made of iron, copper, aluminum, stainless steel, carbon steel, etc. A new wok has to be seasoned before it is used for the first time. Seasoning is said to seal the pores of the metal so that it creates a smooth surface. Food will glide easily on the sides without sticking to the wok.

To season a wok, first wash it thoroughly with hot water and detergent, using a steel wool pad or scouring pad to remove any particles and machine oil used to coat the new wok. Rinse and dry the wok completely. Then use a small piece of paper towel or cheese cloth to apply a very thin layer of vegetable oil (about 1 teaspoon) on the surface of the wok. Heat the wok over a moderate high heat for 2-3 minutes; rinse and dry. Repeat the process several times. The wok is now ready to use.

After cooking, rinse the wok under the water. Rub gently with a wash cloth or sponge if there are food particles on it. Dry the wok thoroughly before storing. The cleaning procedure must be done very carefully, as scrubbing with steel wool or a scouring pad on a seasoned wok should be avoided. The wok will darken with age. A black colored wok proves that the owner is a good Chinese cook. My students suggested that by applying a thin layer of oil on the wok before putting it away, it prevents rust and also reduces the chances of stickiness when cooking. In my opinion, the best way to season a wok is to use it frequently. Cooking matures the wok.

If the wok is teflon-coated (or any other non-stick coating), seasoning the wok is not necessary. A plastic or teflon spatula, instead of a metal one, is recommended to stir and cook the food, so that you will avoid the damaging of the non-stick coating.

Cleaver: This is an all-purpose, rectangular-shaped Chinese cutting knife, made from tempered steel or stainless steel. The rectangular blade is approximately 3 1/2" x 7 1/2" in size. It has a cylindrical wooden or metal handle about 4" long. The blade usually has a 1/8" thick edge on the back and tapers gradually to a thinner and sharper cutting edge. Since every ingredient has to be cut before cooking and serving and since knives are not used at the dinner table, a sharp, good quality cleaver is essential. The Chinese cook depends heavily on the effectiveness of a cleaver to fulfill the job.

The cleaver, just like the wok, was invented a thousand years ago. The shape of the cleaver has never been changed, because it is well designed. With a cleaver one can do all kinds of cutting, also some crushing, pounding, and scrapping. A cleaver can easily split a thin piece of meat or vegetable in two. It can also cut or chop a large piece of food into smaller pieces. The broad blade of the cleaver can also be used as a spatula to shove the already cut ingredients from the cutting board to the pan. In other words, the cleaver acts like a dust pan being held by one hand, and the other hand acts like a broom to sweep the ingredients onto the blade, using the blade of the cleaver to carry the ingredients directly from cutting board to the pan. This eliminates the need for other cooking equipment, thus saving washing and drying time. Some cooks are so attached to the cleaver, that without it they cannot prepare Chinese food.

Cleavers come in two weights, heavy and light. The heavy one is used to chop meat with bones or whole poultry. The lighter one is used to cut soft meat and vegetables. In the American kitchen, a light cleaver is enough to perform all the cutting, as we can always ask the butchers in the supermarkets to cut the meat with bones.

The cleaver should always be kept dry because it rusts easily. Sharpen the cleaver from time to time. A sharp cleaver will cut the ingredient smoothly and neatly without bruising it. Use the conventional method of sharpening the cleaver as you would sharpen regular knives. An electric sharpener or a stone will do the sharpening job.

When cutting the food, put approximately 1/3 of your hand on the blade of the cleaver, and 2/3 on the handle. Your thumb will naturally fall on one side of the blade and the first finger on the other side. The handle is wrapped in the palm and other three fingers. Press the cleaver down in a forward motion (not a sawing motion). Firmly hold the article to be cut with your other hand. For safety's sake, you should never hold your article with flat fingers but curve your fingers. The fingers press hard on the article and the upright curved knuckles serve as a guide to protect the fingers while cutting. The cleaver should not be lifted higher than the knuckles. You might find cutting with a cleaver a little awkward at first, but with some practice, you will enjoy using it.

Cutting board: A larger cutting board is necessary for cutting ingredients because it is heavier and sturdier. A larger board also has more room on which to store the ingredients after they are cut, thus eliminating the need for using extra dishes. When the cutting is completed, the board can be carried to the stove and the ingredients to be cooked are transferred to the wok by the blade of the cleaver, all at one time.

In China, the cutting board is cut from the trunk of a special tree. It is round in shape, about 10 to 24 inches in diameter and 4-10 inches in thickness. The larger ones are for restaurant use. The texture of the wood should be very tight. The large, rectangular, heavy cutting board sold in markets here in the States are good enough to do the job.

Chopsticks: A pair of chopsticks, longer and thicker than the regular ones used for eating will make preparation more convenient. The chopsticks can be used for mixing, beating, sorting, turning, stirring, cutting (from larger to smaller pieces while cooking), piercing, removing cooked food from deep-frying oil, shaking the excess oil from food, and keeping the food from sticking. It is an all-purpose cooking tool.

Chopsticks are easy to wash and clean. They don't occupy too much space, and they are inexpensive. You will find them better than a lot of ordinary metal cooking tools. Chopsticks used for eating are made from different materials, namely, wood, bamboo, plastics, silver, gold, ivory, etc. The best material for chopsticks used for cooking is bamboo. Bamboo chopsticks will not burn or bend easily and will not conduct heat like metal cooking tools do.

Spatula: A long handled metal spatula with a curved edge along the base is nice to have in the kitchen. This spatula is specially designed for stirring and turning the ingredients in the round-bottomed wok.

Ladle: The Chinese ladle is more shallow than the American one. It is not only used to hold liquid ingredients, but it is also used in conjunction with the spatula to stir and turn the ingredients in a lifting and dropping action. It is especially helpful when cooking large amounts of food.

Non-stick pan: a skillet or deep sauce pan with a non-stick coating is very helpful in cooking Chinese food. It avoids sticking which is a big problem in Chinese cooking. When food sticks to a new wok, it oftentimes discourages a beginner. It is advisable for a new explorer of Chinese cooking to start with a non-stick pan.

Large, deep sauce pan or dutch oven: Used for boiling noodles or making stocks. This pan can also be used as a temporary steamer (See the sketch under "Steamer".)

Medium sauce pan: Used for food that requires slow cooking and does not need a large quantity of liquid, such as stewing, simmering or braising.

Strainer: A shallow round, metal wired (usually copper) strainer with a long bamboo handle is nice to have in the kitchen. It is used as a slotted spoon to drain solid food from liquid or drain oil from deep-fried food. The shallowness of the strainer makes it easy to maneuver and lift whole pieces of meat or poultry from hot water or oil.

Steamer: Nearly all the families in China own one or more sets of steamers but an oven is rare. Most of the steamers were made of bamboo years ago. Metal steamers are becoming more popular since they last longer and are easier to keep clean.

A complete steamer contains a base, which is a large deep sauce pan (the wok serves as base for the bamboo steamer), 2-4 tiers of perforated pans, and a cover.

When steaming food: (1) Fill the sauce pan or wok about 1/3 full of water; cover and bring to a boil. (2) Remove the cover from the sauce pan. Set the tier with the food which is going to be steamed on the sauce pan (or wok). Put the cover on the tier and steam as the recipe requires. You can steam several dishes in separate tiers at the same time, saving both time and fuel.

You can make a temporary steamer from a Dutch oven or any kind of large deep sauce pan. Set a rack in the pan and put the dish of food to be steamed on the rack and steam as directed in the recipe. The rack can be made from 1-3 empty tuna fish or fruit cans with both ends removed. Be sure the water level is 2 or more inches below the food being steamed so that the water is not boiled into the food. There should be enough space to allow the steam to circulate freely. The pan should always be covered while steaming.

Chinese Ingredients, Seasonings, Storage and Substitutes

Abalone: A marine snail, sometimes called ear shell. The muscle, which is the part we use in cooking, is sold in cans or in dried forms. The canned ones are precooked and ready to use. The dried ones must be soaked in warm water for 1-2 hours or until softened. The canned and dried abalone can be kept in a dry place for 1-2 years. There are no substitutes.

Agar-Agar: (Also called Ceylon moss) A dried, treated, translucent seaweed. Very light. Used as unflavored gelatin (it hardens at 85°F) in jellied food or in sweet dishes and salads. Comes in long, thin, opaque strips as noodles or rectangular 1"x1"x12" strips. The former is used in salads. the latter is used as gelatin in desserts. Must be soaked when used in cold salads or melted for dessert or sweet dishes. Sold in packages by weight. Can be kept in a dry place indefinitely. Can be substituted by unflavored gelatin.

Almonds: Used in stir-fried dishes for crunchiness and taste. Toasted almonds (blanched or unblanched) are also used for garnish. Sold fried, toasted or raw in cans or packages in supermarkets.

Baby sweet corn: Midget, tender, young ears of corn about 1½-2" long. Crunchy and sweet tasting. Sold canned. Used in stir-fry mixed vegetable and meat dishes or in soups. After opening the can, transfer the baby corns to a clean jar and keep in refrigerator for 4-5 days. Can be substituted by celery, celery cabbage, or Bok Choy stems.

Bamboo shoots: New shoots of bamboo that sprout from the roots of mature plants. They are eaten as vegetables. They are conical in shape. The ivory-colored edible portion is encased in many layers of husk. It has a fresh delicate vegetable taste. Mainly used for crisp texture in a variety of dishes. The fresh ones are occasionally available in the States. Canned ones are sold in Oriental grocery stores and supermarkets. After opening the can transfer the bamboo shoots to a clean, water-filled covered jar and store in the refrigerator for up to two weeks. Change the water once every two days. It does not freeze well. Can be substituted by celery, cabbage stems, Chinese radishes or turnips etc.

The mature bamboo plant symbolizes nobility and is loved by the Chinese. It is one of the "four gentlemen" of the Chinese floral world (others are chrysanthemums, plum flowers and orchids). Bamboo plant stems probably have more uses than any other plants in the Far East countries.

Bean Curd or To Fu: A highly nutritious vegetable protein made from soybeans. It has a smooth, custard-like texture and is ivory in color. To Fu itself is tasteless but easily absorbs the flavor of other food. It is a very delicate, fragil and perishable food, should be handled gently and with care. The Chinese consumption of bean curd is comparable to the meat that is consumed by the Westerner. It is one of the most important sources of protein in their diet. Bean curd is sold fresh in squares (approximately 1 pound per square) or in cans; also can be home-made (recipe on page 318). It should be stored in a water-filled container in the refrigerator at all times. Change water once every two days. Can be kept for ten days.

Bean Curd, dried or To Fu Gan: Fresh bean curd wrapped in cheese cloth and pressed (to reduce water) into a semi-dried flat cake. Can be braised to make a spicy bean curd cake as a snack. Sliced or shredded dried bean curd is stir-fried with meat and vegetables. Sold in Oriental grocery stores.

Bean Curd, fried: Deep-fried fresh bean curd. It is light brown in color, with a crust-like texture outside; whitish and soft inside. Used in soups, braised with soy sauce and meat, or stuffed with ground meat and vegatables. Sold in Oriental grocery stores or can be homemade. See recipes on page 327 and 330. It is also sold in cans, cooked and flavored, and ready to eat.

Bean curd, fermented: Fresh bean curd fermented with cultured bacteria, then seasoned with salt, spices and wine. The texture of the fermented bean curd resembles soft cheese and even tastes like it too. It is used to cook with meat, fish, chicken and vegetables, or served uncooked as a side dish. It is very popular served with rice porridge in the morning as part of breakfast in China. Available in cans or jars. Can be kept in the refrigerator for months.

Bean curd sticks or sheets, dried: Glazed, cream-colored bean curd sticks or sheets are made from layers of soy milk cream and dried. They are high in fat content and rich in flavor. They should be softened by soaking in warm water before using. The extra tough ones need to be soaked with 1-2 tablespoons of baking soda to reduce toughness. Used in braised meat in soup dishes, or stir-fried with vegatables and meats. Dried bean curd sticks or sheets are sold in packages by weight. Can be stored for months in cupboard. Fresh sheets are paper thin and available occasionally in the States, and can be used for wrapping (dumplings, Spring rolls, etc.) in addition to braising and stir-frying. Fresh ones keep only a few days in the refrigerator.

Beans, salted, or black beans, or fermented black beans: These beans are called *Dow See* in Chinese. Small, cooked, fermented, and highly seasoned black soybeans that have a very strong, pungent flavor. Used to season meat, chicken and seafood. Sold in Oriental grocery stores in cans or in plastic bags. After opening, transfer to a tightly covered jar and store in the refrigerator for months. Can also be frozen; thaw before using. Can be substituted by dark and thick soy sauce and mashed garlic.

Bean sprouts: The young sprouts of mung (green) beans or soybeans. Mung beans are more popular in America and easier to grow than soybean sprouts. They are used as vegetables in salads or in stir-fried dishes with shredded meat and other vegetables. Bean sprouts are sold fresh by weight or in cans in supermarkets or in Oriental grocery stores. Can be substituted by shredded cabbage stems or lettuce stems. I would not substitute canned bean sprouts for fresh ones. The texture and flavor are not the same. Bean sprouts can be grown at home. See *Nutrition and Diet with Chinese Cooking* (recipe on page 185).

Bean paste, salted: Fermented cooked soybeans; has a pungent flavor. Used to enhance or heighten the flavor of meat, poultry, seafood, vegetable or noodle dishes. Sometimes it can be used to preserve cucumbers, eggplant, or cabbage. When diluted, it can be used as a table condiment and dip. Sold in cans in Oriental grocery stores. It can be kept for months in a clean jar after it is opened. Can be substituted by oyster sauce and mashed garlic.

Bean paste, Sichuan: Salty, spicy and hot; made from fermented, cooked fava beans. It is an important ingredient in Sichuan cooking.

Bean paste, sweet: Made from cooked and pureed Chinese small red beans stir-fried with brown sugar and fat. Used for stuffing sweet buns, pastries and sweet desserts. Sold in cans in Oriental grocery stores or can be made at home. See *Nutrition and Diet with Chinese Cooking* (recipe on page 269). Transfer the bean paste to a clean jar after the can is opened and keep in refrigerator for one week or frozen for months. American kidney beans or dried dates can be used as a substitute for Chinese red beans.

Bean curd solidifiers: Calcium chloride, magnesium chloride or epsom salt are three kinds of solidifiers used to make firm bean curd. Sold in drug stores. Calcium sulfate is another kind of bean curd solidifier, makes a softer bean curd. Nigari is a Japanese bean curd solidifier dried from sea water after the sea salt is extracted. It makes firm bean curd also.

Bean threads (cellophane noodles, or Chinese vermicelli noodles): These opaque, fine noodles are made from ground green (mung) beans. They are sold dried in bundles of 1-6 ounce packages in Oriental grocery stores or in some supermarkets. Must be soaked in warm water for half an hour and drained before using. After being soaked the noodles become soft, translucent and gelatinous. They easily absorb the flavors of other ingredients. The dried bean threads can be kept for a long time in a dry place.

Bird's nest: The translucent material from the nest of a special sea swallow or swiftlets. Very rare and expensive. Used for soups and sweets. Bird's nest soup is served only at a formal feast. Bird's nest tastes rather bland but absorbs the flavor of other food easily. Sold dried in many grades in boxes. Must be soaked for a few hours and cleaned carefully before using. There are a few tiny twigs and feathers left in the nest. Dried bird's nest can be kept for years. Soaked ones can be stored in the refrigeratgor for a few days or frozen for months. There are no substitutes.

Chestnuts: The sweet, edible nuts of the chestnut tree. The nut has a prickly bur shell, reddish brown in color. They are sold shelled and dried in Oriental grocery stores. Soak in warm water until softened before using (about 1-2 hours). Adds sweet, rich flavor to braised pork and chicken. Also functions as a thickening agent in cooking liquids. Fresh chestnuts can be used in place of dried ones. Boil the fresh chestnuts in water for 30 minutes and shell before adding to the dish. Dried chestnuts can be kept in a cupboard indefinitely. Can be substituted by cubed potatoes or sweet potatoes as thickening agents.

Chinese cabbage: Celery cabbage, Bok Choy, and Napa are collectively called cabbage in China. The celery cabbage has tightly packed stalks (leaves) somewhat resembling celery. Can be eaten raw for salad or stir-fried with meat and other vegetables. Bok Choy has white, firm, loosely packed stalks and large dark green leaves and cannot be eaten raw. Napa has loosely packed, yellowish green wide leaves. Can be used exactly like celery cabbage. Sold fresh by weight in supermarkets.

Cinnamon stick: A spice that has a pleasant taste and aroma, made from the inner bark of branches of the cinnamon laural tree. Used in braised, slow cooked meat or poultry dishes. Sold in supermarkets in jars or cans.

Cooking fat: See fats on page 15.

Curry powder: A spice mixture originally from India. The Chinese adapted it centuries ago. Used in many chicken, meat and fish dishes. Sold in small jars or cans in the spice section of supermarkets. Also sold by weight in plastic bags in Oriental grocery stores.

Cornstarch: Used to coat meat, chicken and shrimp after marinating with soy sauce and other seasonings. The cornstarch seals in the flavor, protecting the texture as well as preventing splattering while stir-frying. Dredging cornstarch on a whole fish before frying can prevent stickiness and keeps the fish intact.

Cornstarch is also used as a thickening agent to thicken gravy and soup. When used as a thickener, it must be blended with cold water before using to avoid lumps.

Dragon's eyes or Que Yuan: A tropical fruit with a brownish, cinnamon-colored, semi-soft shell about 1" in diameter. The pulp inside the shell is opaque and whitish in color, very juicy and sweet. It has a large black pit. Sold fresh in the summer and eaten as fresh fruit. Also sold dried in Oriental grocery stores whole or pitted. The flesh of the dried ones is dark brown in color. Used in many dessert dishes. Must be soaked before using. *Que Yuan* literally means "prosperous." The Chinese love to serve it at weddings or on lunar New Year's days.

Duck, Peking or roasted: Specially roasted duck served with Chinese pancakes, Hoisin sauce and green onions. Originally from the northern part of China (recipe on page 207).

Duck, salted: Duck preserved in salt and spices. Can be dried. Steamed before serving, or served as flavoring in soups. It can be cooked with other meat and vegetables.

Duck, Sichuan: A famous, spicy duck. First marinated with Sichuan peppercorns, then steamed and deep-fried. Originally from Sichuan. For recipe, see page 199.

Eggs, salted: Eggs preserved by soaking in a salted brine for 1-2 months. Duck eggs are used. Chicken eggs can be substituted.

Eggs, thousand year (rubber egg, pine-flower egg): Preserved duck eggs. The egg is first soaked in a mixture of lime brine, then coated with a layer of husk and clay mixture. The alkali of the lime turns the egg white gelatin-textured and amber-colored. The yolk turns to a soft, cheese-like texture. The light grayish shell and the petrified look of the egg white and yolk give an antique appearance from which the name "thousand year egg" comes. Literally in Chinese, we call it "rubber egg" because the egg white turns rubbery when touched, or "pine-flowered egg" to describe the pine needle shaped sparks which appear in the transparent egg white.

Eggs are served as hors d'oeuvres, a cold dish, appetizers, side dishes for breakfast or cooked and steamed with other ingredients. Remove the clay coating and shell before eating. Eaten uncooked. Sold in Oriental grocery stores. In China these eggs are sold in individual plastic bags with the clay coating already removed. Thousand year eggs can be kept in a cupboard for a month or in the refrigerator for months.

Five-spice powder of five-fragrance powder: Already mixed seasoning containing five ground spices: fennel, star anise, clove, cinnamon, and Sichuan peppercorns. A small quantity is used in meat and poultry dishes. Sold by weight in Oriental stores. Can be kept in a dry place indefinitely. Allspice can be used as a substitute.

Garlic: Bulb of the garlic plant with a strong oniony aroma, used as seasoning in all types of dishes. A favorite seasoning of the Northern Chinese. They eat it raw sometimes. Sold in bulbs. Can be kept for months in a dry place. Leeks, onions can be substituted.

Ginger root, fresh: Brownish-tan-skinned, gnarled, knobby, fibrous root of ginger plant, about 2-3 inches long. Has a pungent, hot, spicy taste. Some people discard the ginger root after cooking before the food is served. It is a popular, all purpose seasoning, and can be added to all types of dishes. The Chinese believe that ginger root aroma can cover up or neutralize the unpleasant odors of fish, shrimp or meats etc. Used in a small amount by slicing, shredding or mincing. When slices are called for in a recipe, they should be thin slices, cut across the grain about ⅛" thick. Ginger root doesn't have to be peeled before using, which will save time and reserve nutrients (peeling the skin before using is perfectly all right). The cutting and peeling surface molds easily. If it molds, cut off the molded surface and use the rest of the root. Sold by weight in most supermarkets, or in Oriental grocery stores. Keeps well for 2-3 weeks in the refrigerator in plastic bags. Can be substituted by dried ginger root (must be soaked before using). Never substitute with ginger powder.

Ginger root shoot (tender or young ginger root): Ivory, pinkish colored new ginger root with crisp, fresh, mild ginger taste. Relatively juicy. Can be eaten raw. Finely shredded ginger root shoot is used in dipping sauce or as a garnish. Sold by weight in super markets or in Oriental grocery stores (occasionally). Can be substituted by regular ginger root.

Gingo nuts: Ivory-colored nut meat of a large ornamental tree of China and Japan. Used in soups, stuffing, stir-fried dishes or in desserts. Dried gingo nuts are beige-colored and sold in Oriental grocery stores by weight. Must be soaked for one or two hours before using. They are also available in cans, ready to use. Can be substituted by garbanzo beans, or lotus seeds.

Hoisin Sauce: A thick, dark brownish-red paste made from fermented ground soybeans and spices. Has a sweetish spicy taste. Used in pork, poultry and seafood dishes, as well as for dipping. Sold in bottles or can. After opening, transfer the paste to a clean container or jar and store in refrigerator, covered. Can be kept for a year.

Jelly fish: Soft, boneless, disk-shaped marine creature. Preserved with salt. Used in cold dishes; has a crunchy texture. Must be soaked and shredded before using. Sold by wieght. Can be frozen.

Lard: A cooking fat that is rendered in the process of cooking pork fat or layered fat that surrounds the organs of the hog. First dice the fat, then heat it in a heavy pan over low heat with a small quantity of water. You may press the fat with the back of a spatula or slotted spoon to speed up the process. The lard results when the fat is melted from the meat. Separate the lard from the meat by skimming or straining through a cheesecloth while it is still liquid and fairly warm. The browned, shrunken meat is called "crackling" and can be used in soups for flavor. Lard can be kept at room temperature, but keeping it in the refrigerator is recommended. It is a popular cooking fat in China because it has a rich, meaty flavor. See *fats* on page 15.

Lily buds or golden needles: Flower buds of lily plant, about 2-3 inches long. Freshly dried lily buds are pale gold-colored and semi-soft-textured. They turn brown and brittle when stored for a long period of time but this will not affect the flavor. Used as a vegetable in stir-fried, steamed or meat dishes, they impart a delicate flavor and chewy texture to the dish. Must be soaked 10-

15 minutes in cold water and the hard stem removed (if there is any) before using. Sold dried by weight in packages. Can be kept in a dry place indefinitely. Fresh lily buds (the special edible kind) can be stir-fried and eaten as a vegetable.

Lime: A strong alkali material used to make thousand year eggs.

Litchi or lychee fruit: A tropical fruit with a semi-hardened, rough, reddish shell about the size of a walnut. The pulp is opaque, whitish, juicy and sweet; the pit is small and dark brown. The fresh and canned ones are used as fruit. The preserved pulp (semi-dried) is used in desserts. Sold,(peeled and pitted) in cans or preserved, in Oriental grocery stores. The preserved pulps are dark brown in color; must be soaked before using. Can be substituted by dried dragon's eyes or Que Yuan.

Lotus leaves: Round, tender leaves of water lily plant. Used both fresh or dried as a wrapping for steamed meat, chicken or rice. Imparts a fresh fragrance to food. Dried leaves are sold in Oriental grocery stores; must be soaked briefly in warm water to make them pliable before using. Dried leaves should be kept in a plastic bag in a dry place. Can be substituted by grape leaves.

Lotus root: The long, ivory-colored root of the water lily plant. Each root contains numerous "sweet-potato shaped" sections linked together. About 2"-2½" in diameter and 6"-8" long in each section. The very young roots are served as a fruit, or used in stir-fried dishes, or pickled in sweet and sour sauce. Older roots are used in soups, braised meat, poultry dishes. Or used as a dessert when cooked with sugar or stuffed with glutinous rice and steamed. The older root has a starchy taste after cooking and must be peeled before using. Available canned or dried in Oriental grocery stores. Dried root must be soaked before using and can be kept in a dry place indefinitely. The fresh ones must be wrapped in a plastic wrapper and refrigerated (will keep 1-2 weeks).

Lotus seeds: Filbert nut-shaped seeds of the water lily plant. After flower petals have fadded, the seeds then mature in a funnel-shaped, spongy bed. The young seeds are juicy and sweet, eaten raw as fruit. The ripened seeds are used to make desserts, sweet fillings or are candied. The phonetic name of the lotus seeds means "two hearts joined together." Chinese people love to use it in wedding banquets to emphasize good wishes. In the States, only the dried ones are obtainable. They are sold in Oriental grocery stores by weight. Can be kept in a dry place indefinitely. Must be soaked before using. Can be substituted by garbanzo beans.

Monosodium glutamate (flavoring powder, MSG, Accent): A white crystaline powder manufactured from bacterial fermentation of sugar and plant protein. It is a food additive used to enhance flavor but no significant flavor of its own. Sold in supermarkets in cans and jars under different brand names. (Please see the special section on MSG in Christine Liu's *Nutrition and Diet with Chinese Cooking* pages 7-9).

Mung beans (green beans): Avocado-greenish-colored, tiny dried beans, used to grow bean sprouts. Ground mung beans are used to make bean thread, green-bean gelatin or cakes. Sold by weight in supermarkets or Oriental grocery stores.

Mushrooms, black, dried (Chinese mushrooms, winter mushrooms, flower mushrooms): The Chinese call this brownish dried mushroom "winter mushroom," but it is not necessarily grown in the winter time. From my childhood memories, the dark brown, savory mushroom was served in a rich, tasty hot soup in the bitter winter season more than any other time of the year. Maybe this is the reason called winter mushroom. People in China also call it "fragrant mushroom," to describe the strong mushroomy flavor. There are different kinds and sizes (The caps are from ½"-3" in diameter and ¼"-¾" thick). The large ones which are light brown-colored, thick, with a cracked surface and curled edges, sometimes called "flower mushroom" are considered the best. Sold in Oriental grocery stores. The dried mushroom can be kept in a covered jar in a dry place indefinitely. It should be soaked in warm water for half an hour, or until it becomes spongy, before using. The water used for soaking can be used in soups or other dishes. It will add a subtle mushroom flavor. Can be substituted by fresh mushrooms.

Mushrooms, grasses (straw mushrooms): Tall, thin, umbrella shaped small mushrooms. The black caps are about 1" in diameter. Used in stir-fried dishes. They have a subtle, fresh taste, crisp texture. Sold in cans in Oriental stores. Can be substituted by fresh mushrooms. Dried straw mushrooms come in broken pieces, and are available in Oriental stores. Must be soaked for 30 minutes in warm water before using.

Mustard green: The typical Chinese mustard green is a large, jade green cabbage with thick, lightly curved, tightly packed stems and fan-like leaves. Used in stir-fried dishes and soups. It has a slightly bitter taste and strong fragrance. The Chinese believe that the mustard green cools the body's system and they love it in the summer time.

Mustard green, pickled (sour cabbage, salted cabbage): Fresh Chinese mustard green dried under the sun, semi-dried first, then mixed with salt. Packed firmly in a crock or wooden barrel. Place a weight on the vegetable so that the juice of the vegetable comes up to serve as a brine. The mustard is fermented in the brine for a period of time. The pickled mustard is turned mustard yellow in color and slightly sour in taste (resembles german sauerkraut).Used in stir-fried dishes, soups, noodles. Very tasty. Sold directly from pickling barrel, or in cans and jars. After opening, can be kept for 10 days in refrigerator.

Mustard sauce (mustard dipping): Used as a table condiment, especially for deep-fried food. Made by blending English mustard powder, vinegar, salt and water. Recipe on page 339. Blended sauce can be kept in the refrigerator for weeks.

Napa: See Chinese cabbage.

Noodles, Chinese: The Chinese have used flour as a basis for noodles for centuries. It has been said that Italian pastas were introduced by Marco Polo after his visit to China. However, Chinese noodles are mostly flat and whiter than spaghetti. Used in stir-fried dishes, soups, with vegetables, eggs, meats. Served as a whole meal, part of a meal, or a snack. It is customary with the Chinese to use freshly-made long noodles as a birthday gift. Noodles are served at the birthday party, since the "length" of the noodles is a symbol of longevity and endurance. Sold fresh (soft) or dried in Oriental grocery stores or in some supermarkets. The fresh noodles can be kept for a few days in the refrigerator and can be made at home (recipe on p. 358). Thin spaghetti can be substituted for Chinese noodles.

Noodles, egg: Made with wheat flour and eggs. Used mostly in deep-fried noodle dishes. They have a crunchy texture and nice brownish color after being deep-fried. Sold fresh or dried in Oriental grocery stores. Can be homemade (recipe on page 358). Dried or frozen egg noodles can be substituted for Chinese egg noodles.

Noodles, rice: Thin, brittle, opaque noodles made from cooked, pounded, long grain rice. Loose packed in large yarn-like bundles, or in 1-pound packages. Must be soaked before cooking. Used in stir-fried dishes or soups and have a distinctive texture and flavor. A non-stick pan is recommended if stir-frying the noodle, because it is very sticky. Served as whole meal, snack, or as one course of a meal. Sold dried in Oriental-grocery stores. Can be kept in a dry place indefinitely. Also used deep-fried for garnishing. (For use as a garnish, do not soak the noodles before deep-frying).

Noodles, rice stick: (Ho Fun) Dried, semi-transparent, about ¼" wide, flat noodles made from rice. Used in stir-fried dishes and seasoned with soy sauce. Must be soaked before using. Sold in Oriental grocery stores.

Orange peel, dried: Sold in Chinese herb medicine drug stores or in Oriental grocery stores. Used as a flavoring in some meat, poultry and soup dishes. Made from tangerine peels. Can be home dried.

Oyster, dried: Dark brown-colored dried oyster with a strong taste of smoked oyster flavor. Very delicious when used in braised pork, fried bean curd, and fried wheat gluten. Also can be steamed and stir-fired with vegetables and meat. Must be soaked and cleaned before using. Sold by weight in box or in packages. Can be kept for months in a dry cupboard.

Oyster sauce: A thick, dark brown sauce made from soy sauce and oysters cooked together. It intensifies the flavor of meat, poultry, and even vegetables. Used the same way as soy sauce. The oyster sauce is saltier and tastier. Reduce the quantity when substituting the oyster sauce for soy sauce. Sold in cans and bottles in Oriental grocery stores. Will keep indefinitely in a cupboard.

Parsley, Chinese (coriander, fragrant vegetable): Small, pale green plant with delicate, willowy stems and flat, serrated, fan-like leaves about 4 to 5 inches long. Has a distinctive aroma. Used for garnishing cold dishes, soups etc. Sold fresh by weight in supermarkets or Oriental grocery stores. Will keep 3 to 5 days in the refrigerator.

Pepper, black and white: Hot, spicy, ground peppercorn powder used in all types of dishes as a seasoning. Should be used sparingly. Sold in cans or jars in supermarkets.

Pepper, red and hot: (chili) Small, hot red peppers used in stir-fried or braised dishes. It is the most favorable seasoning of Hunan and Sichuan provinces. Sold whole, fresh or dried, or in dried flakes. The green and yellow hot peppers can be substituted.

Pepper, Sichuan: (See page 47)

Radish: A plant grown for its edible root. There are different varieties with roots which vary in shape, size and color. Those most grown in the United States are spring radishes. In China and Japan, people grow a winter radish called Ro Bo or Daikon.It is white in color, 2"-4" in diameter and 10"-20" long. Used in stir-fried, braised dishes and soups. It is also a favorite vegetable for making pickles. The leaves, rich in Vit. C, A, calcium and iron, are slightly bitter. Can be used in stir-fried dishes.

Red dates, dried (jujubees): A dark-red-colored, oblong-shaped fruit about 1" long, eaten as fruit when it is fresh. Dried ones are used in soups, fish, rice porridge, dessert fillings and also as a garnish. The phonetic name of the date is "having a son as quick as possible." The Chinese serve it at wedding parties to express good wishes, since they favor boys. Must be soaked before using. Sold in Oriental grocery stores by weight. Can be kept in a dry place for years.

Rice, glutinous (sweet rice, sticky rice): Opaque, pearly white, short-grained rice. Becomes very sticky and glutinous after cooking. Used mostly in sweet dishes and desserts. Also used as stuffing for duck and chicken, steamed with meat etc. Served especially in the wedding banquet. The stickiness of the rice gives good wishes to the newlyweds so that they will stick together forever. Ground glutinous rice powder is used for steamed cake and other desserts.It is sold in Oriental grocery stores. Can be kept in a dry place for two years.

Rice powder, spicy (five-spice rice powder): Toasted long grain rice, coarsely ground. Mixed with five-spice powder and salt. Used for steamed meat or chicken. Can be homemade (recipe on page 311). Also available in Oriental grocery stores and sold by weight. Can be kept in a dry place for months.

Sea cucumber or beche-de-mer: A cucumber-shaped, small creature of the sea, 2" – 8" in length. The Chinese consider it a great delicacy. It is served only on special occasions. Sold dried by weight, either whole or in segments. Dark gray or black in color, smooth or spiny in appearance. After soaking it expands to 2 to 3 times its original dried shape and becomes very soft. Used in stir-fried, braised or soup dishes. Dried sea cucumber can be kept for years. Soaked sea cucumber can be kept in clean water in refrigerator for one week, or frozen for months (water drained).

Seaweed (dried purple vegetable): The most commonly used seaweed in soups, salads or as a garnish. It is conveniently prepared in the form of paper-thin, purplish-black sheets, each about 8 inches square and ready to add to dishes without cooking. It is rich in minerals. Sold in Oriental grocery stores by weight. Can be kept in a dry place for years.

Seaweed, rope (sea rope, sea kelp): A greenish-black, flat, long, belt-like seaweed (about 3-6 inches wide and 2 to 6 feet long), used sliced or shredded, in stir-fried or soup dishes. Sold dried in Oriental grocery stores. Must be soaked before using. It doubles in size after soaking and has a fishy smell. It has a slippery texture and is very rich in iodine. Dried seaweed can be kept for years in a dry place. Soaked seaweed can be kept in the refrigerator for one week or frozen for months.

Sesame oil: A strong, aromatic, nutty-flavored, amber-colored oil made from toasted sesame seeds. Used sparingly as flavoring. Adds a delicate taste to any dish. Absolutely not to be used for cooking. Sold in bottles or cans in different sizes in supermarkets or in Oriental grocery stores. Can be kept in well sealed container in cupboard for 1 year.

Sesame seeds: Tiny, flat seeds used for garnishing as well as for flavoring on cookies, steamed cakes, candies or pastries. There are two kinds; black and white. Black ones are used mostly for garnish. Sold in cans, jars or loose by weight. Can be kept in a dry place indefinitely.

Sesame paste: Made from toasted, ground sesame seeds. Has a strong, nutty flavor, but is different from "tahiini" of Middle East. Used in salads, cold dishes or desserts. Sold in cans or bottles in Oriental grocery stores. Can be homemade (recipe on page 315). Will keep for months in the refrigerator.

Shark's fins: A rare delicacy, used in thick, rich stock. Served at special occasions or banquets. Tasty, thread-like and translucent after cooking. There are two kinds sold in Oriental grocery stores. One is loose needles packed in boxes by weight. The other is with needles intact. Both should be soaked before using.

Shrimp chips: Made from a dough of minced shrimp paste, cornstarch, and baking powder, sliced into thin pieces and dried. Deep-fried before serving. Will expand 2-3 times after frying. Resembles potato chips. Serve as garnish on deep-fried dishes or as a snack. Comes in white, pink and green color. Sold in packages by weight. Can be kept indefinitely.

Shrimp, dried: Shelled, dried shrimp in various sizes. Used in stir-fried vegetables and meat dishes to enhance flavor. Sometimes minced and mixed in ground meat (usually, pork) to make meat balls or meat dumpling fillings. Must be soaked before using. Soaking water can be added to soups or gravies. The flavor of the soups and gravies will be enhanced by the shrimp taste. Sold by weight and will keep for months in a dry place in a plastic bag or in a covered jar. There is a very tiny-sized baby shrimp, dried and unshelled, which can be eaten shell and all. Provides a good source of calcium as well as protein in the diet. Can be cooked the same way as shelled dried shrimp.

Shrimp egg soy sauce: A special soy sauce made from cooking shrimp eggs and soy sauce together. It is very tasty, with a delicate shrimp flavor. Can be used in cooking as soy sauce or as a table condiment. Sold in bottles in Oriental grocery stores.

Shrimp paste: Thick, reddish-brown fermented shrimp meat with a strong, pungent aroma. Very salty. Used to enhance the flavor of some stir-fried dishes, and as a table condiment or eaten with rice congee for breakfast. Sold in plastic containers or jars. Will keep a year in the refrigerator. Fermented bean curd can be substituted for shrimp paste.

Sichuan peppercorn: A famous spice originated from Sichuan province. It looks like black peppercorn but is brownish in color and lighter in weight. It has a hollow shell outside and a tough seed inside. Has a very pleasant aroma and mild hot flavor. Used in stir-fried, braised meat and poultry dishes. Also used in Sichuan pickles or for table condiments when ground. Sold in Oriental grocery stores. Will keep indefinitely. No substitutes.

Store Sichuan peppercorn in a basket (or similar container). Do not store in an airtight container or plastic bag. It will lose its flavor without proper circulation.

Snow pea pods (sugar peas): Pale green, flat, crisp young pea pods. A special variety of Chinese origin. Grows very well in the mid-west in the summer. Only a short time is needed to stir-fry and retain the tender, fresh taste and color. Snap off both ends then eat the peas, pods and all. Sold year around in supermarkets. Fresh pea pods will keep for a week in the refrigerator in a plastic wrapper. Frozen pea pods are also available in 10 oz boxes and can be substituted occasionally.

Sodium hydroxide (caustic soda): A strong alkaline chemical used to make thousand-year eggs.

Soy milk: The liquid extract from soaked and ground soybeans. It is the basic material for making bean curd. Also used in other dishes. Very nutritious. Some people use it as a milk substitute if they are allergic to cow's milk.

Soy sauce: A brownish, salty liquid made from fermented cooked soybeans, flour and salt mixture. It is an important and basic seasoning in Chinese cooking. An essential ingredient in 90% of Chinese dishes. It comes in many different types and grades, from thin to thick, light brown to dark. Light-colored soy sauce is thin and delicate and used for flavor. Dark-colored soy sauce is used for color in braised meat and poultry dishes. Both types can be used for gravies, dippings, sauces, soups and marinades. Either soy sauce can be substituted for the other. Good quality, which is made by natural processes, is extremely important. Some soy sauces on the market are a mixture of chemicals and should not be used in Chinese cooking as they will ruin the flavor of the whole dish. Chinese soy sauces that are imported from China are available in Oriental grocery stores. Some domestic-made soy sauces such as La Choy, Chung King or Kikkoman are fairly good. They are available in supermarkets and come in bottles or cans. A small quantity of instant-beef bouillon may be substituted for soy sauce in an emergency.

Squid, dried: Squid preserved by salt and dehydration. Flattened, brownish-colored with a thin layer of salt dust on the surface. Used in quick stir-fried dishes or in soups. Must be soaked in water with 2-3 tablespoons of soda for 1-2 days, or until it is softened. Before using, soak the softened squid in clean water for one day and change water several times in order to get rid of the alkline from the soda. Follow the recipes on how to cut before using. No substitutes.

Star anise: Dried, brownish-colored seeds. The whole star anise contains 6-8 cloves clustered together and shaped like a pointed star. A popular spice used in braised meat and poultry dishes. Sold by weight in Oriental grocery stores. Will keep indefinitely. Cinnamon sticks may be substituted in rare cases.

Stock: Good stocks are the bases of soups, sauces and liquid called for in various dishes. It is made from odds and ends of meat, poultry and bones through slow cooking or simmering. Strain stock through cheese cloth, discard the solids, then season with salt and spices. Good cooks, before MSG and bouillon were invented, always kept a pot of stock at hand to imporve the flavor of the dishes. Can be substituted by canned chicken or beef broth or bouillons.

Taro: Root of taro plant: There are different varieties. They range from small potato-shaped ones to 5"-6" round roots. The small ones are light brown in color; used in stir-fried, braised dishes or in soups. The large ones are reddish in color; used in steamed meats, as desserts or sweet pastry fillings. Sold fresh in some Oriental grocery stores. Will keep a few days in the refrigerator.

Turnips: See radishes.

Vinegar: There are different kinds and qualities of vinegars in China, made from rice wine. They can be sharp, rich, mellow, or light. Also, they come in different colors: clear, red, or black. The best and most famous one is from *Tian-Jing* in the north and which have a rich aroma, has a pungent taste and is dark-reddish in color. Used in sweet and sour dishes, for dipping or as a table condiment. Available in bottles in Oriental grocery stores. Cider vinegar can be substituted.

Water Chestnuts or Ma Ti: Literally "horse hooves" because of the shape and color. The plant grows in a water-flooded field. The edible portion is the root bulb of the plant, about one inch in diameter with a dark brownish skin and white meat. The fresh water chestnuts are available in Oriental grocery stores or supermarkets and are usually covered with mud in order to prevent drying. When the skins are wrinkled, this means the water chestnuts might have been kept on the shelf too long and sometimes are rotten inside. The young, tender water chestnuts are eaten as fruit. The mature ones are used as vegetables in stir-fried dishes, soups or in desserts. Canned water chestnuts are available in supermarkets and Oriental grocery stores. They are peeled and ready to use. After opening, transfer the water chestnuts to a clean, water-filled jar, and store in the refrigerator up to 3 weeks. Change water once every two days. Never freeze water chestnuts. Peeled turnips or radishes can be substituted when cut into 1" round thin pieces.

Water-chestnut flour: Ground fine powder from dried water chestnuts. Used in desserts, water-chestnut tea or steamed cakes, etc. Sold in packages in Oriental grocery stores. No substitutes. Water-chestnut flour can be used to make batter for deep-fried food. If this is the case, cornstarch or flour can be substituted.

Watermelon seeds: Dried, toasted watermelon seeds of special varieties. The seeds are about 1/3" wide, black or dark gray in color. The meat of the seeds has a nutty flavor. Used as snacks accompanied by tea or in sweet dishes after shelled. When eaten as a snack, the Chinese shell the seeds with their teeth.

Winter melon: Large, long melon with a pale-green skin. It resembles watermelon but has a tougher skin and a frosty, white powder on the surface. The edible portion is the snow white, pulpy-textured layer (about 1½" thick), underneath the skin. The seeds, embedded in the spongey yellowish tissue in the center of the melon should be discaded. Winter melon is used in soups, braised meat or dried shrimp. Occasionally used in stir-fried dishes. Sold fresh in Oriental grocery stores whole or in wedges. Can be kept in the refrigerator for a few days when covered with a plastic wrap. Some Chinese believe that the Winter melon cools the body and is an excellent food to be eaten in the summer time.

Wood ears, cloud ears, or tree fungus: Small dried black or dark brown colored, irregular shaped fungus which is grown on trees. After soaking it expands 4-5 times its original size. Used in soups and stir-fried dishes. It adds a pleasant crunchy texture. Put in dishes at the last minute to assure crunchiness. Sold in Oriental grocery stores by weight. Can be kept in a dry place indefinitely. Soak in warm water for at least 10 minutes and then rinse before using. No substitute.

There are other kinds of wood ears. Some are large and grayish in color. Others are large, black in color, mostly from Japan. They are very tough and must be soaked and simmered for 1 hour (or until softened) before using.

Wood ears, white or silver ears or snow ears: An opaque, cream-colored fungus. Larger than black wood ears. Softer in texture after soaking. Becomes gelatinous after cooking. Used in sweets and desserts. Sold in Oriental grocery stores. There is a new instant silver ear for dessert. It is produced and processed in China and is an excellent product.

soup

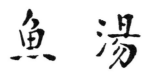

Ingredients:

- 1 T sherry
- ½ t pepper
- ½ t onion power
- ½ t salt
- 2 T cornstarch
- ½ lb fish fillet
- 2 T cornstarch blended with ¼ C of water
- 1 green onion, minced
- 1 oz minced ham
- 2 T oil
- 1 t ginger root
- ¼ lb fresh mushrooms, washed and diced
- ½ C frozen peas and carrots
- ½ C diced bamboo shoot
- 3½ C water
- 3 chicken bouillon cubes

Method:

1. Cut fish into 1" x 2" pieces. Gently mix the fish with the first 4 ingredients in a bowl. Coat with 2 T cornstarch before cooking.

2. Heat oil in a pan or wok; saute ginger root. Add the last 5 ingredients and bring to a boil.

3. Add fish; bring to a boil. Stir gently while cooking.

4. Add blended cornstarch and cook until the sauce thickens. Pour into a large soup bowl and sprinkle minced onion and ham on the soup before serving.

Makes 4-6 servings.

Calories: 747	Iron: 3mg
Carbohydrates: 48gm	Vit. B1: 0.49mg
Protein: 52gm	Vit. B2: 0.77mg
Fat: 36gm	Vit. A: 6910IU
Cholesterol: 238mg	Vit. C: 21mg
Calcium: 64mg	Fiber: 3gm

DRIED SCALLOP SOUP
(Gan Bei Xue Huan Tang)

千貝雪花湯

Ingredients:

3 oz	dried scallops
3 C	hot water
1 T	cornstarch blended with 1 T water
3	slices of ginger root
	Minced coriander for garnishing
1 T	sesame oil
1	egg white, beaten
½ C	shredded bamboo shoot
1 oz	old-fashioned country-style ham, shredded
1/3 t	pepper
2	green onions, minced
1 t	vinegar
2 t	instant chicken bouillon

Method:

1. Soak the dried scallops in hot water for 2 hours or until softened. Drain, but reserve the water.

2. Tear the scallops by hand into fine shreds.

3. Place the scallops in a sauce pan; add reserved water and ginger root with additional water to make 3 C. Cover pan and bring to a boil. Reduce to low heat and simmer for 30 minutes.

4. Add the last 6 ingredients and bring to a boil.

5. Stir in egg white and blended cornstarch; bring to a boil.

6. Stir in sesame oil, then pour the soup into a tureen. Garnish with coriander. Serve hot.

Makes 4-6 servings.

Calories: 474	Iron: 5mg
Carbohydrate: 20gm	Vit. B1: 0.11mg
Protein: 46gm	Vit. B2: 0.20mg
Fat: 22gm	Vit. A: 413IU
Cholesterol: 199mg	Vit. C: 9mg
Calcium: 84mg	Fiber: 1gm

SEA CUCUMBER SOUP
(Hui Hai Sen)

Ingredients:

¼ lb	dried sea cucumber or 1½ C soaked, ready to cook sea cucumber
1/3 lb	chicken breast sliced
1 T	soy sauce
⅛ t	pepper
¼ t	onion or garlic powder
1 t	sherry
1 t	cornstarch
1½ T	cornstarch blended with 1 T water
2-4 T	chopped coriander
1 T	sesame oil
½ C	frozen peas, thawed
2 oz	old-fashioned, country-style ham, thinly sliced
2 C	water
2 t	instant chicken bouillon
1 T	sherry
¼ t	pepper
1 t	vinegar
½ t	sugar
2	green onions, minced
1 C	sliced bamboo shoots

Method:

1. Place ¼ lb dried sea cucumber in a sauce pan and add enough water to cover. Cover pan and bring to a boil. Turn off heat and let the sea cucumber remain in the water for 6 hours. Change water and repeat the same procedure 2-3 times until the sea cucumber has expanded and becomes soft. Wash and discard the loose material from inside of the sea cucumber. Cut the sea cucumber into 2"x½" pieces. Blanch in boiling water for few minutes. Rinse and drain.

2. Mix the chicken slices with the next 5 ingredients. Set aside.

3. Place the sea cucumber in a sauce pan; add the last 8 ingredients and bring to a boil.

4. Add ham and bring to a boil. Add chicken breast and bring to a boil.

5. Add peas and blended cornstarch; bring to a boil.

6. Transfer to a tureen; sprinkle on sesame oil and chopped coriander and serve immediately.

Makes 4-6 servings.

Calories: 545	Iron: 4mg
Carbohydrates: 30gm	Vit. B1: 0.34mg
Protein: 47gm	Vit. B2: 0.36mg
Fat: 25gm	Vit. A: 1137IU
Cholesterol: 121mg	Vit. C: 21mg
Calcium: 54mg	Fiber: 2gm

Sea cucumber is not included in this calculation (see page 10).

With the exception of the newly added Rice Noodle section, the nutritional calculations of all the recipes in this book are for **the whole recipe,** not per serving.

DICED SEA CUCUMBER SOUP
(Hai Sen Nong Tang)

Ingredients:

¼ lb	dried sea cucumber or 1½ C soaked and cleaned sea cucumber
½ C	diced bamboo shoots
4	dried mushrooms, soaked and diced
3 t	instant chicken bouillon
3 C	water
1 T	vinegar
¼ t	pepper
2½ T	cornstarch blended with 2 T water
2 T	oil
½	onion, minced
1 t	minced ginger root
½ C	diced pork mixed with ¼ t salt and ½ t cornstarch
2	green onions, minced
1 t	sesame oil

Method:

1. Place the sea cucumber in a sauce pan and add enough water to cover. Cover pan and bring to a boil. Turn off the heat and let the sea cucumber remain in the water for a few hours. Repeat the same procedure several times until the sea cucumber has expanded and becomes soft.

2. Wash and discard the loose material inside the soaked sea cucumber.

3. Dice the sea cucumber and scald in hot water for 2 minutes. Rinse and drain.

4. Heat oil in a sauce pan; stir-fry pork with onion and ginger root until onion softens.

5. Add the first 8 ingredients; cook until the sauce thickens. Stir while cooking.

6. Add green onions and sesame oil; stir. Serve hot.

Makes 4-6 servings.

Calories: 513	Iron: 2mg
Carbohydrates: 26gm	Vit. B1: 0.68mg
Protein: 15gm	Vit. B2: 0.26mg
Fat: 39gm	Vit. A: 425IU
Cholesterol: 36mg	Vit. C: 12mg
Calcium: 34mg	Fiber: 1gm

Sea cucumber is not included in this calculation (see page 10).

STEAMED SHARK'S FIN THICK SOUP
(Ji Zhi Pai Chi)

Ingredients:

½ lb	whole piece (not the loose needles) shark's fin
½	chicken, cut (bone and all) into 2" pieces
¼ lb	old-fashioned country-style ham, diced
½ lb	pork, cut into 1" cubes
1	onion, quartered
5	slices of ginger root
5	dried mushrooms, soaked
1 T	cornstarch blended with 1 T water
2 t	sesame oil
	Minced coriander leaves for garnishing
	Salt, pepper and vinegar to taste
1½ C	water (liquid that is reserved from steaming the shark's fin)
2 t	instant chicken bouillon
1 T	sherry
½ t	pepper
½ t	sugar

Method:

1. Soak the shark's fin in plenty of water overnight. Wash with a brush to remove all the sand or dirt if there is any.

2. Place the shark's fin in a sauce pan, fill with water 3" above the fin, cover and bring to a boil. Turn to low heat and cook for 1 hour. Rinse and drain.

3. Put the shark's fin in a deep heat-proof bowl; add the next 6 ingredients to the fin. Set the bowl in a boiling steamer and steam for 3-4 hours or until the fin is softened.

4. Reserve the liquid from the steamed shark's fin in a small bowl. Discard the chicken, ham, pork, onion, and ginger root. Quarter the mushrooms. Keep the shark's fin hot.

5. Measure 1½ C reserved liquid from Step 4 (if not enough, add water to make up 1½ C) and pour into a sauce pan. Add the last 4 ingredients and bring to a boil. Add mushroom quarters, blended cornstarch and sesame oil; cook until the sauce thickens.

6. Transfer the steamed shark's fin to a serving platter. Pour the sauce over the shark's fin and garnish with coriander. Serve hot. Makes 4-6 servings.

Calories:	1720	Iron:	19mg
Carbohydrates:	17gm	Vit. B1:	2.5mg
Protein:	191gm	Vit. B2:	3.1mg
Fat:	91gm	Vit. A:	4928IU
Cholesterol:	584mg	Vit. C:	6mg
Calcium:	121mg	Fiber:	0

Shark's fin is not included in this calculation. See page 10.

酸辣湯

SOUR AND HOT SOUP
(Suan La Tang)

Ingredients:

⅛ lb	shredded pork or more
1 T	soy sauce
⅛ t	pepper
⅛ t	onion powder
1 t	sherry
1 t	cornstarch
4	chicken bouillon cubes
4 C	water
1 T	dried black wood ears
20	dried lily buds
2-3	dried mushrooms
¼ C	shredded bamboo shoots
½ lb	bean curd, shredded
1	egg, beaten
2 T	vinegar
2 T	cornstarch blended with 4 T water
1 t	sesame oil or more
¼ t	pepper or more
1 t	hot pepper sauce or oil (optional)
1	green onion, minced

Method:

1. Mix pork with the next 5 ingredients. Set aside.
2. Soak the wood ears, lily buds and mushrooms in hot water in separate bowls for 40 minutes. Wash the wood ears and lily buds.
3. Cut the wood ears and mushrooms in shreds. Have the lily buds knotted, (see below).
4. Place the bouillon and water in a deep sauce pan or wok; cover and bring to a boil.
5. Add pork, wood ears, lily buds, mushrooms and bamboo shoots; bring to a boil.
6. Add bean curd shreds; bring to a boil.
7. Stir in 2 T vinegar and blended cornstarch; cook until the sauce thickens.
8. Reduce to low heat and stir in beaten egg, 1 t sesame oil, hot sauce and ¼ t pepper.
9. Pour into a tureen; sprinkle the minced green onion on the soup and serve hot.

Makes 4-6 servings.

Calories: 535
Carbohydrate: 31gm
Protein: 37gm
Fat: 32gm

There is no nutrition information available on wood ears, lily buds etc. So this calculation is not complete. See page 10.

59

黄瓜湯

Ingredients:

¼ lb   pork butt or chicken breast, thinly sliced
1 T   soy sauce
⅛ t   onion or garlic powder
⅛ t   pepper
1 t   minced ginger root
1 t   sherry
1 t   cornstarch
1   cucumber
4 C   water
3   chicken bouillon cubes
1   green onion, minced
1 t   sesame oil or more

Method:

1. Mix the meat with the next 6 ingredients. Set aside.

2. Peel cucumber and split into halves. Spoon out the seedy portion and cut the cucumber into slices.

3. Place the water, bouillon and cucumber slices in a sauce pan; cover and bring to a boil.

4. Add meat slices one by one, stir and bring to a boil.

5. Reduce heat to medium and cook for 5 minutes. Pour the soup into a tureen and sprinkle the sesame oil and minced onion on the soup. Serve hot.

Makes 4-6 servings.

Calories: 296	Iron: 6mg
Carbohydrate:11gm	Vit. B1: 1mg
Protein: 26gm	Vit. B2: 0.37mg
Fat: 16gm	Vit. A: 717IU
Cholesterol: 80mg	Vit. C: 25mg
Calcium: 80mg	Fiber: 1gm

BEAN CURD SOUP
(Dou Fu Tang)

Ingredients:

½ lb   bean curd, sliced (2"x1"x½")
¼ lb   lean pork butt or chicken breast, sliced (2"x1"x1/8")
1 T   soy sauce
⅛ t   onion or garlic powder
⅛ t   pepper
1 t   sherry
1 t   cornstarch
3 t   instant chicken bouillon
3 C   water
3   slices of ginger root
3-4   dried mushrooms, soaked and sliced (optional)
¼-½ C   sliced bamboo shoot (optional)
¼ lb   or more, celery cabbage or spinach, cut into ½" sections
1 t   sesame oil (optional)

Method:

1. Mix meat with the next 5 ingredients. Set aside.
2. Place the chicken bouillon with the next 4 ingredients in a sauce pan, cover and bring to a boil.
3. Add meat slices one by one; bring to a boil.
4. Add bean curd slices; bring to a boil.
5. Add vegetables and bring to a boil. Pour the soup into a tureen; sprinkle in sesame oil and serve hot.
This soup can be thickened with 1 T blended cornstarch before serving.
Makes 4-6 servings.

Calories:	398	Iron:	9mg
Carbohydrate:	13gm	Vit. B1:	1.2mg
Protein:	43gm	Vit. B2:	0.4mg
Fat:	20gm	Vit. A:	168IU
Cholesterol:	80mg	Vit. C:	16mg
Calcium:	359mg	Fiber:	1gm

三鲜锅巴

THREE-GEM SIZZLING RICE SOUP
(San Xian Guo Ba Tang)

Ingredients:

2 oz	shelled shrimp, split in half lengthwise
2 oz	chicken breasts, sliced
2 oz	pork loin, sliced
	Onion or garlic powder
	Salt
	Pepper
	Sherry
	Cornstarch
	½ recipe of crisp rice (recipe on page 309)
	Oil for deep-frying, about 1 cup
½ C	chopped onion
3	slices of ginger root
4	cloves of garlic, crushed
2 T	cornstarch, blended with ¼ C of water
½ C	frozen peas, thawed or 10-15 snow pea pods, cleaned
4	dried mushrooms, soaked and sliced or ⅛ lb fresh mushrooms, sliced
½ C	thinly sliced carrots
¼ C	sliced water chestnuts
2 t	instant chicken bouillon dissolved in 2 cups of water
2 T	soy sauce
1 t	sugar
2 T	vinegar
¼ t	pepper
2 t	sesame oil
1 C	shredded celery cabbage (optional)

Method:

1. Mix the shrimp with a pinch of onion powder, salt, pepper, sherry and cornstarch. Treat the chicken and pork in the same manner. Set aside.

2. Heat oil in a pan or wok; deep-fry the rice until crisp and crunchy. Keep hot. (If the rice is not hot enough, there will be no sizzling sound.)

3. Pour off all the oil except 2 T; saute onion, ginger root and garlic. Add pork; stir-fry for 1 minute. Add chicken and shrimp; stir-fry with the pork for 1 minute. Remove.

4. Add the last 10 ingredients to the pan; bring to a boil. Add blended cornstarch and bring to a boil.

5. Add cooked shrimp, chicken, pork, peas and bring to a boil. Pour over the hot-fried rice and serve immediately.

Fry the crisp rice just before the sauce is ready. You will get better results.

Makes 6 servings.

Calories:	1389	Iron:	10mg
Carbohydrates:	127gm	Vit. B1:	1.4mg
Protein:	49gm	Vit. B2:	0.9mg
Fat:	75gm	Vit. A:	6300IU
Cholesterol:	157mg	Vit. C:	49mg
Calcium:	200mg	Fiber:	4gm

Calculated with 2 T oil for deep-frying.

WONTON SOUP
(Hung Dun Tang)

馄 饨 湯

Ingredients:

For Fillings
I.

½ lb	ground beef or pork
½ C	coarsely chopped water chestnuts
2 oz	fresh mushrooms, minced, or 2-3 dried mushrooms, soaked and minced
½	onion, minced
1 t	sherry
2 t	finely minced ginger root
¼ t	pepper
1 t	salt
⅛ t	MSG (optional)

II.
- ¼ lb   ground pork
- ¼ lb   shelled shrimp, fresh or frozen, minced
- ½ C   bamboo shoot, minced
- ¼ lb   fresh mushrooms, minced, or 2-3 dried mushrooms, soaked and minced
- ½   onion, minced
- 1 t   sherry
- 1 t   salt
- 2 t   minced ginger root
- ¼ t   pepper
- ⅛ t   MSG (optional)

Seasoned chicken broth, canned
Minced green onions and sesame oil for garnishing
1 pound of Wonton wrappers, home made (recipe on page 343) or ready made from grocery stores at produce sections, about 70-80 per pound. A few spinach leaves, bamboo slices, celery cabbage shreds, greens pea and carrots or meat shreds can be added to the broth before serving (optional).

Method:

Choose either filling I or II for your Wonton soup.

1. Combine all the ingredients in a bowl; mix thoroughly.

2. Put ½ t filling in the center of the skin and fold it up. (See instructions on page 344).

3. Boil 3 cups of chicken broth in a sauce pan. Add 20 Wontons; cover and bring to a boil.

4. Add ¾ C cold water; cover and bring to a boil once more. (Add vegetables)

5. Turn off heat and let the Wontons remain in the covered pan for two minutes.

6. Divide the soup into 4 portions; garnish with minced green onions and few drops of sesame oil before serving. Serve hot. Wonton soup can be served as lunch or as a snack. Each bowl of Wonton soup contains 10-12 Wontons when served as lunch.

To freeze the wrapped Wontons: Arrange the Wontons on a tray and keep in the freezer, uncovered, overnight. Carefully remove the frozen Wontons to a plastic bag; seal and keep frozen. The frozen Wontons can be kept for three months in the freezer and they can be used without thawing.

Calories: 1583   Carbohydrates: 188gm
Protein: 73gm   Fat: 56gm

Calculated with Filling I and one pound of Wonton skin only. Each Wonton contains approximately 21 calories.

EGG DROP SOUP
(Dan Hua Tang)

Ingredients:

2	eggs, beaten with a little salt
3	chicken bouillon cubes
3 C	water
20	or more dried lily buds, soaked and washed (optional)
1 T	cornstarch blended with ¼ cup of water
1	green onion, minced
⅛ t	pepper
1 t	sesame oil

Method:

1. Place the chicken bouillon, water and lily buds in a pan; cover and bring to a boil.
2. Stir in blended cornstarch; bring to a boil.
3. Stir in egg in one direction quickly; turn off heat immediately.
4. Sprinkle minced onion and sesame oil on the surface of the soup and serve hot.

Makes 4-6 servings.

Calories: 309   Iron: 2mg
Carbohydrate: 9gm   Vit. B1: 0.2mg
Protein: 16gm   Vit. B2: 0.3mg
Fat: 23gm   Vit. A: 1180IU
Cholesterol: 468mg   Vit. C: 0
Calcium: 54mg   Fiber: 1gm

ACROSS THE BRIDGE NOODLES
(CHICKEN NOODLE SOUP)
(Guo Qiao Mian)

Ingredients:

1	large hen or roasting chicken
1½	inch ginger root, crushed
4	green onions, washed and cleaned
¼ C	sherry
½ C	thinly sliced cucumber or more
¼ lb	thinly sliced chicken breast or fish
	Salt to taste
½ lb	thin Chinese noodles, cooked and hot

Method:

1. Place the first 4 ingredients in a large sauce pan. Fill pan with water, covering the chicken by 2". Cover pan and bring to a boil. Turn to low heat and simmer for 2-3 hours. Remove chicken, ginger, and onions. Keep the broth hot.

2. Place the hot, cooked noodles, cucumber and chicken breast slices on separate plates. Pour the chicken broth in a tureen or large bowl.

3. Add chicken slices to the hot broth and stir gently. Add cucumber and noodles to the broth and mix well.

4. Divide the noodles with the broth into two Chinese soup bowls; serve hot.

Makes two servings.

This noodle dish can be served in small rice bowls as one of the many course of a dinner or can be served as breakfast, snack, lunch, etc.

One pound of enriched dried egg noodles:

Calories:	1760	Iron:	13 mg
Carbohydrate:	326 gm	Vit. A:	1000IU
Protein:	58 gm	Vit. B1:	4 mg
Fat:	30 gm	Vit. B2:	1.7 mg
Cholesterol:	70 gm	Vit. C.:	0
Calcium:	141 mg	Fiber:	1.5 gm

The Legend of the *"Across-the-Bridge Noodles"*

A family of a mother, her married son, and daughter-in-law lived in the northern part of China. The young couple was deeply in love. They spent so much time together that the son neglected his studies. The young man failed to pass the examination to qualify as a government officer. Consequently, the mother separated the son from his wife by putting him on an island in their own garden, wishing that her son would study hard without any interruptions. The young wife delivered three meals a day to her husband. During the winter time the food was cold by the time she reached her husband so in order to serve hot food, the young lady created this new dish. She chose the plumpest hen to make a chicken broth. The layer of chicken fat on the surface of the broth served as an insulation. With this new idea she was able to keep the broth warm even with a walk of some distance in the bitter winter. There after, the husband could enjoy hot meals all the time in the winter. Love indeed can conquer any difficult task.

Across the bridge to the garden. Garden scenery in Hongzhou.

内丸湯

MEAT BALL SOUP
(Rou Yuan Tang)

Ingredients:

2 oz	bean thread
½ lb	ground pork or beef
¼ t	onion or garlic powder
⅛ t	pepper
1 T	soy sauce
1 t	minced ginger root
1 t	cornstarch
5 C	water
4 t	instant chicken bouillon
½ lb	celery cabbage, Napa, or spinach
½ C	sliced bamboo shoots, or sliced carrots, or both
½-1 t	sesame oil
1	green onion, minced

Method:

1. Soak the bean thread in warm water for 20-30 minutes; drain.
2. Mix the meat with the next 5 ingredients. Set aside.
3. Place the water and bouillon in a sauce pan; cover and bring to a boil.
4. Form the meat mixture into ½" meat balls; drop the meat balls one by one into the boiling soup. Cover and cook for 5 minutes.
5. Cut the bean thread into 2-3" length and add to the soup; cover and cook for 4 minutes.
6. Add cabbage and bamboo shoots; cover and cook for 3 minutes.
7. Add sesame oil and green onion; pour in soup bowl and serve hot.

Makes 6 servings.

Calories: 635	Iron: 12mg
Carbohydrate: 8gm	Vit. B1: 2.3mg
Protein: 60gm	Vit. B2: 0.7mg
Fat: 24gm	Vit. A: 381IU
Cholesterol: 160mg	Vit. C: 33mg

CHINESE FIRE POT
(Shi Jin Huo Guo)

什錦火鍋

The Chinese Fire Pot (Huo Quo) Also called Hot Pot, Mongolian Fire Pot, or Chafing Dish was introduced to China by the invading Mongol's (1280-1368). Chinese adapted it and developed it to suit their own taste.

The Fire Pot is literally a round pot with a built-in brazier at the base and a raising chimney through the center. The fire in the brasier, fueled with either charcoal briquets or sterno, keeps the food in the pot boiling hot and cooking.

Fire Pot cookery is used not for a single dish but for preparing a whole meal. It is a do-it-yourself table stove in which diners cook various combinations of food in the boiling stock. The hostess does not need to do the actual cooking, although she has to do all the advance preparations.

This type of cooking is very enjoyable for family dining or entertaining friends in cold, brisk winter weather. Diners are cozily seated around a table with a pot of bubbling stock in the center. A selection of thinly sliced raw meat, chicken, seafood, and vegetables is cooked in stock (usually less than ½ minute) to suit each persons taste. The cooked food is then dipped into one of a variety of sauces and eaten. No cooking art is involved. The diners eat in a relaxed, party-like atmosphere and at a leisurely pace. Diners seem to enjoy the activity of sorting and checking the ingredients cooking in the pot.

The level of the stock in the pot should be checked and the pot refilled if necessary. The heat will burn the food and the pot if the liquid is not kept at an adequate level. At the end of the meal, the stock becomes richer and more flavorful. Put out the fire by placing a small dish on top of the chimney (to stop the oxygen supply), then scoop out the stock, with all its contents, place in individual bowls, and eat.

If the family does not have a Fire Pot, convenient substitutes are an electric wok, electric frying pan, or simply an earthenware casserole. Even a sauce pan set on an electric hotplate will do the job.

The stock is the absolutely necessary ingredient. Prepare it in advance. The other ingredients listed below are for your choice.

Stock

1	chicken, about 3 pounds, cut into 1½" pieces
1	piece of ginger root (1 inch long), crushed
1	onion, quartered
5 qt	water, more or less
4-5	chicken bouillon cubes
	Salt, light soy sauce (Wan Ja Shan) and pepper to taste

Place the first 4 ingredients in a large sauce pan or dutch oven; cover and bring to a boil. Reduce to low heat and simmer for 2 hours or more. Add bouillon cubes and cook until the cubes are dissolved. Adjust the taste with salt, soy sauce, and pepper and keep hot.

Pork and beef with their bones can be used for stock and can be cooked in the same manner.

Raw meats

Chicken breast, duck breast, lean pork, beef, lamb, etc. Cut the meats paper thin into 1"x2" slices and arrange separately and neatly on plates. (Mix a little soy sauce and cornstarch with the meat before placing it on plates. It will make the meat juicy and tender after being cooked. This is optional).

Raw seafood

Shelled raw shrimp, oysters, clams, lobster, mussels, thinly sliced fish fillets (bass, pike, cod, etc), or cut-up squid. Arrange the seafood separately and neatly on plates.

Raw vegetables

Napa, celery cabbage, Bok Choy, watercress, mustard greens, spinach, etc., washed and cut into 2' sections.

Pea pods, string beans, washed and cut.

Flowerets of broccoli and cauliflower, washed.

Green onions, washed and cut into 2" pieces. Ginger root, finely shredded.

Arrange the vegetables on separate plates or on a large platter.

Dried ingredients

Chinese dried mushrooms, wood ears, lily buds, dried shrimp, bean threads, etc. Soak the ingredients, in separate bowls, with warm water for 30 minutes. Drain and cut the larger pieces into smaller ones. Cut the bean threads into 3" sections. Arrange the ingredients on separate plates.

Cooked Ingredients:

Meat balls (page 139)
Shrimp balls (page 256)
Shrimp patties (page 254)
Egg shreds (page 197)

Salted duck (page 203)
Braised beef shank (page 80)
Braised spareribs (page 145)
Fried bean curd balls (page 330)
Braised fried bean curd (page 327)
Arrange the ingredients on separate plates

Sauce dips

Soy sauce with a few drops of sesame oil is the basic dip. Others are oyster sauce, soybean paste, sesame paste, hot mustard, hot pepper paste, red oil, mashed fermented bean curd, vinegar, sugar, diluted Hoisin Sauce, mashed garlic, and Chinese barbeque sauce (*Sha Cha* sauce).

Place each sauce in separate small bowls or sauce dishes. The diners make their own dip mixtures by taking small amounts from various sauce dips, placing them in their rice bowl and blending to suit their taste.

Fire for the Fire Pot

Charcoal briquets or Sterno can be used as fuels.

Charcoal briquets: Start the charcoal in a grill with charcoal lighter or arrange 10 to 15 charcoal briquets side by side in a baking pan lined with heavy aluminum foil and place under the broiler. Heat for 10 to 15 minutes until a white ash forms on the briquets. Transfer the briquets into the funnel of the Fire Pot. Fill the pot with boiling stock and set the pot on table. Sterno cans only keep the stock warm, not boiling.

Table setting, cooking and serving:

Set the Fire Pot in the center of the dining table on a pad which will protect the table from the heat of the Fire Pot. Place the raw and cooked ingredients and sauce dips around the Fire Pot. (Protecting the tablecloth with a plastic covering is a good idea.)

Each diner is provided with a pair of chopsticks, a rice bowl, a spoon, a plate, and a wire-mesh strainer. The diners take whatever ingredients they like with chopsticks and place them in the strainer (a few pieces at a time) and dip the food in the boiling stock. In less than half a minute the food is cooked. The food is then dipped, with chopsticks, in the combined sauce dip and eaten.

meat

**DRY STIR-FRIED MINCED MEAT,
BEIJING (PEKING) STYLE
(Beijing Sui Rou)**

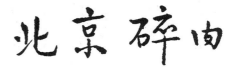

This dish, served with "Sesame Seed Shao Bing" was one of the favorite dishes of empress Dowager, the last empress of China in the Qing (Ch'in) dynasty. We tasted this dish in a special restaurant in Beijing (Peking) called "Imitation of the Imperial Kitchen" or "Fang Shan." All the dishes served in that restaurant were the dishes which used to be served to the imperial families. I gathered the information and wrote this recipe for all my dear friends here in America, so that you can enjoy a little flavor of ancient China, and also as a token of love from my heart to yours.

Ingredients:

1 lb	ground pork or beef, lean
3 T	soy sauce
1 t	brown sugar
3-4	green onions, minced
3-4	slices of ginger root
1 T	sherry
1 T	sesame oil
¼ t	pepper

Method:

1. Place the ground meat in a dry non-stick pan or wok. Over high heat, stir and turn the meat until color turns. Drain off fat.

2. Add soy sauce and brown sugar; stir for 2 minutes.

3. Add green onions and ginger root; stir for 1 minute.

4. Add sherry and stir for ½ minute.

5. Add sesame oil, pepper and mix well. Serve with "Sesame seed Shao Bing."

If you don't want to go to the trouble of making "Sesame Seeds Shao Bing," this dish may be served with rice.

Calories:	1360	Carbohydrates:	7gm
Protein:	84gm	Fat:	110gm

芝麻燒餅

SESAME SEED SHAO BING
(Zi Ma Shao Bing)

Ingredients:

¼ oz   dry yeast (one package)
¼ C   sugar
1 T   sugar dissolved in ¼ C water
       Oil for dipping
       Sesame seeds
2 C   warm water
1 t   salt
¼ C   oil
4 C   all purpose flour
1 C   whole wheat flour
1 T   baking powder

Method

1. Combine the yeast and ¼ C sugar in a large mixing bowl; add water to soften the yeast (takes about 10 minutes).

2. Add the last 5 ingredients to the yeast mixture and blend well.

3. Cover the bowl with a damp towel. Let the dough rise until double in bulk (about 2-4 hours, depending upon the temperature).

4. Place the dough on a floured board and knead for 5-8 minutes.

5. Form the dough into a cylindrical roll about 1" in diameter; cut the roll evenly into 1" pieces.

6. Flatten one piece of the dough into a round cake, about 2" in diameter. Dip another piece of the dough in oil and wrap it in the flattened dough.

7. Roll the wrapped dough into a 2½" diameter cake (Chinese call it Bing) Brush a layer of sugar water on top of the Bing. Sprinkle sesame seeds on the Bing, pressing to make sure the sesame seeds stick on the Bing. Repeat until the dough is used up.

8. Arrange the Bings, sesame seeds side up, on a lightly greased tray or cookie sheet. Bake in a preheated oven at 375° for 20-25 minutes or until light brown and done.

9. Split the Bing horizontally. Pull off a portion of the Bing from the center in order to make room for stuffing the meat.

10. Stuff with "Dry stir-fried minced meat, Beijing style" (page 75) and eat with fingers.

This Shao Bing can be served with Beijing (Peking) duck or Moo-Shu pork in place of Chinese pancakes.

Calories: 2780
Protein: 67gm
Carbohydrates: 490gm
Fat: 61gm

Tai-He-Dian Hall of the Palace Museum (Forbidden City) in Beijing.

加喱牛肉

CURRIED BEEF
(Ka Li Niu Rou)

Ingredients:

2 lb	boneless beef (chuck, shank, beef stew etc.)
1 T	oil
1	large onion, chopped
3-6	slices ginger root
3 T	curry powder blended with 4 T water
	Water
1	large potato (optional)
1 t	sugar
5 T	soy sauce
¼ t	pepper
¼ t	salt

Method:

1. Cut the beef into 1½" cubes.

2. Heat oil in a medium sauce pan; sauté onion, ginger root, and blended curry.

3. Add beef and the last 4 ingredients; stir and cook for 3 minutes.

4. Add enough water to cover the beef; cover pan and bring to a boil. Turn to low heat and cook until the beef is tender and the liquid is reduced to ½ C. Serve hot.

Note: One large potato, peeled and diced, can be added before beef is tender. If the liquid evaporates before the beef is tender, add more water and cook. If too much liquid is left after the meat is tender, turn to high heat and cook, uncovered, until the liquid evaporates to the desirable amount.

Calories:	2514	Iron:	29mg
Carbohydrates:	16gm	Vit. B1:	0.7mg
Protein:	172gm	Vit. B2:	1.7mg
Fat:	190gm	Vit. A:	380IU
Cholesterol:	614mg	Vit. C:	5mg
Calcium:	175mg	Fiber:	0

SICHUAN BRAISED BEEF
(Sichuan Niu Rou)

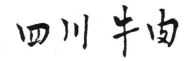

Ingredients:

2-3 lb	boneless lean beef chuck, cut into 1" cubes
4-6	cloves of garlic, crushed
4-6	slices of ginger root
½ C	chopped onion
1 T	red oil (page 313, optional)
1 T	sherry
2-3 T	low sodium or regular soy sauce
2-3 t	brown sugar
½ t	pepper
2-4	cloves of star anise
1 t	or more whole Sichuan peppercorns
1 T	hot bean sauce or paste

Method:

1. Place all the ingredients in a medium sauce pan and bring to a boil. Stir occasionally while cooking.

2. Cover pan, turn to lowest heat and cook for 50 minutes or until the beef is tender.

No water is needed to add to the beef while cooking. Raw beef contains enough juice to make the end product moist. However, if the liquid *does* evaporate before the beef is tender, add some water and continue to cook until it is tender. If too much liquid is left after the beef is tender, turn to high heat and cook, uncovered, until the liquid is reduced to the desirable amount (about ⅓ C). If you wish, discard ginger root, star anise, and Sichuan peppercorns before serving. Serve hot.

Makes 6-8 servings.

Calories: 1586	Cholesterol: 640 mg	Vit. B2: 2 mg
Carbohydrates: 26 gm	Calcium: 211 mg	Vit. A: 140 IU
Protein: 200 gm	Iron: 32 mg	Vit. C: 11 mg
Fat: 69 gm	Vit. B1: 0.9 mg	Fiber: 2 gm

With the exception of the newly added Rice Noodle section, the nutritional calculations of all the recipes in this book are for **the whole recipe,** not per serving.

红烧腱子

Ingredients:

2-3 lb	beef shank, cut across the grain into 3/4" x 2" pieces
1/2 C	chopped onion
1/2 in.	ginger root, crushed
2-4	cloves of garlic
1 T	sherry
2-3 t	brown sugar
2-3 T	low sodium or regular soy sauce

Method:

1. Place all the ingredients in a medium sauce pan; cover and bring to a boil. Stir occasionally while cooking.

2. Cover pan, turn to lowest heat and cook for 50 minutes or until the beef is tender. Turn once while cooking. .

No water is needed to add to the beef while cooking. Raw beef contains enough juice to make the end product moist. However, if the liquid *does* evaporate before the beef is tender, add some water and continue to cook until it is tender. If too much liquid is left after the beef is tender, turn to high heat and cook, uncovered, until the liquid is reduced to the desirable amount (about 1/3 C). Serve hot.

Makes 6-8 servings.

Calories: 1552	Cholesterol: 640 mg	Vit. B2: 2 mg
Carbohydrates: 22 gm	Calcium: 180 mg	Vit. A: 0 IU
Protein: 200 gm	Iron: 32 mg	Vit. C: 9 mg
Fat: 68 gm	Vit. B1: 0.9 mg	Fiber: 2 gm

With the exception of the newly added Rice Noodle section, the nutritional calculations of all the recipes in this book are for **the whole recipe,** not per serving.

OYSTER SAUCE BEEF WITH BROCCOLI
(Hao You Niu Rou Chao Jie Hua)

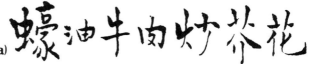

Ingredients:

¾ lb	beef flank steak, sliced
2½ T	oyster sauce
¼ t	pepper
1 t	brown sugar
¼ t	onion powder
1 T	sherry
2	slices of ginger root
1 t	sesame oil
1 T	cornstarch
1 t	cornstarch blended with 1 T water
4 T	oil
2	stalks of broccoli
1	green onion, shredded
1	slice of ginger root
½ t	salt
¼ C	water

Method:

1. Mix the beef slices with the next 8 ingredients.

2. Wash broccoli; break the flowerlets into 1" long small pieces.

3. Heat oil in a pan or in a wok; add beef; stir-fry until color turns. Remove and keep warm.

4. Add broccoli and last 4 ingredients; stir for 1 minute. Cover pan and bring to a boil. Add blended conrstarch; mix well.

5. Place the cooked broccoli on a serving dish and top with the cooked beef. Serve hot.

Makes 4-6 servings.

Calories:	1218	Iron:	16mg
Carbohydrates:	37gm	Vit. B1:	0.6mg
Protein:	86gm	Vit. B2:	1.4mg
Fat:	80gm	Vit. A:	7983IU
Cholesterol:	307mg	Vit. C:	353mg
Calcium:	401mg	Fiber:	5gm

蠔油牛肉炒蘆筍 **OYSTER SAUCE BEEF**
WITH ASPARAGUS
(Hao You Niu Rou Chao Lu Sun)

Ingredients:

1 lb	beef, sliced (flank, loin, round, etc.)
3 T	oyster sauce
1 t	sherry
1 t	sesame oil
½ t	onion powder
¼ t	pepper
2	slices of ginger root, shredded
½ t	brown sugar
1 T	cornstarch
2-4	green onions, shredded
4 T	oil
½ lb	fresh asparagus
⅛ t	salt (or to taste)

Method:

1. Mix beef with the next 7 ingredients. Add 1 T cornstarch and mix well.

2. Wash and cut off the tough parts of the asparagus. Slant-slice the asparagus into ⅛" slices. If the asparagus spears are small, cut into 1" sections.

3. Heat 3 T oil in a non-stick pan or wok; stir-fry the beef until color turns (about 1-2 minutes). Add shredded green onions and mix well. Transfer to a dish.

4. Add 1 T oil to the pan; stir the asparagus with ⅛ t salt for 1-2 minutes. Add cooked beef; mix well and serve hot.

Makes 4-6 servings.

Calories: 1262		Iron: 16mg	
Carbohydrates: 14gm		Vit. B1: 0.4mg	
Protein: 99gm		Vit. B2: 1.0mg	
Fat: 87gm		Vit. A: 1200gm	
Cholesterol: 307mg		Vit. C: 45mg	
Calcium: 90mg		Fiber: 1.5gm	

OYSTER SAUCE BEEF WITH MUSHROOMS
(Don Gu Hao You Niu Rou)

冬菇蠔油牛肉

Ingredients:

1 lb	beef, sliced (flank, sirloin, round, etc.)
1 T	sherry
2 T	oyster sauce
¼ t	pepper
¼ t	onion powder
1 t	brown sugar
2	slices of ginger root
1 T	cornstarch
1-2	green onions, shredded
1 T	cornstarch blended with ⅛ C of water
4 T	oil
	Salt and pepper to taste
½ lb	or more fresh mushrooms, sliced
1 C	celery, sliced diagonally
½ C	water
1 T	oyster sauce

Method:

1. Mix beef with the next 6 ingredients. Add cornstarch and mix well.

2. Heat oil in a non-stick pan or wok; sauté onion. Add beef and stir-fry until color turns (about 2 minutes). Remove.

3. Put the last four ingredients into the pan and bring to a boil.

4. Add blended cornstarch, salt and pepper to taste; cook until the sauce thickens.

5. Add cooked beef; mix well. Serve immediately.

Step 1 can be prepared in advance. It can be kept in the refrigerator for a few days or in the freezer for a few weeks.

Makes 6 servings.

Calories: 1300	Cholesterol: 320mg	Vit. B2: 2.0mg
Carbohydrates: 35gm	Calcium: 159mg	Vit. A: 495IU
Protein: 108gm	Iron: 19mg	Vit. C: 19mg
Fat: 80gm	Vit. B1: 0.7mg	Fiber: 2gm

青蔥牛肉

BEEF WITH GREEN ONIONS
(Qing Cong Niu Rou)

Ingredients:

- 2 T soy sauce
- ¼ t pepper
- 1 T sherry
- 1 t brown sugar
- 1 T cornstarch
- 2/3 lb beef (flank, round, chuck, sirloin, etc., sliced)
- 1 T sesame oil
- 3-4 T oil
- 1 t ginger root, shredded
- 2 bunches of green onions (about 10-15) or ½ pound of leeks
- 2 T soy sauce

Method:

1. Mix the beef with the first 5 ingredients.
2. Wash and shred onions.
3. Heat oil in a pan or wok; sauté ginger root; add beef; stir-fry until color turns (about 1½-2 minutes). Remove.
4. Add onions and 2 T soy sauce to the remaining oil; stir and cook until onions are wilted.
5. Add cooked beef and sesame oil; mix well. Serve hot.
Makes 4-6 servings.

Calories: 1070
Carbohydrates: 28gm
Protein: 69gm
Fat: 75gm
Cholesterol: 204mg
Calcium: 141mg

Iron: 13mg
Vit. B1: 0.3mg
Vit. B2: 0.7mg
Vit. A: 2030IU
Vit. C: 32mg
Fiber: 1gm

DRY COOKED BEEF WITH CELERY
(GAN BIAN NIU ROU)

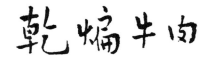

Ingredients:

2/3 lb	beef; (flank steak, loin, round, chuck etc.)
2 T	soy sauce
¼ t	pepper
½ t	onion or garlic powder
1 t	sherry
1 T	cornstarch
1 T	sesame oil
3-4 T	oil
2-3	slices of ginger, shredded
2-4	fresh or dried hot pepper, shredded
4	ribs of celery, shredded (about 2 C)
2 T	soy sauce
1 t	sugar
1	carrot, shredded (optional)
1	onion, shredded

Method:

1. Cut beef into fine shreds, then mix with the next 5 ingredrients.

2. Heat oil in a pan or a wok; add beef, ginger root, hot pepper and stir-fry for 4 minutes.

3. Add the last 5 ingredients, stir and cook until the cooking juice dries. Add 1 T sesame oil; mix well. Serve hot.

Makes 4-6 servings.

Calories: 1070	Cholesterol: 204mg	Vit. B2: 0.8mg
Carbohydrates: 30gm	Calcium: 200mg	Vit. A: 661IU
Protein: 70gm	Iron: 13mg	Vit. C: 27mg
Fat: 75gm	Vit. B1: 0.4mg	Fiber: 2gm

雪豆牛肉 OYSTER SAUCE BEEF WITH SNOW PEA PODS
(Xu Dou Niu Rou)

Ingredients:

¾ lb   beef, flank, round, sirloin etc., sliced
3 T   oyster sauce
¼ t   pepper
1 t   brown sugar
¼ t   onion powder
1 T   sherry
1 t   finely minced ginger root
1 T   sesame oil
1 T   cornstarch
½ lb   fresh snow pea pods
½ C   sliced bamboo shoots
4 T   oil
2   green onions, shredded
2   slices of ginger root
¼ t   salt

Method:

1. Cut the beef into 1½-inch long, ½-inch wide and ⅛-inch thick slices. Marinate the beef with the next 7 ingredients. Mix the beef with the 1 T cornstarch before cooking.

2. Wash and remove the stems and strings from the snow pea pods. Pat dry.

3. Heat 1 T oil in a pan or wok; add snow pea pods and ¼ t salt. Stir quickly for ½ minute. Remove.

4. Wipe the pan clean. Add 3 T oil; sauté onion and ginger root. Add beef, stirring constantly until color turns (about 2 minutes). Add bamboo shoots and snow pea pods; mix well. Serve hot.

Calories: 1250   Carbohydrates: 30gm
Protein: 80gm   Fat: 80gm

BEEF WITH OYSTER SAUCE
(Hao You Niu Rou)

Ingredients:

- 1 T   oyster sauce
- 1 t   brown sugar
- ¼ t   salt
- 1 T   sherry
- ¼ t   pepper
- 1 T   cornstarch
- 1 lb   beef (flank, round, chuck or sirloin steak etc.)
- 4   green onions, shredded
- 2 t   shredded ginger root
- 2 T   oyster sauce
- 1 T   sesame oil
- 3-4 T   oil

Method:

1. Cut the beef into 1½"x1"x⅛" slices. Marinate the beef for 30 minutes or more with the first 5 ingredients. Add cornstarch and mix well.

2. Heat 2-3T oil in a non-stick pan or in a wok. Add beef; stir-fry until color turns (about 1-1½ minutes). Remove.

3. Add 1T oil, sauté onion and ginger root. Add beef, sesame oil, and oyster sauce; mix well. Serve hot.

Makes 4-6 servings.

Calories:	1220	Iron:	15mg
Carbohydrates:	14gm	Vit. B1:	0.4mg
Protein:	98gm	Vit. B2:	0.9mg
Fat:	94mg	Vit. A:	845IU
Cholesterol:	307mg	Vit. C:	13mg
Calcium:	88mg	Fiber:	0.4gm

中式牛排

BEEF STEAK, CHINESE STYLE
(Zhong Shi Niu Pai)

Ingredients:

1 lb   boneless beef (sirloin or tenderloin)
2 T   soy sauce
1 t   sesame oil
1 t   sherry
¼ t   pepper
½ t   onion powder
½   egg, beaten
3 T   cornstarch
3 T   oil
1   onion, shredded
1 T   soy sauce
¼ t   pepper
½ t   sugar

Method:

1. Cut the beef across the grain into ¼" thick pieces. Mix the beef with the next 6 ingredients. Let stand for a half hour or more.

2. Coat the beef with 3 T cornstarch.

3. Heat oil in a pan or wok. Fry beef pieces, first on one side, then the other, until done (about 2 minutes). Remove to a dish and keep warm.

4. Add the last 4 ingredients; stir and cook until the onion is done. Spread the onion on the beef steak or surround the beef with it and serve hot.

Steps 1 and 2 can be prepared in advance.
Makes 4-6 servings.

Calories:	2066	Iron:	14mg
Carbohydrates:	43gm	Vit. B1:	0.41mg
Protein:	83gm	Vit. B2:	0.87
Fat:	172gm	Vit. A:	609IU
Cholesterol:	435mg	Vit. C:	22mg
Calcium:	131mg	Fiber:	1.4gm

STIR-FRIED BEEF WITH VEGETABLES
(Su Cai Cho Niu Rou)

素菜炒牛肉

Ingredients:

¾ lb	beef, shredded (flank, loin, round, etc.)
2 T	soy sauce
2 t	sherry
¼ t	pepper
½ t	onion powder
1 t	minced ginger root
1 t	sesame oil
2 t	cornstarch
4 T	oil
½	or more, onion shredded
1 t	or more, shredded ginger root
2-4	hot peppers, shredded (optional)
1	green pepper, shredded
2/3 C	carrots, shredded
¼ lb	or more, shredded celery cabbage
1½ T	soy sauce
½ t	brown sugar
¼ t	salt or to taste

Method:

1. Combine the beef with the next 6 ingredients. Add 2 t cornstarch and mix well.

2. Heat oil in a pan or wok. Add beef; stir-fry until color turns. Remove.

3. Sauté onion, ginger root, and hot peppers in the remaining oil.

4. Add carrots, stir and cook for 1 minute.

5. Add shreds of green pepper, and celery cabbage; mix well.

6. Add the last 3 ingredients; stir and cook until the vegetables are wilted.

7. Add cooked beef and mix well. Serve hot.

Step 1 can be prepared in advance.

Makes 4-6 servings.

Calories: 1201
Carbohydrates: 37gm
Protein: 81gm
Fat: 81gm
Cholesterol: 230mg
Calcium: 271mg

Iron: 16mg
Vit. B1: 0.6mg
Vit. B2: 1mg
Vit. A: 10029IU
Vit. C: 199mg
Fiber: 5gm

SHISH KEBAB, CHINESE STYLE
(Zhong Shi Kao Rou)

Ingredients:

1 lb	beef (flank steak, chuck, or sirloin etc.)
3 T	soy sauce
⅛ t	pepper
1 t	sherry
1 t	brown sugar
1 T	cornstarch
1	onion, cut into 1" squares
1-2	green pepper, cut into 1" squares
1	1" diameter carrot, cut into ⅛" slices (crosswise)
½ lb	medium sized fresh mushrooms, washed and dried
	Five inch long bamboo skewers
2 T	soy sauce
½ t	salt
¼ t	pepper
2 T	sherry
1 T	vinegar
2 T	oil
½ C	water
1 t	sesame oil

Method:

1. Cut the beef into 1″ cubes. Mix the beef with the next 5 ingredients. Set aside.

2. Combine the last 8 ingredients in a bowl. Set aside. Assemble the ingredients on skewers in the following order: Mushrooms, carrots, onion, green pepper, and meat. Repeat 2-3 times.

4. Heat a skillet over medium heat; add the assembled skewers several at a time. Brush with the sauce mixture from Step 2; cover and grill over high heat for 1 minute. Turn to other side, brush with sauce, and cook in the same manner. Serve immediately.

Makes 4-6 servings.

Calories: 1206	Cholesterol: 307mg	Vit. B2: 2.1mg
Carbohydrates: 48gm	Calcium: 179mg	Vit. A: 5936IU
Protein: 109gm	Iron: 21gm	Vit. C: 129mg
Fat: 59gm	Vit. B1: 0.8mg	Fiber: 4gm

Life-sized terra cotta warrior and horse from the Imperial Tomb of Qin-Shi Huang (the first emperor of China, 221-206 BC) in Xian, the western part of China.

嫩瓜炒肉片

ZUCCHINI WITH BEEF
(Nen Gua Chao Rou Pian)

Ingredients:

¾ lb	beef (flank, loin, round etc.)	
2 T	soy sauce	⎫
¼ t	pepper	
½ t	sugar	
1 t	sherry	
½ t	onion or garlic powder	
1 T	cornstarch	⎭
1 t	sesame oil	
1 T	cornstarch blended with 2 T water	
4 T	oil	
2	green onions, shredded	
2	slices of ginger root	
1 lb	small size zucchini (green summer squash)	⎫
1 T	soy sauce	
½ C	water	
	Salt and pepper to taste	
⅛ t	MSG (optional)	⎭

Method:

1. Slice the beef, then mix with the next 6 ingredients.

2. Wash zucchini and cut off both ends. Slant slice into 1/6" thick slices.

3. Heat oil in a pan or wok; sauté onion and ginger root. Add beef; stir-fry until color turns (about 2 minutes). Remove.

4. Put the last 5 ingredients into the pan and bring to a boil. Add blended cornstarch (salt and pepper if necessary). Cook until the sauce thickens.

5. Add cooked beef and sesame oil; mix well. Serve hot.

Makes 4-6 servings.

Calories: 1315	Iron: 18mg
Carbohydrates: 27gm	Vit. B1: 0.64mg
Protein: 104gm	Vit. B2: 1.37mg
Fat: 87gm	Vit. A: 1877IU
Cholesterol: 221mg	Vit. C: 82mg
Calcium: 230mg	Fiber: 3gm

ORANGE DRY COOKED BEEF
(Jie Xiang Niu Rou)

Ingredients:

1 lb	beef flank steak, sliced
½ t	salt
1 T	oil
3 T	fresh orange peel or more, shredded
2-4	slices of ginger root
2-4	green onions, shredded
2-4	fresh or dried hot peppers, diced
1 T	orange extract (optional)

⎧ 2 T   soy sauce
⎪ 2 T   brown sugar
⎨ 1 T   sherry
⎩ 1 T   water

Method:

1. Mix the beef with the salt.

2. Heat oil in a pan or a wok; brown orange peel and ginger root.

3. Add beef, onion, and pepper; stir and mix over medium heat until it dries. Remove.

4. Add the last 4 ingredients to the pan; cook over medium heat until the sugar is melted. Add cooked beef (orange extract) and mix well. Serve hot or cold.

This meat can be served as a main or side dish; also as a snack, lunch meat, or appetizer.

Makes 4-6 servings.

Dried orange peels can be used in this dish. They can be purchased in Oriental grocery stores or dried at home. To dry orange peels is very simple, just put the fresh orange peels in 275° oven for ½ hour or until they become dried.

Calories: 922		Iron:	16mg
Carbohydrates: 32gm		Vit. B1:	0.4mg
Protein: 99gm		Vit. B2:	1mg
Fat: 40gm		Vit. A:	1956IU
Cholesterol: 307mg		Vit. C:	32mg
Calcium: 95mg		Fiber:	1gm

茄汁牛肉　　　　**BRAISED BEEF WITH TOMATO SAUCE**
　　　　　　　　　　　　　　　　　　(Qie Zhi Niu Rou)

Ingredients:

2 lb　　boneless beef (shank, chuck, or beef stew, etc.)
5 T　　soy sauce
4　　slices of ginger root, minced
1　　onion, diced
1 t　　brown sugar
　　　Water
1　　6oz can tomato paste

Method:

1. Cut the beef into 1½" cubes.
2. Put the beef and the next 4 ingredients into a medium sauce pan. Stir and cook until the liquid is evaporated.
3. Add water to cover the meat. Cover pan and bring to a boil.
4. Reduce to low heat and cook until the meat becomes tender and the liquid is reduced to 1 C.
5. Add tomato paste and cook until the sauce thickens. Serve hot. Add water if the liquid evaporates too quickly before the meat becomes tender. If there is too much liquid left after the meat becomes tender, remove the lid; turn to high heat and cook until the liquid is reduced to desirable amount.

Makes 4-6 servings.

Calories:　2556　　　　Iron:　36mg
Carbohydrates:　54gm　　Vit. B1:　1.1mg
Protein:　179gm　　　　Vit. B2:　1.9mg
Fat:　177gm　　　　　　Vit. A:　6914IU
Cholesterol:　614mg　　　Vit. C:　102mg
Calcium:　232mg　　　　Fiber:　2gm

BEEF WITH FRESH TOMATOES
(Fan Qie Niu Rou)

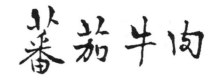

Ingredients:

1 lb   beef flank steak, sliced
3 T   soy sauce
1 T   sherry
¼ t   pepper
½ t   onion powder
1 t   sugar
1 T   cornstarch
4 T   oil
1   onion, diced
3   slices of ginger root
3   medium sized fresh tomatoes, diced (about 1 pound)
¼ t   salt
1 t   sesame oil

Method:

1. Combine the first 6 ingredients in a bowl; mix well. Mix the beef with 1 T cornstarch before cooking.

2. Heat oil in a non-stick pan or wok; saute' onion and ginger root.

3. Add beef; stir-fry for 2 minutes. Add tomato dices; stir and cook for 2 minutes.

4. Add sesame oil and mix well. Serve immediately.

Calories: 1400   Carbohydrates: 42gm
Protein: 105   Fat: 86gm

沙茶牛肉

Ingredients:

1 lb	beef (flank steak or other cuts)
2 T	soy sauce
3 T	or more, Sa Cha sauce
1 t	sherry
½ t	onion powder
1 t	minced ginger root
½ t	brown sugar
1 t	sesame oil
1 T	cornstarch
3-4 T	oil
5	slices of ginger root, finely shredded
3-6	green onions, shredded
	Salt to taste

Method:

1. Cut the beef into 1½"x½"x1/6" slices. Thoroughly mix the beef with the next 7 ingredients. Add cornstarch and mix well.

2. Heat oil in a non-stick pan or wok; saute ginger root. Add beef; stir-fry until color turns (about 2 minutes).

3. Add onion shreds and salt; stir and mix until the green onion is wilted. Serve hot.

Makes 4-6 servings.

Calories:	1170	Iron:	16mg
Carbohydrates:	16gm	Vit. B1:	0.4mg
Protein:	100gm	Vit. B2:	1mg
Fat:	76gm	Vit. A:	645IU
Cholesterol:	307mg	Vit. C:	9mg
Calcium:	112mg	Fiber:	0

STIR-FRIED BEEF LIVER
(Qing Chao Niu Gan)

清炒牛肝

Ingredients:

    1 lb   beef liver
    3 T   soy sauce
    1 t   onion or garlic powder
    ¼ t   pepper
    1 T   sherry
    ½ t   sugar
    1 T   cornstarch
    4 T   oil
    4   cloves of garlic, sliced
    4-6   slices of ginger root
    1   onion, diced
    ½ lb   fresh mushrooms, sliced
    1 T   soy sauce
    ½ C   water
    1 T   cornstarch blended with 1 T water
    2 t   sesame oil
        Salt and pepper to taste

Method:

1. Remove and discard all the membranes of the liver and split slice into 1"x1½"x1/6" slices. Pat dry with a towel.

2. Mix the sliced liver with the next 6 ingredients.

3. Heat oil in a non-stick pan or a wok. Add beef; stir-fry until color turns. Remove.

4. Saute garlic, ginger, and onion in the remaining oil. Add the last 6 ingredients and bring to a boil. Stir gently while cooking.

5. Add the cooked liver and mix well. Serve immediately.

Steps 1 and 2 can be prepared in advance.

Makes 4-6 servings.

Calories: 1448	Cholesterol: 1433mg	Vit. B2: 15mg
Carbohydrates: 65gm	Calcium: 117mg	Vit. A: 199, 130IU
Protein: 100gm	Iron: 34mg	Vit. C: 153mg
Fat: 86gm	Vit. B1: 1.4mg	Fiber: 2gm

中式牛肉餅

GROUND BEEF STEAK, CHINESE STYLE
(Zhong Shi Rou Bing)

Ingredients:

1 lb	ground beef
2 T	soy sauce
¼ t	salt
1 t	sugar
1 t	sesame oil
1	large onion, chopped
1 T	cornstarch
1 T	oil
2	green onions, minced
1 C	water
1 t	sherry
2 T	soy sauce
¼ t	pepper
½ t	sugar

Method:

1. Mix the first 7 ingredients together thoroughly.
2. Form the meat mixture into 2" balls. Flatten the meat balls into ½" thick patties.
3. Heat oil in a pan or wok; brown both sides of the meat.
4. Add last 5 ingredients; cover and cook until the liquid is reduced to ¼ C. Turn the patties two or three times while cooking for even flavor. Add minced green onion; mix well. Serve hot.

Makes 4-6 servings.

Calories: 1486	Cholesterol: 313mg	Vit. B2: 0.9mg
Carbohydrates: 23gm	Calcium: 119mg	Vit. A: 601IU
Protein: 85gm	Iron: 15mg	Vit. C: 12mg
Fat: 114gm	Vit. B1: 0.4mg	Fiber: 0.6gm

SWEET AND SOUR BEEF BALLS
(Tian Suan Niu Rou Wan)

甜酸牛肉丸

Ingredients:

- 1 lb ground beef
- 1 egg
- 2 T soy sauce
- ¼ t salt
- ½ t pepper
- ½ onion, finely minced
- 1 t sesame oil
- 2 T cornstarch
- Oil for deep-frying
- 1-3 green onion, minced
- 1 t minced ginger root
- 1 t minced garlic
- ¼ C sugar
- ¼ C catsup
- ¼ C vinegar
- ¼ C water
- 1 T soy sauce
- 1 t cornstarch

Method:

1. Mix the first 8 ingredients together thoroughly.
2. Combine the last 6 ingredients in a small bowl. Set aside.
3. Make ¾" meat balls with a teaspoon or with your hands.
4. Heat oil in a pan or wok. Fry the meat balls until golden brown. Transfer to a dish and keep warm.
5. Pour off all the oil except 1 T. Sauté minced onion, garlic and ginger root. Add sauce mixture from Step 2, and cook until the sauce thickens.
6. Add the fried meat balls and mix well. Serve hot.

Makes 4-6 servings.

Calories: 2192	Cholesterol: 547mg	Vit. B2: 1mg
Carbohydrates: 91gm	Calcium: 136 mg	Vit. A: 1927IU
Protein: 91gm	Iron: 16mg	Vit. C: 15mg
Fat: 162gm	Vit. B1: 0.5mg	Fiber: 0.6 gm

Calculated with 3 T oil for deep-frying.

牛肉泡饃

MUTTON OR BEEF PAO MO
(Niu Rou Pao Mo)

Ingredients:

1 lb	mutton or beef shank, chuck, or stew meat.
½ oz	dried bean thread
1	small onion, chopped
2-3	slices of ginger root
2-3	cloves of garlic, crushed
4-5 T	soy sauce
2 C	water
2-3	cloves of star anise
½ lb	fresh vegetable such as spinach, celery cabbage or Bok Choy, washed and cut into 1" pieces
3	Bings (recipe on page 101)

Method:

1. Cut the meat into 1" cubes.
2. Soak the bean thread in warm water for ½ hour; drain and cut the bean thread into 3" lengths.
3. Heat oil in a sauce pan; sauté onion, ginger, and garlic.
4. Add meat and soy sauce; sauté for 2 minutes.
5. Add water and star anise; cover pan and bring to a boil.
6. Reduce to low heat and simmer until the meat is tender.
7. Add bean thread and vegetables; bring to a boil before serving.
8. Break the Bing (recipe on page 101) into small pieces in a soup bowl. Add cooked meat Pao Mo to the Bing and serve immediately. This dish can be served as a complete meal, for lunch or dinner. The cooked meat Pao Mo can be served on cooked noodles.

English muffins can be substituted for Bings.

Calories: 1620   Carbohydrates: 96gm
Protein: 109gm   Fat: 86gm

PAO MO BING
(Pao Mo Bing)

Ingredients:

- ⅛ oz   dry yeast (about half package)
- 2 T   sugar
- 1 C   warm water
- 2 T   oil
- 1 C   whole wheat four
- 1½ C   all purpose flour
          Pinch of salt

Method:

1. Place the first 3 ingredients in a large mixing bowl; let stand for 10 minutes.

2. Add the rest of the ingredients to the yeast mixture; mix well to form a dough.

3. Cover the bowl with a damp towel. Let the dough rise for one hour.

4. Place the dough on a floured board and knead for 5-8 minutes, or until smooth. The dough should be hard; flour may be added while kneading.

5. Divide the dough into 10 portions. Roll the dough into Bings, 3" in diameter.

6. Arrange the Bings on a cookie sheet and bake in a preheated 400° oven until brown (about 25 minutes).

The baked Bings can be used for Beef Pao Mo. or they can also be used as a bread or snack.

English muffins are a good substitute for Bings.

Calories: 1390   Carbohydrates: 242gm
Protein: 37gm   Fat: 32gm

139 calories per Bing

Mongolian tent of Chinese nomads in Xing-Jiang province.

XIN JIANG BEEF OR MUTTON
(Shou Zhua Yang Rou)

Ingredients:

- 1 lb beef or mutton
- 1 t salt
- 2 T oil
- 1 onion, shredded
    Cumin powder
    Hot pepper powder

Method:

1. Place the meat in a sauce pan, add water to cover meat. Cover pan and bring to a boil. Reduce to low heat and simmer until the meat is tender.

2. Tear the meat into strips.

3. Toast 1 T cumin in a wok until aromatic. Grind the cumin into a fine powder.

4. Heat oil in a pan or wok, add salt, and onion shreds; sauté for 1 minute.

5. Add meat and stir for 2 minutes. Transfer the meat to a plate. Spread ¼ t or more cumin powder and little hot pepper powder on the meat and serve hot.

This is a dish from the Chinese minority tribes who live in Xing Jiang, the northwest area of China.

Calories: 1450
Carbohydrate: 9 gm
Protein: 86 gm
Fat: 117 gm
Cholesterol: 320 mg
Calcium: 77 mg

Iron: 13 mg
Vit. B1: 39 mg
Vit. B2: 0.79 mg
Vit. A: 229IU
Vit. C: 10 mg
Fiber: 0.5 gm

Calculated with beef chuck.

醸辣椒

MEAT STUFFED HOT PEPPERS
(Nian La Jiao)

Ingredients:

¼ lb	ground pork or beef
1	green onion, minced
1 t	ginger root, minced
1 T	soy sauce
1 t	sherry
¼ t	pepper
1 t	cornstarch
1 t	sesame oil
½ lb	fresh yellow or green hot peppers
2 T	oil
1	green onion, shredded
2	slices of ginger root
11/3 T	soy sauce
1 t	sugar
1 C	water
	Salt & pepper to taste

Method:

1. Thoroughly mix the first 8 ingredients in a bowl.
2. Cut off the stems of the peppers. Remove seeds with a sharp, narrow knife.
3. By hand, stuff the peppers with the meat mixture.
4. Heat oil; sauté onion and ginger root. Add the meat-stuffed peppers and the last 4 ingredients. Cover pan and cook over medium heat until the liquid is reduced to ¼ C. Serve hot.

Makes 4-6 servings.

Calories: 649		Iron: 6mg	
Carbohydrates: 46gm		Vit. B1: 0.8mg	
Protein: 18gm		Vit. B2: 0.7mg	
Fat: 46gm		Vit. A: 1270IU	
Cholesterol: 71mg		Vit. C: 826mg	
Calcium: 72mg		Fiber: 5gm	

MOO-SHU MEAT
(Mu Xu Rou)

木樨肉

Ingredients:

¼	lb	shredded pork or beef
1	T	soy sauce
1	t	sherry
1	t	cornstarch
30-40		dried lily buds (golden needles)
¼	C	small dried wood ears (cloud ears)
1-2	C	fresh bean sprouts, shredded celery, or bamboo shoots
2-3		dried mushrooms, soaked and shredded
3-4	T	oil
3		eggs beaten with ¼ t salt
2	t	shredded ginger root
2		or more green onions, shredded
2	T	soy sauce
½	t	sugar
1	T	sesame oil (optional)
¼	t	pepper

Method:

1. Marinate meat with the next 3 ingredients. Set aside.

2. Soak dried lily buds in hot water for 15 minutes. Drain and knot (see sketch on page 59).

3. Soak dried wood ears in hot water for 15 minutes. Wash and drain.

4. Heat half of the oil in a nonstick pan or wok. Scramble eggs and break them into fine pieces. Remove.

5. Add remainder of oil; stir-fry pork or beef with ginger root and onions for 2 minutes.

6. Add lily buds, wood ears, bean sprouts (or shredded celery, etc.) mushrooms, and the last 4 ingredients; stir and mix for 3 minutes.

7. Add scrambled eggs and mix well.

Serve hot with Chinese pancakes (recipe on page 209) or rice. With Chinese pancakes, spoon some of the Moo-Shu meat onto a pancake, roll and eat with your fingers.

Makes 6 servings.

Calories: 880	Cholesterol: 860mg	Vit. B2: 1mg
Carbohydrates: 16gm	Calcium: 141mg	Vit. A: 1987 IU
Protein: 46gm	Iron: 9mg	Vit. C: 20mg
Fat: 71gm	Vit. B1: 1.3mg	Fiber: 1gm

Calculated with pork butt. The lily buds and wood ears are not included.

豆豉炒肉絲

FERMENTED
BLACK BEANS WITH MEAT
(Dou Chi Chao Rou Si)

Ingredients:

2-4 T   fermented black beans, minced
1 t   minced ginger root
2-4   fresh or dried hot pepper, diced (optional)
1 T   soy sauce
½ lb   pork or beef, sliced

1 t   cornstarch
3 T   oil

½ lb   leeks
¼ t   salt or to taste
½ t   sugar
1 t   sesame oil (optional)

Method:

1. Mix the meat with 1 t cornstarch.

2. Wash leeks. Split the leeks in half lengthwise, then cut into 1" sections.

3. Heat oil in a pan or wok; add meat and the first 4 ingredients. Stir and mix for 2-3 minutes.

4. Add the last 4 ingredients; stir and mix until the leeks are wilted. Serve hot.

Step 1 can be prepared in advance.

Makes 3-4 servings.

Calories: 870	Cholesterol: 136mg	Vit. B2: 0.7mg
Carbohydrates: 36gm	Calcium: 157mg	Vit. A: 1601IU
Protein: 53gm	Iron: 10mg	Vit. C: 64mg
Fat: 57gm	Vit. B1: 2.5mg	Fiber: 4gm

SPRING FESTIVAL SOFT ROLLS, BEIJING STYLE
(Zhun Juan)

Ingredients:

- ½ lb   pork or beef, shredded
- 2 T   soy sauce
- 1 T   cornstarch
- 4 T   oil
- 3   thin slices of ginger root, finely shredded
- 2-3   cloves of garlic, crushed
- ½ C   bamboo shoots, shredded
- 1 C   egg shreds (page 197)
- ¼ lb   fresh spinach, shredded
- 1 T   sesame oil
- 2 T   soy sauce, or to taste
- 1 t   sugar
- ¼ t   pepper
- ½ lb   fresh bean sprouts, washed and drained
- 6   green onions, shredded
- 2 t   cornstarch blended with 2 T water

Method:

1. Mix the first 3 ingredients in a small bowl and set aside.
2. Heat oil in a pan or wok; add ginger root, garlic and meat; stir and toss until the color of the meat turns.
3. Add bamboo shoots and egg shreds; stir for 1 minute.
4. Add the last 6 ingredients; stir and cook for 1-2 minutes.
5. Add spinach and sesame oil; mix well.

Serve hot as a filling for Chinese pancakes (page 209). To serve, place about 1 T of the filling across the center of the cake. Roll the cake around the filling and eat with fingers.

This dish can be served as Spring Roll filling (page 337).

Calories: 1450   Carbohydrates: 40gm
Protein: 67gm   Fat: 116gm

甜酸·肉

Ingredients:

2 lb	pork chops, boned
½ t	onion powder
1 t	minced ginger root
5 T	soy sauce
1 T	sherry
⅛ t	pepper
1	egg white
2-3 T	cornstarch
1 C	or more oil for deep-frying
3	green onions, shredded
3	slices of ginger root
½ C	brown sugar
1 T	soy sauce
1 T	sherry
½ C	vinegar
2 T	cornstarch blended with 2 T water
1 C	water
1 T	sesame oil

Method:

1. Bone the pork chops. Cut the meat into ½"x2" pieces.

2. Mix the pork thoroughly with the next 6 ingredients. Mix with 2-3 T cornstarch and set aside.

3. Combine the last 7 ingredients in a bowl. Set aside.

4. Heat oil in a pan or wok; deep-fry the pork (drop the meat in to the oil carefully piece by piece) until brown and crisp. Tranfer to a serving dish.

5. Pour off all but 1 T of oil. Saute' onion and ginger root. Add well stirred sauce mixture from Step 3; stir and cook until the sauce thickens.

6. Add fried pork and mix well. Serve hot.

Calories: 2830	Carbohydrates: 130gm
Protein: 132gm	Fat: 193gm

Calculated with 4 T oil for deep-frying.

SWEET AND SOUR PORK LOIN
(Tian Suan Li Ji)

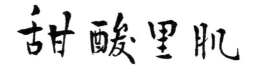

Ingredients:

¾ lb	pork loin
2 T	soy sauce
⅛ t	salt
¼ t	pepper
½ t	onion powder
1 t	sherry
1	egg
2 T	cornstarch
½ C	green pepper dices and a few tomato wedges (optional)
3-4 T	oil
1-2 T	minced ginger root
2-4	gloves of garlic, minced
1-2	green onion, minced
¼ C	sugar
2 t	cornstarch
¼ C	catsup
¼ C	vinegar
1 T	soy sauce
½ C	water

Method:

1. Cut the pork into ¼" thick slices. Pound slices until thin.

2. Mix the pork with the next 6 ingredients. Let stand for 1 hour or more. Mix the pork with 2 T cornstarch before cooking.

3. Combine the last 6 ingredients in a bowl. Set aside.

4. Heat oil in a pan or wok; fry the pork over medium heat until light brown. Transfer to a serving dish to keep warm.

5. Saute ginger root, garlic, and onion in the remaining oil. Add the sauce mixture from Step 3 and bring to a boil. Add green pepper dices and tomato wedges, if you prefer to use them. Pour the sauce over the cooked pork. Serve hot.

Makes 4-6 servings.

Calories: 1479	Iron: 14mg
Carbohydrates: 96gm	Vit. B1: 3.4mg
Protein: 78gm	Vit. B2: 1mg
Fat: 86gm	Vit. A: 1742IU
Cholesterol: 446mg	Vit. C: 14mg
Calcium: 118mg	Fiber: 0.6gm

SWEET AND SOUR PORK
(Gu Ru Rou)

Ingredients:

1 lb	pork, cubed (butt, shoulder or loin etc.)
1 T	sherry
3 T	soy sauce
¼ t	pepper
½ t	garlic or onion powder
1	egg
1/3 t	baking powder
4-6 T	cornstarch
	Oil for deep-frying, about 1 cup

Method:

1. Mix pork with the next 6 ingredients.

2. Add 4 T cornstarch to pork and mix well. If the coating is too drippy, add more cornstarch.

3. Heat oil in a wok or pan; carefully drop the pork pieces into the hot oil one by one and fry until golden brown. Remove to a serving plate and keep hot. Serve with sweet and sour sauces I or II. Steps 1 and 2 of the method can be prepared in advance. The fried pork can be refrigerated or frozen. Before serving, reheat the pork in a 300° oven until hot.

Sweet and Sour Sauce I (Cantonese Style)

¼ C   catsup
2 T   cornstarch
½ C   sugar
¼ C   vinegar
1 C   canned pineapple tidbits or chunks in heavy syrup
1 C   pineapple syrup from the can (add water to make up 1 cup if it is necessary.)
1 T   soy sauce
½   green pepper, cut into bite-sized pieces (optional)
1   tomato, cut into bite-sized pieces (optional)

Place all the ingredients (except green pepper and tomato) in a small sauce pan and mix well. Bring the sauce to a boil; stir constantly while cooking. Turn off heat; add green pepper and tomato to the sauce. Pour the sauce over pork immediately and serve.

Sweet and Sour Sauce II (Peking Style)

1 T   oil
2   green onions, shredded
3   slices of ginger root
2   cloves of garlic, crushed
1 T   cornstarch blended with ½ C of water
5 T   brown sugar
4 T   vinegar
2 t   sesame oil
1 T   soy sauce

Pour off all but 1 T of the oil used for deep-frying the pork. Saute onion, ginger root and garlic; add the last 5 ingredients and bring to a boil. Stir while cooking. Add fried pork and mix well. Serve hot.

Calories:	2360	Iron:	19mg
Carbohydrates:	257gm	Vit. B1:	4.5mg
Protein:	96gm	Vit. B2:	1.4mg
Fat:	105gm	Vit. A:	1923IU
Cholesterol:	530mg	Vit. C:	107mg
Calcium:	211mg	Fiber:	2gm

Calculated with sauce I and 4 T oil for deep-frying.

糖醋肉球

SWEET AND SOUR SCORED PORK
(Tang Cu Rou Qiu)

Ingredients:

- 1 lb   pork (loin, butt, etc.)
- 2 T   soy sauce
- ⅛ t   salt
- ¼ t   pepper
- ½ t   onion powder
- 1 T   sherry
- 1 T   cornstarch
- 4 T   oil
- 1   onion, minced
- 1 t   ginger root
- 1/3 C   sugar
- 1 T   cornstarch
- ¼ C   vinegar
- ¼ C   catsup
- ½ C   water
- 1 t   instant chicken bouillon
- 1 T   soy sauce
- ¼ t   pepper
- 1 T   sesame oil
- 3-4   dried mushrooms, soaked and sliced or ½ C bamboo shoots
- 10   water chestnuts, sliced
- ½ C   frozen peas, thawed

Method:

1. Slice the pork into ¼″ thick slices. Score the pork on one side in a crisscross pattern ⅛″ apart. Cut the meat into 1½″ squares.

2. Mix the meat with the next 5 ingredients. Let stand for 1 hour or more. Mix with 1 T cornstarch.

3. Combine the last 12 ingredients in a small pan. Set aside.

4. Heat oil in a pan or wok; sauté onion and ginger root. Add pork. (At the same time, in a separate pan, bring the sauce mixture from Step 3 to a boil; stir while cooking.) Stir and cook pork until color turns, about 2-3 minutes. Transfer to a serving plate.

5. Pour the cooked sauce over the pork; serve immediately.

Calories: 1867	Iron: 17mg
Carbohydrates: 116gm	Vit. B1: 4.6mg
Protein: 97gm	Vit. B2: 1.3mg
Fat: 113gm	Vit. A: 1246IU
Calcium: 128mg	Fiber: 2gm

Calculated with pork loin.

PRESERVED AND FRESH PORK
(Yan Man Xian)

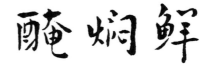

Ingredients:

2 lb	pork
1 lb	old-fashioned, country-style, dried ham
1 T	sherry
1	onion, chopped
2-4	slices of ginger root
3 C	water

Method:

1. Cut the pork and ham into 1" cubes.

2. Put all the ingredients in a medium sauce pan; cover and bring to a boil. Continue boiling for 10 minutes.

3. Reduce to medium heat; cook until the liquid is reduced to ½ C and the meat becomes tender. Serve hot.

If the water evaporates before the meat becomes tender, add ½-1 C water.

One pound of rolling-cut bamboo shoots can be added when the meat is half done. Add soy sauce if necessary.

Makes 4-6 servings.

Calories: 2919	Iron: 25mg
Carbohydrates: 8gm	Vit. B1: 8.1mg
Protein: 256gm	Vit. B2: 2mg
Fat: 197gm	Vit. A: 22IU
Cholesterol: 754mg	Vit. C: 7mg
Calcium: 114mg	Fiber: 0.3gm

PORK WITH WOOD EARS AND BAMBOO SHOOTS
(Hu Cai)

Ingredients:

½ lb	pork, sliced
1 t	sherry
1 T	soy sauce
¼ t	pepper
¼ t	onion powder
½	egg white
1 T	cornstarch
3 T	oil
1 t	finely minced ginger root
1 t	minced garlic or more
¼ C	minced pickled hot pepper
2	green onions, minced
1 C	sliced bamboo shoots
1 C	soaked wood ears
1 T	sherry
1 t	sugar
⅛ t	Sichuan peppercorn powder
1 T	vinegar
1 T	soy sauce
1 T	water
2 t	cornstarch

Method:

1. Mix the pork thoroughly with the next 5 ingredients. Add cornstarch and mix well.

2. Mix the last 7 ingredients in a small bowl. Set aside.

3. Heat oil in a pan or wok; saute' ginger root, garlic, pickled pepper, and minced onions.

4. Add meat; stir until color turns. Add wood ears and bamboo shoots; stir for 1 minute.

5. Add the sauce mixture from Step 2; stir and cook for 1 minute. Serve hot.

Calories: 745   Protein: 50gm
Carbohydrates: 27gm   Fat: 48gm

SESAME PORK
(Zi Ma Su Rou)

芝麻酥肉

Ingredients:

- 1 lb   pork (loin, butt etc.)
- 1 t   sherry
- ½ t   onion powder
- 1 t   ginger root, minced
- ¼ t   pepper
- ½ t   Sichuan peppercorn powder for dipping (page 314)
- 2 T   soy sauce
- ½ t   sugar
- ½   egg, beaten
- ¼ C   sesame seeds
- 2 T   cornstarch
- 1-2   green onions, minced or ¼ C minced parsley or coriander
- 4 T   oil
- 1 C   water
- 1 t   instant chicken bouillon
- ½ t   sugar
- 1 T   fresh lemon juice
- 2 t   cornstarch blended with 2 T water.

Method:

1. Cut the pork into 2"x1½"x¼" slices. Mix the pork with the next 9 ingredients. Let stand for 1 hour or more. Coat the pork with cornstarch before cooking.

2. Heat oil in a pan or wok. Place the pork slices one by one into the pan; fry over medium heat until brown. Transfer to a plate. Keep warm.

3. Add the last 5 ingredients to the pan and bring to a boil. Stir while cooking. Pour the cooked sauce over the fried pork. Garnish with the minced onion, parsley or coriander. Serve hot.

Makes 4-6 servings. Without the sauce, the pork may be served as an appetizer.

Calories:	1756	Cholesterol:	389mg	Vit. B2:	1.3mg
Carbohydrates:	40gm	Calcium:	572mg	Vit. A:	332IU
Protein:	103gm	Iron:	20mg	Vit. C:	13mg
Fat:	130gm	Vit. B1:	4.8mg	Fiber:	3gm

甜 醬 燉 肉

BRAISED PORK WITH BEAN PASTE
(Tian Jiang Dun Rou)

Ingredients:

½ C	Hoisin sauce
2 T	soy sauce, dark
1 T	sherry
2 lb	boned fresh ham or shoulder with the skin on
2-3	green onions, cut into 3-inch sections
4	slices of ginger root
1 t	brown sugar
3 C	water
1 T	sesame oil
	Parsley leaves for garnishing

Method:

1. Mix the first 3 ingredients in a small bowl.

2. Rub the mixture over the pork and let set for a few hours or overnight in the refrigerator.

3. Place the pork in a medium sauce pan; add water and brown sugar, green onions, and ginger root. Cover and bring to a boil.

4. Reduce to low heat and simmer until the pork is tender and the liquid is reduced to ¼ C.

5. Cut the pork into ½" thick slices. Arrange neatly on a serving dish. Discard the green onions and ginger root; add sesame oil. Pour the sauce over the pork. Garnish with parsley and serve hot.

In China, people serve this dish with the skin. If you do not like the skin, simply discard before cooking or use pork butt instead of fresh ham or shoulder.

Calories:	2400	Carbohydrates:	25gm
Protein:	135gm	Fat:	195gm

HU-NAN PRESERVED MEAT AND LEEKS
(Hu Nan La Rou)

Ingredients:

¾ lb   Hu-Nan preserved pork or old fashioned, country-style dry ham

1-2 T   oil

2-4   fresh hot peppers or dried peppers, shredded (optional)

1 lb   leeks

1 T   sherry

1 t   brown sugar

      Soy sauce or salt to taste

Method:

1. Cut the meat into 1½"x½"x⅛" slices.
2. Wash off the sand and mud from the leeks. Discard the roots. Cut the leeks in half lengthwise, then cut into 1" sections.
3. Heat oil in a pan or wok; sauté pepper and ginger root. Add meat; stir and cook for 5 minutes over medium heat.
4. Add leeks; stir and cook until the leeks are wilted and tender.
5. Add sherry and brown sugar; mix well. Serve hot.

The flavor of old-fashioned, country-style ham resembles the Hu-Nan preserved pork. It is one of the most popular dishes of the Hu-Nan province.

Calories:	1417	Iron:	5mg
Carbohydrates:	56gm	Vit. B1:	0.5mg
Protein:	75gm	Vit. B2:	0.3mg
Fat:	99gm	Vit. A:	172IU
Cholesterol:	141mg	Vit. C:	76mg
Calcium:	237mg	Fiber:	6gm

FRESH HAM, SICHUAN STYLE
(Xiang Su Yuang Ti)

Ingredients:

1	fresh ham or shoulder, about 3-5 pounds
2 T	Sichuan peppercorn powder for dipping (page 314)
½ t	onion powder
½ t	ginger powder
1 T	cornstarch
1 C	Oil for deep-frying
½ C	minced coriander leaves for garnish.

Method:

1. Mix 1½ T of the Sichuan peppercorn powder with ½ t onion powder and ½ t ginger powder. Rub the mixture thoroughly over the fresh ham. Keep in the refrigerator, covered, for 6 hours or overnight.

2. Place the ham in a deep heat-proof bowl, then steam in a boiling steamer for 3 hours. Check the water in the steamer and add more if needed.

3. Transfer the ham to a plate. Reserve the juice left in the bowl.

4. Gently remove the bones without disturbing the meat.

5. Mix 1 T cornstarch together with 1½ t Sichuan peppercorn powder for dipping; rub the mixture evenly on the steamed ham.

6. Heat oil to 375° in a wok. Deep-fry the ham until brown and crisp on the outside.

7. Slice the ham and arrange on a platter. Garnish with coriander. Serve hot with Chinese steamed bread, rice, or buns.

Makes 4-6 servings.

Calories: 2499		Iron: 41mg	
Carbohydrates: 7gm		Vit. B1: 13.3mg	
Protein: 274gm		Vit. B2: 0 mg	
Fat: 145gm		Vit. A: 0	
Cholesterol: 816mg		Vit. C: 0	
Calcium: 161mg		Fiber: 0	

Calculated with lean ham.

ZUCCHINI WITH PORK
(Rou Pian Chao Nen Gua)

Ingredients:

½ lb	pork (fresh ham, butt, loin, etc.)
1½ T	soy sauce
½ t	sugar
¼ t	pepper
1 t	sherry
½ t	onion powder
1 t	sesame oil
2 t	cornstarch
3 T	oil
¼	onion, chopped
3	slices of ginger root
	Salt and pepper to taste
1 lb	zucchini (green summer squash)
1 T	soy sauce or more

Method:

1. Slice the pork into 1½"x¾"x1/6" pieces. Marinate the pork with the next 7 ingredients.

2. Wash the zucchini; remove both ends. Slant slice it into 1/6" slices. If the zucchini is larger than 1½" in diameter, split lengthwise before slicing.

3. Heat oil in a pan or wok; sauté onion and ginger root. Add pork; stir-fry for 3 minutes.

4. Add zucchini and soy sauce; stir with the pork for two minutes. Add a little water if it is too dry while cooking. Serve hot.

Makes 4-6 servings.

Calories:	1003	Iron:	12mg
Carbohydrates:	46gm	Vit. B1:	2.49mg
Protein:	54gm	Vit B2:	1.39mg
Fat:	69gm	Vit. A:	3275IU
Cholesterol:	142mg	Vit. C:	175gm
Calcium:	309mg	Fiber:	5gm

Ingredients:

1 lb	pork loin
3 T	soy sauce
1 t	sherry
1	small egg
¼ t	pepper
½ t	onion powder
1 t	minced ginger root
4-6 T	cornstarch
	Sichuan peppercorn powder or horseradish for dipping
4 T	oil
	Boston lettuce or parsley for garnishing

Method:

1. Cut the pork into 1/6″ slices.

2. Marinate the pork slices with the next 6 ingredients for 2 hours or more.

3. Mix the pork with 4 T cornstarch. If the batter is too drippy, add more cornstarch.

4. Heat oil in a non-stick pan or wok. Add pork and fry until golden brown over medium heat. Serve hot with a small dish of Sichuan peppercorn powder or horseradish for dipping. Boston lettuce or parsley may be used for garnish.

Makes 4-6 servings.

Calories: 1578		Iron: 17mg	
Carbohydrates: 34gm		Vit. B1: 4.4mg	
Protein: 99gm		Vit. B2: 1.3mg	
Fat: 113gm		Vit. A: 590IU	
Cholesterol: 506mg		Vit. C: 1mg	
Calcium:118mg		Fiber: 0.5gm	

QUI HUA PORK
(Gui Hua Rou)

桂花肉

Ingredients:

¾ lb   pork loin
- 2 T   soy sauce
- ½ t   pepper
- ½ t   onion powder
- 1 t   sherry

2   eggs
½ C   glutinous rice powder
¼ t   salt
½ t   sugar
      Oil for deep-frying
1-2   green onions, minced for garnishing
- 1 T   cornstarch
- 1 T   sugar
- 1 T   vinegar
- 2 T   soy sauce
- 1 t   sesame oil
- 2/3 C   water

Method:

1. Cut pork across the grain in ¼" thick pieces. Mix with the next 4 ingredients. Let it set for 20 minutes or more.

2. Mix the eggs, glutinous rice powder, ¼ t salt, and ½ t sugar in a mixing bowl. Add pork pieces and mix well.

3. Mix the last 6 ingredients in a small bowl. Set aside.

4. Heat oil in a pan or wok on high heat. Turn to medium heat; add pork and fry until brown. Remove to a serving plate.

5. Pour off all the oil. Add the sauce mixture (from Step 3) and bring to a boil. Stir while cooking. Pour the sauce over the pork; garnish with minced onions. Serve hot.

Makes 4-6 servings.

Calories: 1819	Cholesterol: 680mg	Vit. B2: 1.6mg
Carbohydrates: 108gm	Calcium: 171mg	Vit. A: 1380IU
Protein: 90gm	Iron: 18mg	Vit. C: 3mg
Fat: 111gm	Vit. B1: 3.8mg	Fiber: 0

Calculated with 4 T oil for deep-frying.

 STIR-FRY VEGETABLES WITH EGG HAT
(Ho Cai Dai Mao)

Ingredients:

- ½ lb pork, shredded (butt, fresh ham etc.)
- 1 T soy sauce
- 1 t sherry
- ¼ t pepper
- ¼ t onion powder
- 1 t cornstarch
- 2 oz bean threads
- ½ lb leeks
- ¼ lb fresh spinach
- ¼ lb bean sprouts
- 5 T oil
- 3 slices of ginger root
- 3 eggs
- ½ t salt
- 1 t sugar
- 2 T soy sauce
- ¼ t pepper
- 1 t sesame oil

Method:

1. Mix the first 6 ingredients in a small bowl. Set aside.
2. Soak bean threads in hot water for 10 minutes, drain and cut into 3" sections.
3. Wash leeks and spinach; pat dry, then cut into shreds. Wash and clean the bean sprouts.
4. Beat eggs with ¼ t salt, a pinch of pepper and onion powder.
5. Heat 3 T oil in a pan or wok; sauté ginger root. Add pork and stir-fry until color turns.
6. Add leeks; stir and mix for 1 minute.
7. Add bean threads and the last 5 ingredients; stir and mix for 2 minutes.
8. Add bean sprouts and spinach; stir and mix until the bean sprouts are wilted (about 1 minute). Remove to a serving plate.
9. Heat 2 T oil in the pan; add eggs. Tip the pan so that a layer of egg covers the bottom of the pan. Cook until surface dries. Turn to the other side and cook for ½ minute. Place the egg sheet over the cooked vegetables. Serve hot.

Makes 6 servings.

Calories:	2152	Iron:	19mg
Carbohydrates:	91gm	Vit. B1:	3.9mg
Protein:	104gm	Vit. B2:	1.9gm
Fat:	154gm	Vit. A:	20025IU
Cholesterol:	830mg	Vit. C:	173gm
Calcium:	500gm	Fiber:	6gm

红 白 肉 片

RED AND WHITE STIR-FRY PORK
(Hong Bai Rou Pian)

Ingredients:

½ lb   pork loin, sliced

I
- 1½ T   soy sauce
- ¼ t   five-spice powder
- 1 t   sherry
- ¼   egg, beaten
- 2 T   cornstarch

II
- 1/3 t   salt
- ⅛ t   pepper
- ¼ t   onion or garlic powder
- 1 t   sherry
- ½   egg white
- 2 T   cornstarch

- 6 T   oil
- 2-4   green onions, minced
- 1 T   ginger root, minced
- 2 T   garlic, minced
- 1 C   sliced cucumber
- 1 C   sliced bamboo shoot
- 1 C   celery cabbage or napa, cut into ¾" pieces
- 1 C   thinly sliced carrots
- 1 C   soaked wood ears
- 2 T   soy sauce
- 1 T   sesame oil
- Salt and pepper to taste

Method:

1. Slice the pork into 1" x 1½" x ⅛" thick slices. Divide the pork into two portions.

2. Mix one portion of the pork with the first group of ingredients (I) and the other portion with the second group of ingredients (II).

3. Heat 2 T oil in a pan or wok; sauté onions, ginger root and garlic. Add the last 8 ingredients; stir and mix for 2 minutes. Remove.

4. Heat 2 T oil; add one portion of the pork and stir for 2 minutes. Add half of the cooked vegetables and mix well. Arrange on one side of a serving plate.

5. Heat 2 T oil and cook the other portion of the pork in the same manner. Transfer this cooked portion to the other side of the serving plate. Serve hot.

Calories: 1800	Cholesterol: 230 mg	Vit. B1: 1.9 mg
Carbohydrate: 37 gm	Calcium: 63 mg	Vit. B2: 0.56 mg
Protein: 42 gm	Iron: 7 mg	Vit. C: 100 mg
Fat: 160 gm	Vit. A: 11000IU	Fiber: 1 gm

豆豉和菜

**FERMENTED BLACK BEANS
WITH MEAT AND VEGETABLES**
(Dou Shi Hu Cai)

Ingredients:

½ lb	pork loin or beef flank steak
⅛ t	salt
½ t	sherry
½ t	onion powder
⅛ t	pepper
1 t	cornstarch
1 T	or more, fermented black beans, minced
1 t	minced ginger root
1 T	soy sauce
½ t	sugar
3 T	oil
1	carrot, peeled and thinly sliced
⅛ lb	or more, snow pea pods
1 C	bamboo shoot slices
2-3	green onions, shredded
¼ t	pepper
1 T	sherry
1 T	soy sauce
1 T	sesame oil (optional)

Method:

1. Slice the meat into slices (1½"x½"x⅛"). Mix the meat with the next 5 ingredients.

2. Wash and remove the stems and string from both ends of the snow pea pods.

3. Heat oil in a pan or wok; add seasoned meat and the next 4 ingredients. Stir and mix for 3-4 minutes.

4. Add the last 8 ingredients; stir and mix for 1-2 minutes. Serve hot.

Makes 4-6 servings.

Calories: 884	Cholesterol: 136mg	Vit. B2: 0.7mg
Carbohydrates: 19gm	Calcium: 95mg	Vit. A: 787IU
Protein: 50gm	Iron: 8mg	Vit. C: 19mg
Fat: 68gm	Vit. B1: 2.4mg	Fiber: 1gm

FISH FLAVORED MEAT SHREDS
(Yu Xiang Rou Si)

No fish or its by products are used in this dish. The seasonings used in this dish are used for cooking most of the fish dishes. This is where the reference to "fish flavor" comes from.

Ingredients:

- 1 lb   pork, shredded (meat from pork chops, loins, etc.)
- 1 T   sherry
- 2 T   soy sauce
- ¼ t   pepper
- 1   egg white
- 2 T   cornstarch
- 4 T   oil
- 2 t   finely shredded ginger root, or more
- 4-5   green onions, shredded
- ½ C   or more shredded pickled pepper (Del Monte or other brand yellow or green hot pickled peppers are available at stores.)
- 1 C   shredded bamboo shoots
- 1 T   sherry
- 2 t   sugar
- 2   cloves of garlic, minced
- ½ t   Sichuan peppercorn powder for seasoning (page 314)
- 1 T   red oil or more (page 313)
- 1 T   vinegar
- 1 T   soy sauce
- 1 T   Hot bean sauce or paste (available at Oriental grocery stores)
- 1 T   water
- 1 T   cornstarch

Method:

1. Combine the first 5 ingredients in a bowl and mix thoroughly. Add cornstarch and mix well.

2. Place the last 10 ingredients in a small bowl; blend well.

3. Heat oil in a pan or wok; sauté ginger root. Add meat; stir and toss until the meat shreds separate.

4. Add onions, pickled pepper and bamboo shoots; stir with the meat for 1-2 minutes.

5. Add the sauce mixture from Step 2; stir for 1-2 minutes.   Serve hot.

Calories:	1720	Carbohydrates:	32gm
Protein:	68gm	Fat:	145gm

This Sichuan-style shredded pork recipe won the first prize in a Shanghai city-wide cooking contest in 1980.

Giant panda of Sichuan Province

LOTUS LEAF STEAMED PORK
(He Ye Zheng Rou)

Ingredients:

2-3 lb	pork (butt, spareribs, loin, fresh ham, boneless shoulder etc.)
2-3	lotus leaves, fresh or dried
1-2 T	cornstarch
4	green onions, minced
2 t	minced ginger root
1 t	Sichuan peppercorn powder for dipping (page 314)
2 T	soy sauce
1 T	sherry
¼ t	pepper
1 t	sugar

Method:

1. Cut the meat into 1" cubes. Marinate the meat with the last 7 ingredients for two hours or more. Mix with 1 T cornstarch.

2. Soak the dried lotus leaves in warm water until softened. Wash and dry. If using fresh leaves, wash and dry them

3. Divide the pork into 2-3 portions. Wrap one portion of the pork in one leaf. Repeat.

4. Put the wrapped pork in a shallow dish and steam in a boiling steamer for 1-1½ hours.

5. Unwrap the pork and arrange, with its juices, on a serving dish. Serve hot. Thicken the juice with l t cornstarch blended with 1 T water before serving if desired.

Makes 4-6 servings.

Calories:	1591	Iron:	27mg
Carbohydrates:	19gm	Vit. B1:	8mg
Protein:	169gm	Vit. B2:	2mg
Fat:	85gm	Vit. A:	800IU
Cholesterol:	566mg	Vit. C:	13mg
Fiber:	0.5gm	Calcium:	144mg

蒜苗炒粉絲

BEAN THREADS
WITH HAM AND LEEKS
(Suan Miao Cho Fen Si)

Ingredients:

3 T	oil
2	slices of ginger root
½ lb	old-fashioned country-style ham, shredded
2 oz	bean thread
1	medium sized carrot, shredded
½ lb	leeks
2 T	soy sauce
½ t	sugar
1 t	sesame oil

Method:

1. Soak bean thread in warm water for 30 minutes. Drain and cut into 3″ sections.

2. Wash the leeks (be sure to remove all the mud and sand), then cut into shreds.

3. Heat oil in a pan or wok; saute ginger root. Add ham; stir and turn for 2 minutes.

4. Add bean thread; stir and mix for 3 minutes. Add carrots, stir and mix for 1 minute.

5. Add leeks, soy sauce and sugar; stir and mix until the leeks are wilted.

6. Add sesame oil; mix well. Serve hot.

Makes 4-6 servings.

Calories: 1131	Iron: 3mg
Carbohydrates: 33gm	Vit. B1 0.3mg
Protein: 49gm	Vit. B2: 0.2mg
Fat: 89gm	Vit. A: 5589IU
Cholesterol: 94mg	Vit.C: 42mg
Calcium: 135mg	Fiber: 3gm

(Bean threads not included in this calculation, see page 10)

HOISIN SAUCE HAM WITH NUTS
(Jiang Bao Rou)

Ingredients:

- 1 T soy sauce
- 1 T sherry
- ¼ t pepper
- 1 t finely minced ginger root
- ¼ t onion or garlic powder
- 1 T cornstarch
- 1 lb fresh ham, diced
- 4 T Hoisin sauce
- 1 T water
- ¼ t salt
- 1 T sesame oil
- 3 T oil
- ½ C or more walnuts, peanuts, almonds or cashews, freshly roasted
- 2 green onions, minced
- 2 slices of ginger root
  Coriander (Chinese parsley) for garnishing

Method:

1. Mix the diced ham thoroughly with the first 5 ingredients. Add cornstarch and mix well.

2. Heat oil in a non-stick pan or wok; sauté onion and ginger root.

3. Add ham and stir constantly for 4 minutes.

4. Add nuts, Hoisin sauce, water, salt and sesame oil; stir and mix for 1-2 minutes.

5. Transfer to a serving plate and garnish with a few coriander leaves. Serve hot.

Calories: 1625   Carbohydrates: 25gm
Protein: 105gm   Fat: 123gm

甜醤炒肉 HOISIN SAUCE PORK WITH GREEN ONIONS
(Tian Jiang Chao Rou)

Ingredients:

- 2 T soy sauce
- 2 t sherry
- ¼ t pepper
- 3 slices of ginger root
- 1 T cornstarch
- 1 lb pork fresh ham, or pork butt
- 4 T Hoisin sauce or more
- 1 T water
- 1 can (8 oz) water chestnuts, sliced
- 3 T oil
- 2 bunches of green onions, shredded
- 1 T sesame oil, or more

Method:

1. Cut the pork into 1½x1"x1/6" pieces. Mix with the first 4 ingredients. Mix the pork with 1 T cornstarch before cooking.
2. Combine the Hoisin sauce and water in a small bowl. Set aside.
3. Heat oil in a pan or wok. Add pork; stir-fry for 3-5 minutes; add water chestnuts and sauce mixture from Step 2 and mix well.
4. Add onion shreds; stir and cook until the onions are wilted.
5. Add sesame oil and mix well. Serve hot.
Makes 4-6 servings.

Calories: 1218
Carbohydrates: 27gm
Protein: 97gm
Fat: 77gm
Cholesterol: 283mg
Calcium: 143mg.

Iron: 17mg
Vit. B1: 4.5mg
Vit. B2: 1.2mg
Vit. A: 2000IU
Vit. C: 32mg
Fiber: 2gm

SICHUAN PICKLE WITH MEAT
(Zha Cai Rou Si)

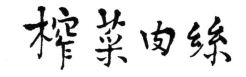

Ingredients:

- 1 T soy sauce
- ½ t onion powder
- ¼ t pepper
- 2 t cornstarch
- 1 T sherry
- ¾ lb pork butt, loin, fresh ham etc., finely shredded
- 4 T oil
- 2 green onions, shredded
- 2 t shredded ginger root
- ¾-1 C bamboo shoots, shredded
- ¾ C Sichuan pickle, (mustard pickle), shredded
- ½ t sugar

Method:

1. Mix the pork shreds with the first 5 ingredients. Set aside.
2. Heat oil in a pan or wok; sauté onion and ginger root
3. Add pork; stir-fry for 5 minutes. Separate pork shreds while cooking.
4. Add bamboo shoots, Sichuan pickle and sugar; stir and mix for 2-3 minutes. Salt to taste. Serve hot.

Step 1 can be prepared in advance.
Makes 4-6 servings.

Calories: 1190		Iron: 15gm	
Carbohydrates: 23gm		Vit. B1: 3.2mg	
Protein: 69gm		Vit. B2: 0.9mg	
Fat: 90gm		Vit. A: 420IU	
Cholesterol: 212mg		Vit. C: 10mg	
Calcium: 127mg		Fiber: 2gm	

粉蒸肉

STEAMED PORK WITH SPICY-RICE POWDER
(Fen Zheng Rou)

Ingredients:

1 lb	pork (butt, fresh ham, or shoulder, etc.)
½ C	spicy rice powder (buy the ready made rice powder found in Oriental grocery stores or follow the recipe on page 311). Chopped parsley or coriander for garnishing
1 t	onion powder
2 t	minced ginger root or more
¼ t	pepper
2 T	oyster sauce
1 T	sherry
1 t	brown sugar

Method:

1. Cut the pork into slices, 1/6" thick. Mix the pork with the last 6 ingredients. Let stand for 1 hour or more.

2. Put the rice powder on a plate. Coat the pork slices one by one with a layer of rice powder. Arrange the rice coated pork in a heat-proof serving dish and steam in a boiling steamer for 1½ hours.

3. Garnish with chopped parsley or coriander before serving. Serve hot.

Cut up spareribs can be used for this dish also.

Makes 4-6 servings.

Calories: 1155		Iron: 17mg	
Carbohydrates: 87gm		Vit. B1: 4.5mg	
Protein: 92gm		Vit. B2: 1.4mg	
Fat: 43gm		Vit. A: 0	
Cholesterol: 283mg		Vit. C: 0	
Calcium: 102mg		Fiber: 0.4gm	

MEAT BALLS IN LEMON SAUCE
(Ning Meng Rou Wan)

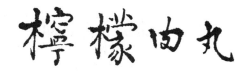

Ingredients:

- 1 lb   ground pork or beef
- 6   water chestnuts or more, coarsely minced
- ¼   onion, finely minced
- 1 t   minced ginger root
- 1   dried mushroom, soaked and minced (optional)
- 1   egg white
- 3½ T   soy sauce
- 1 t   sherry
- ¼ t   pepper
- ½ t   sugar
- 1 T   cornstarch
- 2   green onions, shredded
- 1   fresh tomato, cut into wedges (optional)
-     Lemon slices for garnishing
-     Oil for deep-frying
- 2/3 C   water
- 1 t   instant chicken bouillon
- ½ C   sugar
- ½ T   soy sauce
- ⅛ t   salt
- 3-4 T   fresh lemon juice
- ¼ C   vinegar
- 2 t   cornstarch
- ⅛ t   pepper
- 1 t   lemon extract
- 1   carrot, sliced
- ½-¾ C   pineapple tidbits

Method:

1. Mix the first 11 ingredients together thoroughly. Form the meat into 1" balls.

2. Combine the last 12 ingredients in a bowl. Set aside.

3. Heat oil in a pan or wok to 375°-400°. Fry meat balls until brown and done. Transfer to a serving dish and keep warm.

4. Pour off all the oil except 1 T. Add the sauce mixture from Step 2 and bring to a boil. Stir while cooking. Add tomato. Pour the sauce over cooked meat balls. Garnish with green onion and lemon slices.
Makes 4-6 servings.

Calories:	2103	Iron:	18mg
Carbohydrates:	211gm	Vit. B1:	4.4mg
Protein:	97gm	Vit. B2:	1.4mg
Fat:	98gm	Vit. A:	7383IU
Cholesterol:	283mg	Vit. C:	89mg
Calcium:	170mg	Fiber:	2gm

Calculated with 3 T oil for deep frying

LUCKY MEAT BALLS
(Ru Yi Rou Wan)

Ingredients:

- 1 lb — pork or beef
- 3-4 — dried mushrooms, soaked and minced
- 6 — water chestnuts, coarsely minced
- 1 — green onion, minced
- 1 t — finely minced ginger root
- 1 T — soy sauce
- 1½ t — salt
- ¼ t — pepper
- 1 T — sherry
- 1 — egg
- 2 t — cornstarch
- 6 — egg sheets (recipe, page 197)
- 2 t — cornstarch
- 1/3 C — sugar
- 1 C — milk
- 4 T — vinegar
- Parsley leaves for garnishing

Method:

1. Combine the first 11 ingredients in a mixing bowl; mix well.
2. Form the meat mixture into 24 balls. Cut each egg sheet into quarters. Wrap each meat ball in a piece of egg sheet. Repeat.
3. Arrange the wrapped balls, seam side down, in the tier of a steamer and steam over boiling water for 30 minutes.
4. Place the sugar and 2 t cornstarch in a small sauce pan, mix well. Add milk to the mixture, stir and cook until the sauce thickens. Add vinegar, 1 T at a time; stir and mix well.
5. Arrange the meat balls neatly on a platter. Pour the sauce on the meat balls. Garnish with parsley and serve hot.

The meat balls can be served plain without sauce.

The meat balls:
Calories: 1470   Carbohydrates: 10gm
Protein: 120gm   Fat: 100gm

The sauce:
Calories: 365   Protein: 9
Carbohydrates: 82gm   Fat: 0

Calculated with skim milk

獅子頭

Ingredients:

- 2 lb ground pork
- 5 T soy sauce
- 1 T sherry
- ¼ t pepper
- 2 green onions, minced
- 1 t finely minced ginger root
- 1 t brown sugar
- 3 Chinese dried mushrooms, soaked and coarsely minced
- 6 water chestnuts, coarsely minced
- 2 T cornstarch
- 1 C oil for deep-frying
- 1½ C water
- 1 lb Napa (Chinese cabbage), cut the leaves lengthwise in half
- 1 green onion, cut in half
- 3 thin slices of ginger root
- 1 T soy sauce
- 1 t brown sugar

Method:

1. Mix the first 10 ingredients together thoroughly. Divide the meat into 4 large meat balls.

2. Heat oil; brown meat balls.

3. Pour off oil. Add 1½ C water, green onions, ginger root, and 1 T soy sauce. Cover and bring to a boil.

4. Reduce to low heat and simmer the meat balls for 1 hour.

5. Add Chinese cabbage and 1 t brown sugar. Cover and cook over medium heat until the cooking liquid is reduced to one half cup.

6. Line a serving dish with the Chinese cabbage (the cabbage should be very soft and tender). Arrange meat balls on the cabbage and serve hot.

This dish does not require constant attention while cooking. The meat balls (Steps 1-4) can be cooked in advance and also can be frozen. Before serving, add vegetable and cook (follow Steps 5-6).

Calories: 2425   Carbohydrates: 40gm
Protein: 145gm   Fat: 185

Calculated with 1 T oil for deep-frying.

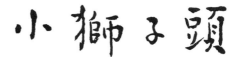

MINIATURE LION'S HEAD
(SMALL MEAT BALLS)
(Xiao Si Zi Tou)

小 獅 子 頭

Ingredients:

3 lb	ground pork
4 T	soy sauce
1 t	salt
½ t	pepper
1 T	finely minced ginger root
2-3	green onions, minced or ½ onion, finely minced
1 T	sherry
3-4	dried mushrooms, soaked and minced
2 T	cornstarch
1½ C	water or more
	Oil for browning the meat balls
1 lb	bamboo shoots, cubed
1-3	green onions, shredded
4	slices of ginger root
1 T	soy sauce or to taste
1 t	brown sugar or more

Method:

1. Mix the first 8 ingredients together thoroughly. Add cornstarch; mix well. Make 1½" meat balls with the palms of your hands.

2. Heat oil in a pan or wok; brown the meat balls.

3. Pour off oil. Add 1½ C water and the last 5 ingredients to the meat balls cover and bring to a boil.

4. Reduce to low heat and simmer for 1 hour or until the liquid is reduced to ¼ C. Serve hot.

This dish does not require constant attention while cooking. The meat balls (Steps 1-4) can be cooked in advance and also can be frozen. Before serving, add vegetable and cook (follow Step 5).

Makes 8-10 servings.

Calories:	2600	Cholesterol:	960mg	Vit. B2:	3.4mg
Carbohydrates:	44gm	Calcium:	250mg	Vit. A:	700IU
Protein:	263	Iron:	12.5mg	Vit. A:	30mg
Fat:	144gm	Vit. B1:	12.5mg	Fiber:	3mg

Calculated with lean ground pork butt and 1 T oil for browning.

**STEAMED SPARERIBS
WITH FERMENTED BLACK BEANS**
(Dou Chi Zheng Pai Gu)

Ingredients:

2 lb	baby spareribs (ask your butcher to cut the ribs)
2 T	fermented salted black beans, minced
2-4	cloves of garlic, minced
1 T	sherry
4 T	soy sauce
1 T	brown sugar
1 t	finely minced ginger root
1	fresh hot pepper, or more, diced (optional)
1 T	cornstarch

Method:

1. Ask your butcher to cut spareribs across the bone into 1-inch wide strips. Separate the ribs into small pieces with a cleaver or knife by cutting between bones.

2. Marinate the ribs with rest of ingredients (except for the cornstarch) for 2-4 hours or overnight in refrigerator. Turn from time to time for even flavor.

3. Mix the ribs thoroughly with 1 T cornstarch before steaming.

4. Steam the ribs over boiling water in a covered steamer for 30 minutes or until they are done. Serve hot.

Calories:	1800	Carbohydrates:	22gm
Protein:	80gm	Fat:	153gm

HUNG SHAO SPARERIBS, WU-SIH STYLE
(Hung Shao Pai Gu)

Ingredients:

¾ C	soy sauce (dark soy sauce is better for this dish)
2 T	sherry
4	green onions, shredded
½-in	ginger root, crushed
8-10	cloves of star anise
1	cinnamon stick
3-4 lb	pork spareribs, regular or country style
3 T	brown sugar
	Water to cover the spareribs
1 T	cornstarch blended with ¼ C water (optional)

Method:

1. Ask your butcher to cut the spareribs, across the bone into 2-3-inch wide strips. Separate the ribs into small pieces with a cleaver or knife by cutting between bones.

2. Place the spareribs in a large bowl, add the first 6 ingredients to the ribs and mix well. Let it set for few hours or overnight. Turn occasionally for even flavor.

3. Put the spareribs and the marinade in a medium sauce pan; add water and sugar; cover and bring to a boil.

4. Reduce to low heat and simmer until the meat is tender and the liquid is reduced to ¼ cup.

5. Transfer the meat to a serving dish. Stir the blended cornstarch into the liquid and cook until it thickens; pour it over the cooked meat and serve hot.

If the cooking liquid dries before the meat is tender, add water and continue to cook. If the meat becomes tender and too much liquid remains, remove the lid and cook over high heat until the liquid is reduced to the desired amount.

Sliced fresh mushrooms or soaked dry lily buds can be added to the cooking liquid before it thickens.

Calories: 2700
Protein: 118gm
Carbohydrates: 53gm
Fat: 225gm

甜酸排骨

Ingredients:

- 2 lb   spareribs
- 4 T   soy sauce
- ½ t   onion powder
- ¼ t   pepper
- 1 T   sherry
- 1 T   cornstarch
- 1 C   oil for deep-frying
- 2-3   green onions, cut into 2-inch sections
- 3-4   slices of ginger root
- 1 T   sesame oil
- 1 C   water
- ¼ C   catsup
- ¼ C   sugar
- 1 T   soy sauce
- 2 T   vinegar

Method:

1. Ask the butcher to cut the spareribs across the bone into 1½" sections. Separate spareribs into small pieces by cutting between bones.

2. Place the first 5 ingredients in a mixing bowl and mix well. Let set for 4 hours or more. Mix the spareribs with 1 T cornstarch before cooking.

3. Heat oil in a pan or wok; fry the spareribs for 2 minutes. With a slotted spoon, transfer the spareribs to a platter.

4. Pour off all but 1 T of the oil. Sauté onion and ginger root. Add spareribs and the last 5 ingredients; cover and bring to a boil.

5. Reduce to medium heat and cook until the liquid is reduced to ¼ C.

Add sesame oil and mix well. Serve hot.

Calories: 2390		Carbohydrates: 76gm	
Protein: 81gm		Fat: 195gm	

Calculated with 1 T oil for deep-frying.

SPARERIBS WITH GREEN ONIONS
(Cong Bao Pai Gu)

Ingredients:

2 lb	pork spareribs
1 t	salt
1 t	onion powder
¼ t	pepper
1 T	sherry
1 T	oil
4	slices of ginger root
6-10	green onions, shredded
1 t	cornstarch
1 t	sugar
¼ t	pepper
2 T	soy sauce
1 T	sherry
½ C	liquid from steaming the ribs
1 T	sesame oil (optional)

Method:

1. Ask the butcher to cut the spareribs across the bones into 1" wide strips. Separate the spareribs into small pieces by cutting between the bones. Mix the ribs with the next 4 ingredients. Steam in a boiling steamer for 50 minutes.

2. Mix the last 7 ingredients in a small bowl. Set aside.

3. Heat oil in a pan or wok; sauté ginger root. Add ribs; stir and cook for 4 minutes.

4. Add green onion, mix well.

5. Add the sauce mixture from Step 2; stir and cook until the sauce thickens. Serve hot.

Makes 4-6 servings.

Calories: 1860	Iron: 13mg
Carbohydrates: 15gm	Vit. B1: 3.56mg
Protein: 75gm	Vit. B2: 0.95mg
Fat: 165gm	Vit. A: 1200IU
Cholesterol: 464mg	Vit. C: 19mg
Calcium: 100mg	Fiber: 1gm

生焗排骨

Ingredients:

{ ½ t   salt
  ¼ t   pepper
  ½ t   onion or garlic powder
  2 lb   spareribs
{ 5-6 T Hoisin sauce
  3   slices of ginger root
  3 T   sherry
  1 T   soy sauce

Method:

1. Combine the first 3 ingredients in a small bowl. Rub the mixture on the spareribs evenly. Let stand for 1 hour.

2. Place the spareribs in a dish and steam in a boiling steamer for 1 hour or until the meat is tender.

3. Combine the last 4 ingredients in a dish. Set aside

4. Preheat broiler. Place the spareribs on a rack in a shallow pan, 6" from the broiler. Brush the sauce mixture from Step 3 evenly on the spareribs. Broil the spareribs for 8-10 minutes.

5. Turn the spareribs and brush with sauce mixture on the spareribs once more and continue to broil for 8-10 more minutes. (The door of the broiler should be open a little while broiling.)

6. Cut the spareribs with a knife in between the bones into smaller pieces. Serve hot.

The spareribs can be barbecued outdoors in the summertime.

Calories: 1800   Carbohydrates: 30gm
Protein: 80gm   Fat: 153gm

RED BRAISED SPARERIBS
(Tian Jiang Pai Gu)

Ingredients:

2	lb	extra lean spareribs
		Water to cover the spareribs
2	T	sherry
1/4	t	pepper
4	T	Hoisin sauce
1	T	soy sauce
1	T	honey
2-4		green onions, cut into 1-inch sections
3-6		slices of ginger root
4-6		cloves garlic, crushed

Method:

1. Ask your butcher to cut the spareribs across the bone into 1-inch wide strips. Separate the ribs into small pieces with a cleaver or knife by cutting between the bones.

2. Place the spareribs in a medium sauce pan. Add water and the rest of the ingredients; stir to mix. Cover pan and bring to a boil. Reduce to low heat and simmer until the liquid is reduced to 1/4 C and the meat is tender, about 1 hour. Check spareribs occasionally. If the liquid cooks down before the meat is tender, add additional water.

If too much liquid remains, turn to high heat and cook, uncovered, until liquid is reduced to 1/4 C. Skim off fat and serve hot. Skimming off the fat further reduces calories and fat content of the whole recipe. Remember, reducing 1 T of fat will reduce calories by 120 grams and fat by 14 grams.

Makes 6-8 servings.

Calories: 2228	Cholesterol: 639 mg	Vit. B2: 2 mg
Carbohydrates: 33 gm	Calcium: 181 mg	Vit. A: .1 IU
Protein: 95 gm	Iron: 16 mg	Vit. C: 3 mg
Fat: 167 gm	Vit. B1: 7 mg	Fiber: 4 gm

红烧猪耳

BRAISED PORK EAR, TRIPE AND LIVER
(Hong Shao Zhu Er)

Ingredients:

- 1 lb   pork ear
- 1 lb   tripe or pork stomach
- 1 lb   pork, beef or chicken liver
- Sesame oil for brushing
- 4-5 C   water
- ½   onion, diced
- 6   slices of ginger root
- 2   whole star anise or more
- 1-2   cinnamon sticks
- 1 T   brown sugar
- 6 T   soy sauce or more

Method:

1. Wash and clean the first 3 ingredients.
2. Put the last 7 ingredients in a deep sauce pan. Cover pan and bring to a boil.
3. Turn to low heat and simmer for 10 minutes.
4. Add the first 3 ingredients and bring to a boil on high heat. Turn to low heat and cook until meats are tender and the liquid is reduced to 1 C. Chill.
5. Remove fat. Cut the meat with the jellied liquid into thin strips. Brush on a layer of sesame oil before serving. Serve cold or warm. Can be served with dishes of soy sauce, vinegar and hot pepper oil as dippings.

This meat can be served as a main dish, appetizer, side dish or sandwich meat.

Makes 4-6 servings.

Calories: 2004	Iron: 54mg
Carbohydrates: 46gm	Vit. B1: 5.3mg
Protein: 265gm	Vit. B2: 16.4mg
Fat: 77gm	Vit. A: 199130IU
Cholesterol: 2250mg	Vit. C: 138mg
Calcium: 763mg	Fiber: 0

SAUTÉED PORK KIDNEY
(Chao Yao Hua)

炒腰花

Ingredients:

1 lb	pork kidneys (total edible portion)
½ C	vinegar
4 T	oil
½ t	salt
3	slices of ginger root
4-6	cloves of garlic, sliced
½ C	thinly sliced carrots
½ C	sliced bamboo shoots
15	snow pea pods, cleaned
1 T	cornstarch
1 T	soy sauce
¼ t	pepper
1 t	brown sugar
1 t	vinegar
1 t	instant chicken bouillon
¾ C	water
2 t	sesame oil
1 t	sherry
⅛ t	MSG (optional)

Method:

1. Split the kidneys in half, horizontally. With the cut side up, remove all the whitish knobs, membranes, and fat of the kidneys.

2. Turn the kidney halves to the other side; score the surface 1/6" deep and ⅛" apart in a crisscross pattern.

3. Soak the kidney pieces in cold water, changing water from time to time until no bloody string is left in the water. Cut the kidneys into 1½"x¾" pieces. Rinse and drain.

4. Boil 5 C of water in a pan. Pour the boiling water over the kidney pieces. Drain.

5. Put the kidney pieces in a bowl. Pour the vinegar into the bowl. Gently mix the vinegar and kidneys for 1 minute. Rinse and drain.

6. Mix the last 10 ingredients in a bowl. Set aside.

7. Heat oil in a pan or wok; add salt, ginger root, and garlic; stir for ½ minute. Add kidneys and stir for ½ minute. Remove.

8. Add carrots to the remaining oil; stir for ½ minute. Add bamboo shoots, snow pea pods, and the sauce mixture (Step 6); cook and stir until the sauce thickens.

9. Add kidneys; mix well. Serve immediately.

Kidney is the organ that filters wastes from the blood. It discharges the waste in a fluid called urine. The kidney has a sharp odor. In order to remove the odor and clean the kidneys, you must soak the kidneys in water and mix with vinegar before using.

Makes 4-6 servings.

Calories: 1217	Iron: 32mg
Carbohydrates: 41gm	Vit. B1: 2.9mg
Protein: 80gm	Vit. B2: 7.9mg
Fat: 81gm	Vit. A: 6499IU
Cholesterol: 1701mg	Vit. C: 78mg
Calcium: 145mg	Fiber: 2gm

Gate of Dispelling Clouds, Summer Palace, Beijing

poultry

BONED CHICKEN, SICHUAN STYLE
(Jiao Ma Ji)

Ingredients:

1	chicken, about 2-3 pounds
1 T	oil
1 T	Sichuan peppercorns, or more
4	green onions, shredded
4	slices of ginger root
3-4	hot peppers, dried or fresh, diced
½ C	sliced carrots
1	small bunch of coriander, cleaned and washed
4 T	soy sauce
1 T	sherry
1 t	sugar
1 t	sesame oil
1 T	vinegar
¼ C	or more water

Method:

1. Place the ready-to-cook chicken in a deep sauce pan. Fill water to half the depth of the chicken. Cover pan and bring to a boil.

2. Continue to boil the chicken for 15 minutes. Turn and cook for 10 more minutes. Remove and cool.

3. Bone the chicken and cut into 1" chunks (the skin may be left on). Makes about ¾ lb cooked chicken meat.

4. Heat oil in a pan or wok; brown the peppercorns until dark. Turn off heat and discard the peppercorns.

5. Heat oil again and saute onion, ginger root and hot pepper. Add carrot slices and stir for 1 minute.

6. Add chicken and the last 6 ingredients; cook for 3-5 minutes. Stir gently while cooking. Transfer to a serving plate and garnish with coriander. Serve immediately.

Makes 4-6 servings.

Calories: 644	Iron: 9mg
Carbohydrates: 24gm	Vit. B1: 0.26mg
Protein: 85gm	Vit. B2: 0.88mg
Fat: 20gm	Vit. A: 9626IU
Cholesterol: 268mg	Vit. C: 68mg
Calcium: 12mg	Fiber: 3gm

加喱鷄丁

STIR-FRY CURRIED CHICKEN
(Ka Li Ji Ding)

Ingredients:

1 lb	chicken breast, diced
2 T	soy sauce
	pinch of salt
¼ t	pepper
1 t	sherry
1 t	garlic powder
1 T	cornstarch
1 t	cornstarch blended with 2-4 T water
2-3 T	oil
1 T	minced ginger root
1-2 t	minced garlic
½ C	diced onion
1-2 T	or more curry powder, blended with 2-4 T water
2 T	or more soy sauce
½ lb	fresh mushrooms, washed and diced
3-6	hot peppers, minced (optional)
¾ C	water

Method:

1. Mix the diced chicken with the next 6 ingredients.

2. Heat oil in a non-stick pan or wok; sauté ginger root and garlic. Add chicken and stir-fry until the color turns (about 1-2 minutes). Remove.

3. Add onion to the remaining oil and stir for 1-2 minutes. Add blended curry powder; stir and mix for a few seconds.

4. Add the last 4 ingredients; bring to a boil.

5. Add blended cornstarch and cooked chicken; mix well. Serve hot.

Makes 4-6 servings

Calories: 1000	Cholesterol: 295mg	Vit. B2: 2mg
Carbohydrates: 39gm	Calcium: 153mg	Vit. A: 3650 IU
Protein: 101gm	Iron: 11mg	Vit. C: 69mg
Fat: 47gm	Vit. B1 0.52mg	Fiber: 4gm

With the exception of the newly added Rice Noodle section, the nutritional calculations of all the recipes in this book are for **the whole recipe,** not per serving.

SNOW WHITE CHICKEN
(Xue Bai Ji Rou)

雪 白 雞 肉

Ingredients:

½ lb	chicken breast
½ t	salt
¼ t	white pepper
½ t	onion powder
1 t	sherry
1 t	cornstarch
3 T	oil
1 oz	regular or country style ham, minced
1	green onion, minced
6	egg whites
1 t	sesame oil
½ t	salt

Method:

1. Cut the chicken into thin slices and mix with the next 5 ingredients.
2. Beat the egg whites with sesame oil and salt in a bowl.
3. Heat 2 T oil in a pan or wok; stir-fry chicken until color turns (about 1½ minutes). Separate the chicken pieces while stirring. Remove.
4. Heat 1 T oil; add egg whites and cooked chicken; stir and cook until the egg whites dry. Transfer to a serving dish. Garnish with minced onion and ham. Serve hot.

Makes 4-6 servings.

Calories:	885	Iron:	3mg
Carbohydrates:	5gm	Vit. B1:	0.11mg
Protein:	71gm	Vit. B2:	0.89mg
Fat:	61gm	Vit. A:	491IU
Cholesterol:	159mg	Vit. C:	3mg
Calcium:	47mg	Fiber:	0

花椒鷄丁

SICHUAN PEPPERCORN CHICKEN
(Hua Jiao Ji Ding)

Ingredients:

1 lb	chicken breast, sliced
1 t	Sichuan peppercorn powder for dipping (page 314)
1 T	sherry
¼ t	pepper
½ t	onion or garlic powder
1 T	cornstarch
4 T	oil
½	onion, chopped
2	slices of ginger root
½ C	bamboo shoot slices
1 C	sliced Bok Choy
1 T	soy sauce
1 t	sugar
1 t	sesame oil
1 T	vinegar
1 t	instant chicken bouillon
	Sichuan peppercorn powder for dipping to taste
1 t	cornstarch blended in ½ C water

Method:

1. Mix the chicken slices with the next 5 ingredients.

2. Heat oil in a pan or wok; add chicken and stir-fry until color turns. Remove.

3. Sauté onion and ginger root in the remaining oil; add the last 7 ingredients and bring to a boil.

4. Add bamboo shoots and Bok Choy and bring to a boil. Add cooked chicken and mix well. Serve hot.

Makes 4-6 servings.

Calories:	1192	Iron:	8mg
Carbohydrates:	22gm	Vit. B1:	0.39mg
Protein:	95gm	Vit. B2:	0.89mg
Fat:	78gm	Vit. A.:	769IU
Cholesterol:	289mg	Vit. C:	21mg
Calcium:	135mg	Fiber:	1gm

PALACE CHICKEN
(Gong Bao Ji Ding)

宫保鷄丁

Ingredients:

³/₄	lb	chicken breast, diced
2	T	or more soy sauce
¹/₄	t	pepper
¹/₄	t	onion or garlic powder
1	T	sherry or cooking wine
1	T	cornstarch
1-2	T	or more oil
4		or more dried or fresh hot peppers, diced (optional)
2	t	or more minced ginger root
2		or more cloves of garlic, minced
1	t	cornstarch blended with 1 T of water
		Soy sauce or salt and pepper to taste
¹/₄	C	or more roasted peanuts,* walnuts, almonds, or cashews
2	t	or more sesame oil
1	C	diced red bell pepper
1	C	diced celery
¹/₄	C	chopped onion
¹/₂	C	water chestnuts, diced
1	T	or more soy sauce
1	t	sherry or cooking wine
¹/₃	C	water

* Palace Chicken is traditionally made with peanuts.

Method:

1. Mix and marinate the diced chicken with the next 5 ingredients. Set aside.

2. Heat oil in a non-stick wok or pan. Sauté hot pepper, ginger root, and garlic. Add chicken and stir-fry until color turns (about 1 ½ -2 minutes). Remove.

3. Add the last 7 ingredients; bring to a boil and add soy sauce or salt and pepper to taste. Add blended cornstarch; mix well.

4. Add cooked chicken, nuts, sesame oil and mix well. Serve hot.

Step 1 of the Method can be prepared in advance. The marinated chicken can be frozen for weeks. Before using, thaw completely. When you have time, I suggest you do this first step ahead of time. You will have less work and pressure while preparing this dish and will enjoy it more.

Makes 6 servings.

Calories: 998	Cholesterol: 196 mg	Vit. B2: 0.7 mg
Carbohydrates: 50 gm	Calcium: 173 mg	Vit. A: 548 IU
Protein: 94 gm	Iron: 8 mg	Vit. C: 246 mg
Fat: 47 gm	Vit. B1: 0.7 mg	Fiber: 10 gm

With the exception of the newly added Rice Noodle section, the nutritional calculations of all the recipes in this book are for **the whole recipe,** not per serving. 1 or 2 tablespoons of oil can be reduced from each recipe if desired. A reduction of 1 tablespoon of oil will reduce the calories of the recipe by 120, and the fat by 14 grams.

怪味鷄腿

DRUMSTICKS IN ODD SAUCE
(Quai Wei Ji Tui)

Ingredients:

8	medium-sized chicken drumsticks
2 t	or more curry powder blended with 1 T water
¼ C	catsup
½ C	chopped onion
2	cloves of garlic, crushed
2 t	or more minced ginger root
1 t	brown sugar
1 t	sherry
2 T	low sodium or regular soy sauce
¼ t	pepper
½ C	water

Method:

1. Place all the ingredients in a sauce pan; cover and bring to a boil.

2. Reduce to medium heat and cook until liquid is reduced to ¼ C. Turn several times while cooking. Serve hot.

Makes 8 servings.

Calories: 1091	Cholesterol: 384 mg	Vit. B2: 1 mg
Carbohydrates: 34 gm	Calcium: 148 mg	Vit. A: 220 I
Protein: 118 gm	Iron: 10 mg	Vit. C: 18 mg
Fat: 50 gm	Vit. B1: .4 mg	Fiber: 4 gm

MEAT STUFFED DRUMSTICKS
(Ji Tui Niang Rou)

鷄 腿 釀 肉

Ingredients:

- ½ lb   ground pork or beef
- 1 T   soy sauce
- ¼ t   onion powder
- ⅛ t   pepper
- 1 t   sherry
- 2   water chestnuts, minced
- ½ t   minced ginger root
- 1 t   cornstarch
- 6   chicken drumsticks
- 1   green onion, or more, minced
- 2-3 T   oil
- 1 T   cornstarch
- 2 T   soy sauce or to taste
- 2   slices of ginger root
- 1 t   brown sugar
- 1 t   sherry
- ¾ C   water

Method:

1. Mix the first 8 ingredients together thoroughly in a small bowl.

2. Cut a slit lengthwise on a drumstick to the bone. Use a paring knife to remove the meat from the bone.

3. Discard a ¾" portion (from the narrow end) of the drumstick. Repeat procedure on the remaining drumsticks.

4. Flatten the drumsticks, meat side up, and score.

5. Sprinkle 1 T cornstarch on the scored sides and pat. Spread a layer of the meat mixture on the chicken and press.

6. Score again through the meat mixture down to the chicken so that the meat mixture will stick to the chicken while frying.

7. Heat oil in a non-stick pan; fry the meat stuffed chicken drumsticks, meat sides down, until brown.

8. Turn drumsticks to skin side; add the last 5 ingredients and cook until the liquid is reduced to a few tablespoons.

9. Remove to a serving plate, garnish with minced onion. Serve hot.   Makes 6 servings.

Calories: 1653
Carbohydrates: 60gm
Protein: 171gm
Fat: 76gm

Cholesterol: 500mg
Calcium: 193mg
Iron: 20mg
Vit. B1: 2.4mg

Vit. B2: 2.7mg
Vit. A: 1000IU
Vit. C: 3mg
Fiber: 0

红烧鸡腿

SOY SAUCE BOILED DRUMSTICKS
(Hong Shao Ji Tui)

Ingredients:

2-3 lb	chicken drumsticks or wings
½	onion, diced
6	slices of ginger root
2	whole star anise
2	cinnamon sticks
1½ C	soy sauce
1 T	brown sugar
4 C	water

Method:

1. Score the drumsticks.

2. Put the last 7 ingredients in a sauce pan; cover and bring to a boil. Reduce to low heat and simmer for 10 minutes.

3. Add chicken and bring to a boil. Continue boiling for 5-7 minutes. Remove chicken. Serve hot or cold.

The resulting sauce can be served as a dip for the chicken or can be saved and reused for cooking additional pieces of chicken in the same manner. (Add a little more soy sauce if a saltier taste is wanted.) The sauce can be kept in a clean jar in the refrigerator for a few days or in the freezer for a month.

Makes 4-6 servings.

Calories: 1256
Carbohydrates: 39gm
Protein: 182gm
Fat: 38gm
Cholesterol: 478mg
Calcium: 332mg

Iron: 26mg
Vit. B1: 0.59
Vit. B2: 3.4mg
Vit. A: 1086IU
Vit. C: 2mg
Fiber: 0

160

DRUMSTICKS SICHUAN STYLE
(Xiang Su Ji Tui)

Ingredients:

- 2 lb   chicken drumsticks
- 2 T   Sichuan peppercorn powder for dipping (page 314)
        Flour for coating
        Oil for deep-frying
- 1 T   sherry
- 2   green onions, shredded or half onion, shredded
- 1 T   soy sauce
- 3   slices of ginger root

Method:

1. Mix 1½ T Sichuan peppercorn powder with the last 4 ingredients, then rub the mixture on the drumsticks. Let stand for 2 hours at room temperature or overnight in the refrigerator.

2. Place the drumsticks in a heatproof bowl and steam in a boiling steamer for 40 minutes.

3. Brush off the ginger root and onion from the drumsticks.

4. Place ½ C flour in a sturdy plastic bag. Place the steamed drumsticks in the flour, one or two at a time. Shake until a layer of flour coats the drumsticks. Shake off the excess flour.

5. Heat oil in a pan or wok; fry the drumsticks until brown and crisp. Serve hot with a small dish of Sichuan peppercorn powder for dipping.

Approximately 4 T oil and 2 T flour were used.

Makes 4-6 servings.

Calories: 1615	Iron: 15mg
Carbohydrates: 16gm	Vit. B1: 0.55mg
Protein: 171gm	Vit. B2: 2.92mg
Fat: 91gm	Vit. A: 1475IU
Cholesterol: 478mg	Vit.C: 6mg
Calcium: 141mg	Fiber: 0

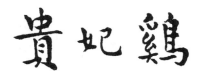

GUI FEI CHICKEN
(Gui Fei Ji)

Ingredients:

2 lb	chicken wings
2 T	oil
1 T	sugar
1 C	bamboo shoot slices
¼ lb	fresh mushrooms, quartered
1 T	sherry
1 T	cornstarch blended with 1 T water
4 T	soy sauce or to taste
3	green onions, minced
¼ t	salt
½ C	water
3	slices of ginger root

Method:

1. Cut the chicken wings through the joints; discard the tips.

2. Heat oil in a pan or wok; add sugar and stir until the sugar is melted.

3. Add chicken wings; stir and cook for 2 minutes.

4. Add the last 5 ingredients; cover and cook over medium high heat for 3-5 minutes.

5. Add the bamboo shoots, mushrooms and sherry; cover and cook for 3-5 minutes. Add blended cornstarch and mix well. Serve hot.

Makes 4-6 servings.

Calories:	1773	Iron:	18mg
Carbohydrates:	41gm	Vit. B1:	0.71mg
Protein:	176gm	Vit. B2:	2.03mg
Fat:	100gm	Vit. A:	2777IU
Cholesterol:	620mg	Vit. C:	18mg
Calcium:	178mg	Fiber:	2gm

OYSTER SAUCE CHICKEN WINGS
(Hao You Ji Chi)

Ingredients:

2 lb	chicken wings
4 T	oyster sauce
1 t	sugar
1 T	sherry
¼ t	pepper
1 T	oil
2-4	slices of ginger root
2-4	cloves of garlic, crushed
½ C	water
2 t	cornstarch blended with 1 T water
3-4	green onions, shredded
1 t	sesame oil

Method:

1. Wash and dry the chicken wings. Cut off and discard the tips. Cut the chicken wings into two parts through the joints.

2. Heat oil in a pan or wok; sauté ginger root and garlic. Add chicken wings and the next 4 ingredients; stir and cook for 3-4 minutes.

3. Add water; cover and bring to a boil, and continue to cook for 2-3 minutes.

4. Add blended cornstarch and cook until the sauce thickens.

5. Add shredded onions and sesame oil; mix well. Serve hot.

Makes 4-6 servings.

Calories:	1753	Iron:	16mg
Carbohydrates:	64gm	Vit. B1:	0.4mg
Protein:	170gm	Vit. B2:	1.4mg
Fat:	85gm	Vit. A:	2750IU
Cholesterol:	620mg	Vit. C:	10mg
Calcium:	156mg	Fiber:	0

笑蓉鶏

Ingredients:

1 oz	chicken breast
¾ t	salt
1 T	sherry
¼ C	milk
5	egg whites
¼ C	milk
2 T	cornstarch blended with 2 T water
1	large bowl of hot water
	Oil for deep-frying
¼ C	chopped onion
2	slices of ginger root
1	chicken bouillon cube dissolved in 1 C water
¼ C	minced ham (optional)
¼ C	frozen peas
¼ C	sliced bamboo shoot
2 T	cornstarch blended with 2 T water

Method:

1. Mince the chicken breast into a paste. Add the salt and sherry; mix well.

2. Gradually add ¼ C milk to the chicken paste, stirring in one direction. Continue stirring until the chicken and milk are well blended.

3. Stir the egg white, ¼ C milk, and 2 T blended cornstarch together (do not beat).

4. Pour the egg white into the chicken, gradually, stirring in one direction while pouring (do not beat).

5. Have a large bowl of hot water ready and near the stove.

6. Heat oil for deep-frying in a wok; add 1/3 portion of the egg mixture to the oil. Fry the egg white until it coagulates. Remove the cooked egg with a slotted spoon and drop into the hot water. Repeat until all egg whites are cooked. Drain off the water.

7. Pour off oil except for 1 T. Sauté onion and ginger until black. Discard.

8. Add the last 5 ingredients to the pan and bring to a boil. Add the cooked egg whites; mix and bring to a boil. Transfer to a serving plate and serve hot.

Calories: 725	Iron: 2 mg
Carbohydrate: 17 gm	Vit. A: 650IU
Protein: 30 gm	Vit. B1: 0.41 mg
Fat: 59 gm	Vit. B2: 0.32 mg
Cholesterol: 17 mg	Vit. C: 20 mg
Calcium: 184 mg	Fiber: 2 gm

Calculated with 4 T oil

脆皮炸鷄

CRISPY SKIN CHICKEN
(Cui Pi Zha Ji)

Ingredients:

- 2 cinnamon sticks
- 2 or more whole star anise
- 2 t Sichuan peppercorns
- 4 bay leaves
- 4 slices of ginger root
- 1 C soy sauce
- 4 C water
- 1 chicken, about 2-3 pounds
  Oil for deep-frying
  Sesame oil for brushing
- 2 T honey or corn syrup
- 2 T sherry
- 2 t cornstarch
- 2 T water

Method:

1. Tie the first 5 ingredients in a piece of cheese cloth. Put this package with the soy sauce and water into a deep sauce pan; cover and bring to a boil. Simmer over low heat for 15 minutes.

2. Put the chicken into the pan and bring to a boil. Reduce to medium heat and cook for 15 minutes. Turn the chicken and cook over medium heat for 15 minutes.

3. Remove chicken from the liquid and cool. (Liquid in which the chicken was cooked may be reused again for making the same dish.)

4. Mix the last 4 ingredients in a small bowl. Brush the mixture on the chicken evenly. Put the chicken on a rack and keep it in the refrigerator overnight.

5. Heat oil in a pan or wok. Deep-fry the chicken until the skin becomes crisp. Brush a layer of sesame oil on the chicken while it is still warm.

6. Cut the chicken, bone and all, into bite-size pieces. Arrange on a platter and serve hot or cold.

Makes 4-6 servings.

Calories:	1353	Iron:	21mg
Carbohydrates:	50gm	Vit. B1:	0.66mg

Protein: 171gm   Vit. B2:   3.61mg
Fat: 45gm   Vit. A: 6572IU
Cholesterol: 716mg   Vit. C: 2mg
Calcium: 173mg   Fiber: 0

Calculated with 5 T oil for deep-frying.

THOUSAND DOLLAR CHICKEN
(Qian Jing Ji)

Ingredients:

1	chicken, about 2-3 pounds
1 T	oil
1	onion, chopped
6	slices of ginger root
1 T	sesame oil
5 T	soy sauce
1 T	sherry
1 T	sugar

Method:

1. Cut the chicken, bone and all, into 1" pieces.

2. Heat oil; brown onion and ginger root. Add chicken and the last 3 ingredients; stir and cook over medium heat for 10-15 minutes.

3. Stir 2-3 times while cooking for even flavor. Add sesame oil and mix well. Serve hot.

Makes 4-6 servings.

This dish only requires 15 minutes to cook. In China there is an old saying, "Fifteen minutes of sweet moments are worth $1000." This is where the name of the recipe comes from.

Calories: 1286   Iron: 21mg
Carbohydrates: 25gm   Vit. B1   0.65mg
Protein: 171gm   Vit. B2   3.6mg
Fat: 49gm   Vit. A: 6563IU
Cholesterol: 716mg   Vit. C: 5mg
Calcium: 184mg   Fiber: 0

雪豆鶏片

CHICKEN WITH SNOW PEA PODS
(Xue Dou Ji Pian)

Ingredients:

½ lb	chicken breast, boned
1½ T	soy sauce
½ t	onion powder
¼ t	pepper
1 t	cornstarch
½ lb	snow pea pods
¼ t	salt
3 T	oil
2	green onions, minced
1 t	minced ginger root
½ t	chicken bouillon dissolved in ½ C water
1 t	cornstarch blended with 1T water
1 T	sesame oil

Method:

1. Slice chicken into 1½"x½"x1/6" slices, then mix with the next 4 ingredients. Set aside.

2. Wash and snap off the stem and strings from both ends of the snow pea pods. Set aside.

3. Heat oil in a pan or wok. Add chicken; stir-fry until color turns white. Remove.

4. Add snow pea pods and salt; stir for a few seconds or until the pea pods turn bright green. Remove.

5. Add the last 5 ingredients and cook until the sauce thickens. Add cooked chicken and pea pods. Serve immediately.

The amount of chicken breast used may be increased to 1 lb. If this is done, increase the soy sauce to 3 T.

Makes 4-6 servings.

Calories: 787		Iron: 5mg	
Carbohydrates: 33gm		Vit. B1: 0.74mg	
Protein: 52gm		Vit. B2: 0.63mg	
Fat: 51gm		Vit. A: 2241IU	
Cholesterol: 147mg		Vit. C: 53mg	
Calcium: 174mg		Fiber: 3gm	

CHICKEN IN EIGHT PIECES
(Zha Ba Kuai)

Ingredients:

1	ready to cook chicken, about 2-3 pounds
3 T	soy sauce
2 t	minced ginger root
¼ t	pepper
4-6	cloves of garlic, crushed
1 T	sherry
2-3	green onions, parsley, or coriander, minced
	Oil for deep-frying
¼ C	flour
¼ C	cornstarch
¼ t	baking powder
¼ t	baking soda
1 t	instant chicken bouillon
4-5 T	water

Method:

1. Cut the chicken into 8 pieces: 2 wings, 2 thighs, 2 drum-sticks and breast halves.

2. Mix the chicken with the next 5 ingredients. Let stand for 1 hour or more.

3. In a medium bowl mix the last 6 ingredients into a smooth batter.

4. Heat oil in a pan or wok. Mix the chicken with the batter.

5. Deep-fry the chicken pieces one by one until light brown. Remove.

6. Heat the oil and fry the chicken once more until dark brown.

7. Arrange the fried chicken on a platter; garnish with minced green onions. Serve hot.

Makes 4-6 servings.

Calories: 2021	Cholesterol: 716mg	Vit. B2: 3.5mg
Carbohydrates: 60gm	Calcium: 162mg	Vit. A: 6941IU
Protein: 173gm	Iron: 19mg	Vit. C: 7mg
Fat: 115gm	Vit. B1: 0.68mg	Fiber: 0

Calculated with 6 T oil for deep-frying.

杏仁鶏

Ingredients:

1 lb	chicken breast
3 T	soy sauce
1 T	sherry
¼ t	onion powder
¼ t	pepper
1 t	finely minced ginger root
1	egg white
1 t	sesame oil
3 T	cornstarch
1 C	oil for deep-frying
½-¾ C	sliced almonds
2	cloves of garlic, crushed
2	green onions, shredded
2 t	finely shredded ginger root
1	medium sized carrot, sliced
¼ lb	fresh mushrooms, sliced
1	8oz can sliced bamboo shoots, drained
2	celery cabbage or napa leaves, sliced into 1-inch sections
¼ lb	snow pea pods
1	chicken bouillon cube dissolved in 1 cup of water
1 T	soy sauce
1 T	vinegar
1 t	sugar
1 T	sesame oil
1 T	cornstarch
¼ t	pepper
1 T	sherry

Method:

1. Cut the chicken into ½" thick x 2" long pieces. Wash and remove stems and strings from the snow pea pods. Cut the larger ones in half.

2. Mix the chicken slices and the next 8 ingredients together thoroughly. Set aside.

3. Combine the last 8 ingredients in a bowl. Set aside.

4. Heat oil in a pan or wok. Place the chicken slices into the oil one by one and deep-fry until light brown and crisp. Remove from oil and drain.

5. Pour off all but 3 T of the oil. Sauté almonds for a few seconds; remove.

6. Sauté garlic, green onions, and ginger root; add carrots and stir for ½ minute.

7. Add mushrooms and bamboo shoots; stir for ½ minute.

8. Add celery cabbage or napa leaves and the sauce mixture from Step 3 (stir the sauce before using); bring to a boil.

9. Add snow pea pods and mix well.

10. Add chicken and mix well. Transfer to a serving dish; spread the sautéed almonds over the chicken and serve hot.

Calories: 1580   Carbohydrates: 60gm
Protein: 98gm   Fat: 108gm

Calculated with 3 tablespoons of oil for deep-frying.

SOY SAUCE BOILED CHICKEN
(Jiang You Ji)

Ingredients:

1	chicken, about 3 pounds
1	onion, chopped
1-inch	ginger root, crushed
2	whole star anise
2	cinnamon sticks
1½ C	dark soy sauce
4 T	brown sugar
¼ C	sherry
4 C	water
	Sesame oil for brushing

Method:

1. Wash and dry the chicken.

2. Place the next 8 ingredients in a sauce pan large enough to hold the chicken. Cover and bring to a boil. Turn to low heat and simmer for 10 minutes.

3. Add chicken, cover and cook over medium heat for 10 minutes. Turn the chicken and cook in the same manner for 10 more minutes. Turn off heat and let the chicken remain in the sauce for 30 minutes. Turn once during that time.

4. Cut the chicken, bone and all, into pieces by first disjointing the wings, legs, and thighs. Separate the back and breast with a cleaver. Chop the back crosswise into 1½ inch pieces. Chop the breast lengthwise in half, then chop crosswise into 1 inch pieces.

5. Arrange the back on the center of the platter lengthwise. Place the chicken breast on the back. Put the wings, legs, and thighs in the original positions, so that when served, the chicken looks like a breast-up whole chicken. Brush with sesame oil before serving.

The sauce resulting from the cooking liquid can be reused for the same pupose at a later time or as a dipping sauce. Add more soy sauce if a saltier taste is desired.

This chicken dish can be frozen. Thaw completely before serving.

Calories: 1489	Iron: 28mg
Carbohydrates: 31gm	Vit. B1: 0.67mg
Protein: 180gm	Vit. B2: 4mg
Fat: 61gm	Vit. A: 6540IU
Cholesterol: 716mg	Vit. C: 0
Calcium: 304mg	Fiber: 0

CHICKEN WITH MUSHROOMS
(Kou Mo Ji)

Ingredients:

1 lb   chicken breast, boned
3 T   soy sauce
1 T   sherry
¼ t   onion powder
¼ t   pepper
1 t   finely minced ginger root
1 t   sesame oil
2 T   cornstarch
½ lb   fresh mushrooms
¼ lb   celery cabbage or about 20 snow pea pods
3 T   oil
2-3   cloves of garlic, crushed or 2 green onions, shredded
2-3   slices of ginger root
1 T   light soy sauce
1 T   sherry
1 t   cornstarch blended with 2 T water
1 T   sesame oil

Method:

1. Slice the chicken into pieces, ¾"x2"x1/6". Slice the mushrooms into ¼" thick slices. Slice the celery cabbage, crosswise, into 3/4" pieces (or clean and string the pea pods).

2. Mix the first 7 ingredients together thoroughly. Add 2 T cornstarch and mix well.

3. Heat oil in a pan or wok; sauté garlic and ginger root. Add chicken and stir constantly until color turns (about 2 minutes). Remove.

4. Add mushrooms and celery cabbage or pea pods and the last 4 ingredients; stir and cook for 1-2 minutes. Add cooked chicken and mix well. Serve hot.

Calories: 1090
Protein: 84gm
Carbohydrates: 34gm
Fat: 69gm

Participants in a cooking competition in Shanghai.

Market scene near Beijing.

CHICKEN WITH GREEN PEPPER
(Jing Jiao Ji Ding)

青椒鷄丁

Ingredients:

- 2 T soy sauce
- ¼ t salt
- ½ t onion powder
- ⅛ t pepper
- 1 T sherry
- ½ egg white
- 2 T cornstarch
- 1 lb chicken breast, diced
- 4 T oil
- 1 large green pepper, diced
- 2 green onions, minced
- 3 thin clices of ginger root, minced
- 3 cloves of garlic, minced
- 1 T sherry
- 1 T soy sauce
- ½ t chicken bouillon
- ½ C water
- 1 t cornstarch

Method:

1. Cut the chicken breast into ½" dices. Mix the chicken with the first 7 ingredients. Dice the green pepper into ½" squares.

2. Combine the last 5 ingredients in a small bowl. Set aside.

3. Heat oil in a pan or wok; sauté onion, ginger and garlic. Add chicken and stir for 1 minute.

4. Add green pepper and stir for 2 minutes or more.

5. Add sauce mixture from Step 2; stir and cook until the sauce thickens. Transfer the chicken to a serving plate and serve hot.

Calories: 1100		Iron: 5.5 mg	
Carbohydrate: 20 gm		Vit. A: 670IU	
Protein: 95 gm		Vit. B1: 0.28 mg	
Fat: 66gm		Vit. B2: 0.80	
Cholesterol: 270 mg		Vit. C: 94 mg	
Calcium: 60 mg		Fiber: 1.6 gm	

雪白雞片

MINCED CHICKEN IN EGG WHITE
(Xue Bai Ji Pian)

Ingredients:

4 oz	chicken breast, minced
1 t	salt
¼ t	white pepper
1 t	sherry
1 t	cornstarch
3 T	water
6	egg whites
4 T	oil
2	green onions, minced
1 t	minced ginger root
20	fresh pea pods, stringed and cleaned
1 t	sesame oil
1 C	milk, whole
1 t	chicken bouillon
1 T	cornstarch blended with 2 T water
3-4	dried mushrooms, soaked and diced or ¼ lb fresh mushrooms, sliced
½ C	sliced bamboo shoots

Method:

1. Mince the chicken with a cleaver or knife into a paste. Add the next 5 ingredients, stir, in one direction, until they are well blended.

2. Beat the egg whites slightly with a pair of chopsticks or fork. Add the chicken and stir in one direction until they are well blended.

3. Heat 3 T oil over medium high heat in a non-stick skillet. Add egg mixture and cook until the egg dries, turn and cook for a few seconds. Remove and cut into 1"x2" pieces.

4. Add 1 T oil to the skillet, saute onion and ginger root. Add the last 5 ingredients and bring to a boil.

6. Add cooked chicken, pea pods, and sesame oil and mix well. Serve hot.

Calories: 980
Protein: 50gm

Carbohydrates: 28gm
Fat: 70gm

CHICKEN IN LEMON SAUCE
(Ning Meng Ji)

檸檬鷄

Ingredients:

2	chicken breasts, boned and skinned
3 T	soy sauce
1 T	sherry
1 t	sesame oil
½ t	onion powder
1 t	minced ginger root
¼ t	pepper
1	egg white, slightly beaten
1/3 C	flour
1/3 C	cornstarch
2	green onions, shredded
1	lemon, cut into thin slices for garnishing
5 T	oil
1 t	chicken bouillon
2/3 C	water
1/3 C	sugar
1 T	soy sauce
⅛ t	salt
¼ C	fresh lemon juice
¼ C	vinegar
2 t	cornstarch
⅛ t	pepper
¼ t	lemon extract
1	small carrot, slant sliced
½ C	pineapple tidbits

Method:

1. Cut chicken breasts in half; pound to a ½" thickness. Marinate the chicken with the next 7 ingredients for ½ hour or more.

2. Combine the last 12 ingredients in a small bowl. Set aside.

3. Mix the flour and cornstarch in a plate. Coat the chicken with a layer of flour mixture. Press to make the flour stick firmly on the chicken. Shake off the excess flour.

4. Heat oil in a pan or wok, fry the chicken until golden brown. Remove.

5. Cut the chicken into 1″ sections, arrange on a serving platter and keep warm.

6. Cook the sauce mixture from Step 2 until it boils, stir while cooking. Add shredded green onions.

7. Pour the sauce over the cooked chicken, garnish with lemon slices on the edges of the platter. Serve hot.

Makes 6 servings

Calories: 1988	Cholesterol: 295mg	Vit. B2: 1.04mg
Carbohydrates: 182gm	Calcium: 160mg	Vit. A: 6563IU
Protein: 102gm	Iron: 10mg	Vit. C: 48mg
Fat: 94gm	Vit. B1: 0.43mg	Fiber: 1gm

SICHUAN PEPPERCORN
AND SESAME CHICKEN
(Ma La Ji)

Ingredients:

¼ lb	bean or alfalfa sprouts
½ C	finely shredded carrots
½ C	finely shredded celery cabbage
½	onion, shredded (optional)
½	chicken, about 2 pounds
½-1 t	Sichuan peppercorn powder for seasoning (page 314)
1 T	or more toasted sesame seeds
¼-½ C	chopped coriander or parsley
3 T	soy sauce
1 T	sugar
2 T	vinegar
1 t	Sichuan peppercorn powder for dipping (page 314)
2 T	sesame oil
1 t	or more, red hot pepper oil or paste
1 t	minced ginger root

Method:

1. Boil 3-4 cups of water in a sauce pan. Drop the bean sprouts in the boiling water and cook for 5 seconds. Rinse in cold water until the bean sprouts are chilled. Drain.

2. Arrange the bean sprouts (or alfalfa sprouts) with the shredded carrots, celery cabbage, and onion on a platter. Chill.

3. Place the chicken in a deep sauce pan; add water until the chicken is half covered. Cover pan and bring to a boil. Reduce to medium heat and cook for 10 minutes. Turn chicken over and cook for 10 more minutes. Remove and chill.

4. Cut chicken, bone and all, into bite-size pieces, or bone the chicken and cut. Arrange the chicken over the vegetables.

5. Mix the last 7 ingredients in a small bowl. Pour this sauce mixture over the chicken evenly. Sprinkle sesame seed, peppercorn powder and coriander over the chicken before serving. Mix the chicken and vegetables before eating. Serve cold.

Makes 4-6 servings.

Calories: 1574	Cholesterol: 716mg	Vit. B2: 3.77 mg
Carbohydrates: 36gm	Calcium: 359mg	Vit. A: 12369IU
Protein: 177 gm	Iron: 22mg	Vit. C: 44mg
Fat: 78gm	Vit. B1: 0.96mg	Fiber: 3gm

ONION SATURATED CHICKEN
(Cong Jiang Yiu Ji)

葱薑油鷄

Ingredients:

	1	chicken, about 2-3 pounds
⎧	¼ t	pepper
⎨	2 T	salt
⎩	1 T	sherry
	1 C	shredded green onions, about 5-6
	⅛ C	shredded ginger root
	½ C	oil

Method:

1. Wash and dry the chicken.

2. Mix the next 3 ingredients together. Rub the mixture on the chicken evenly, inside and out. Allow to stand for a few hours or overnight in the refrigerator.

3. Place the chicken in a heat-proof dish, then set in a boiling steamer and steam for 40 minutes or until the chicken is cooked.

4. Cut chicken into 1½x1½" pieces while it is warm. Arrange the chicken pieces neatly on a serving platter.

5. Spread the onions and ginger root shreds over the chicken.

6. Heat oil in a small sauce pan to 375°-400°. Pour the hot oil evenly over the shreds. Tip the platter and let the oil flow back to the pan.

7. Heat the oil until hot and pour over the shreds once more. Pour off the oil again before serving. Serve hot or cold.

Makes 4-6 servings.

Calories:	1151	Iron:	17mg
Carbohydrates:	6gm	Vit. B1:	0.65mg
Protein:	167gm	Vit. B2:	3.4mg
Fat:	44gm	Vit. A:	7540IU
Cholesterol:	716mg	Vit. C:	16mg
Calcium:	133mg	Fiber:	1gm

Calculated with 3 T oil

STUFFED CHICKEN ROLLS
(Hu Tao Ji Juan)

胡 桃 鷄 卷

Ingredients:

- 2 T chopped roasted walnuts
- 2 oz shelled shrimp, fresh or frozen, minced
- 2 oz ground pork
- ½ small onion, minced
- 2 T soy sauce
- ¼ t pepper
- ¼ t sugar
- 1 t sherry
- 1 t cornstarch
- 1 lb chicken breast
- 4 2"x4" thin slices of old fashioned ham
- 1 t sesame oil
- 3-4 T oil
- 1 green onion, shredded
- ½ lb celery cabbage, cut into 2" pieces
- 1 chicken bouillon cube
- 1 T soy sauce
- 3 dried mushrooms, soaked and quartered
- 1 C water

Method:

1. Mix the first 9 ingredients together thoroughly. Divide the mixture into 4 portions.

2. Divide the chicken breast into four portions. Between sheets of wax paper, pound each portion with a mallet to a 1/6" thickness.

3. Place a piece of ham on the chicken; spread a portion of the meat mixture on the ham. Roll the chicken breast into a cylinder. Secure the roll with tooth picks. Repeat.

4. Heat oil in a pan or a wok. Powder the chicken with cornstarch; brown the chicken roll. Remove.

5. Add the last 6 ingredients in the pan. Place the chicken rolls on the vegetables, cover and bring to a boil. Turn to medium heat and cook until the liquid is reduced to ¼ C. Add sesame oil and serve hot.

Makes 4 servings.

181

Calories: 1375
Carbohydrates: 23gm
Protein: 124gm
Fat: 86gm

Cholesterol: 378mg
Calcium: 221mg
Iron: 13mg
Vit. B1: 1.4mg

Vit. B2: 1.3mg
Vit. A: 1133IU
Vit. C: 40mg
Fiber: 2gm

RICE FLOURED STEAMED CHICKEN
(Fen Zheng Ji)

Ingredients:

    1   chicken, about 2-3 pounds
    ½ C   flavored rice powder, (recipe on page 311)
    3 T   soy sauce
    1 T   sherry
    1 T   sesame oil
    ½ t   onion or garlic powder
    2 t   minced ginger root
    ½ t   pepper
    1 t   sugar

Method:

1. Cut the chicken, bone and all, into 1" cubes or bone chicken.

2. Mix the chicken with the last 7 ingredients. Let stand for 1 hour or more. Stir from time to time for even flavor.

3. Coat chicken pieces with a layer or rice powder, then arrange them in a heat-proof bowl.

4. Steam the chicken in a boiling, covered steamer for 1 hour. Serve hot.

Makes 4-6 servings.

Calories: 1664
Carbohydrates: 90gm
Protein: 176gm
Fat: 59gm
Cholesterol: 716mg
Calcium: 176mg

Iron: 22mg
Vit. B1: 1mg
Vit. B2: 3.9mg
Vit. A: 6552IU
Vit. C: 3mg
Fiber: 0

HOT AND SOUR CHICKEN
(Suan La Ji)

酸 辣 鷄

Ingredients:

- 1 frying chicken, about 2-3 pounds
- 2 T soy sauce
- ½ t pepper
- ½ t onion powder
- 1 T cornstarch
- 1 T oil
- 3 slices of ginger root
- 1 small onion, chopped
- 2-3 cloves of garlic, crushed
- 1 C water
- 1 C sliced bamboo shoots (1 8oz can)
- ½ C sliced carrot
- 1 T soy sauce or to taste
- 1 t dried pepper flakes or cayenne powder
- 2-4 pickled hot pepper, diced (Del Monte, or other brand of yellow or green pickled peppers are available at the supermarket.)
    - Salt or soy sauce to taste
- 1 green pepper, diced
- 3 T vinegar
- 1 T sherry
- 1 T cornstarch blended with 2 T water

Method:

1. Cut the chicken, bone and all, into 1-inch pieces (or bone the chicken and cut into 1-inch pieces). Mix the chicken thoroughly with the next 3 ingredients. Mix the chicken with 1T cornstarch before cooking.

2. Heat oil in a sauce pan or wok; saute ginger root, onion and garlic. Add chicken and stir for 3-4 minutes.

3. Add water, bamboo shoots, carrots and soy sauce; cover pan and bring to a boil.

4. Add dried pepper and pickled pepper; cover and cook for 2 minutes.

5. Add the last 4 ingredients and cook for 1-2 minutes. Serve hot.

Calories: 1030   Carbohydrates: 33gm
Protein: 121gm   Fat: 44gm

豆豉鷄丁

FERMENTED BLACK BEAN
CHICKEN WITH NUTS
(Dou Shi Ji Ding)

Ingredients:

1 lb	chicken breast, diced
1 t	sherry
½ t	onion or garlic powder
⅛ t	pepper
1 t	minced ginger root
1 T	soy sauce
½ t	sugar
3-4 T	minced fermented black beans
1 T	cornstarch
1 t	cornstarch blended with 1 T water
4 T	oil
¼-½ C	nuts (walnuts, cashews, almonds, peanuts, etc.)
1	onion, diced
1-2	carrots, sliced
1	green pepper, diced
½ C	water
1 T	soy sauce
Salt and pepper to taste	

Method:

1. Mix the diced chicken with the next 7 ingredients together in a bowl. Add 1 T cornstarch and mix well.

2. Heat oil in a pan or wok; fry nuts until light brown (takes less than 1 minute). Remove.

3. Add chicken and stir-fry in the remaining oil until color turns (about 1-1½ minutes). Remove.

4. Saute onion and carrots in the remaining oil for 1-2 minutes. Add the last 4 ingredients and bring to a boil.

5. Add blended cornstarch, cooked chicken and mix well. Transfer to a serving dish; spread the nuts evenly on the chicken. Serve hot.

Makes 4-6 servings.

Calories: 1459   Cholesterol: 295mg   Vit. B2: 1.01mg
Carbohydrates: 55gm   Calcium: 189mg   Vit. A: 6510IU
Protein: 105gm   Iron: 12mg   Vit. C: 125mg
Fat: 91gm   Vit. B1: 0.62mg   Fiber: 4gm

SWEET AND SOUR SCORED CHICKEN
(Tang Cu Ji Pian)

糖醋鷄片

Ingredients:

1 lb	chicken breast
1 T	sherry
½ t	onion powder
¼ t	pepper
3 T	soy sauce
1 t	sesame oil
1 T	cornstarch
	Oil for deep-frying
½ C	frozen peas and carrots, thawed
2	green onions, minced
1 t	minced ginger root
½ C	sugar
1 T	cornstarch
¼ C	vinegar
¼ C	catsup
½ C	water
¼ t	salt
¼ t	pepper
1 t	soy sauce
1 t	sesame oil
3-4	dried mushrooms, soaked and diced
¼ C	diced water chestnuts

Method:

1. Split the chicken breast horizontally into ½" thick pieces and score lightly in a crisscross pattern. Cut the chicken into 1½" squares.

2. Mix the chicken gently with the next 5 ingredients. Let stand for 1 hour. Stir occasionally for even flavor. Mix with 1 T cornstarch before cooking.

3. Mix the last 11 ingredients in a small bowl. Set aside.

4. Heat oil in a pan or wok. Deep-fry the chicken over medium heat until the chicken turns white (about 2 minutes). Transfer to a serving dish.

5. Pour off all the oil except 1 T. Heat the oil; saute onions and ginger root. Add sauce mixture from Step 3 and bring to a boil. Add peas and carrots; mix well. Pour the sauce on the cooked chicken. Serve hot.

Makes 4-6 servings.

Calories:	1598	Iron:	10mg
Carbohydrates:	151gm	Vit. B1:	0.42mg
Protein:	96gm	Vit. B2:	1.03mg
Fat:	78gm	Vit. A:	5282IU
Cholesterol:	295gm	Vit. C:	21mg
Calcium:	130mg	Fiber:	1gm

Calculated with 4 T oil for deep-frying

CHICKEN WITH PORK LOIN
(Ji Pian Li Ji)

鷄片里肌

Ingredients:

- ½ lb   chicken breast, sliced
- ½ lb   pork loin, sliced
- 3 T   soy sauce
- ¼ t   pepper
- ½ t   onion powder
- 1 t   sherry
- 1 t   minced ginger root
- ⅛ t   MSG (optional)
- 1 T   cornstarch
- 1 t   sesame oil (optional)
- 1 C   frozen peas, thawed
- ¼ t   salt
- 4 T   oil
- ½   onion, minced

Method:

1. Mix the first 9 ingredients together thoroughly.

2. Heat oil in a pan or wok. Sauté onion; add chicken and pork. Stir-fry for 2-3 minutes. Separate the meat while stirring.

3. Add peas and ¼ t salt; stir until the peas are heated. Add sesame oil and mix. Serve hot.

Makes 4-6 servings.

Calories: 1383
Carbohydrates: 35gm
Protein: 101gm
Fat: 91gm
Cholesterol: 289mg
Calcium: 128mg

Iron: 15mg
Vit. B1: 2.83mg
Vit. B2: 1.18mg
Vit. A: 1390IU
Vit. C: 33mg
Fiber: 3gm

Yi-Xing pottery steamer of Qi Guo. The steamer was made from a special type of clay from Yi Xing, Jiangsu. It is claimed that food steamed in this steamer will retain its flavor, aroma and nutrients.

STEAM CHICKEN IN YI-XING POTTERY STEAMER
(Qi Guo Ji)

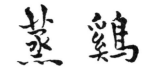

Ingredients:

1	chicken, about 2-3 pounds
10	dried mushrooms, soaked
1 C	sliced bamboo shoots (1 8 oz can)
1 T	salt
¼ C	sherry
4-6	slices of ginger root
2-4	green onions, cut into 2" sections
1 T	sesame oil

Method:

1. Soak the dried mushrooms in hot water for 1 hour or until expanded completely. Squeeze out the water and cut them into quarters.

2. Cut the chicken, bone and all, into 1" pieces.

3. Combine all the ingredients in a bowl and mix thoroughly. Transfer the chicken to a Yi-Xing pottery steamer and cover.

4. Place the Yi-Xing pottery steamer in a tier of a steamer, cover and steam over boiling water for 1 hour or until the chicken is tender. Serve hot in the Yi-Xing pottery steamer or transfer the chicken to a serving plate and serve.

If you don't have a Yi-Xing pottery steamer, the chicken may be placed in a covered heat-proof dish and steamed in the same manner.

Calories: 940	Iron: 14 mg
Carbohydrate: 9 gm	Vit. A: 4600IU
Protein: 120 gm	Vit. B1: 0.59 mg
Fat: 45 gm	Vit. B2: 2.8 mg
Cholesterol: 716 mg	Vit. C: 10 mg
Calcium: 88 mg	Fiber: 2 gm

成 都 鶏

CHENG DU CHICKEN
(Cheng Du Ji)

Ingredients:

1	chicken, boned (about 3 pounds)
1 T	sherry
2 T	soy sauce
½ t	pepper
2 T	cornstarch
3-4 T	oil
2-4	dried hot peppers or 1 T dried pepper flakes
4	cloves of garlic, crushed
3-4	slices of ginger root
¼-½ C	roasted peanuts
1	green pepper, diced
1 T	vinegar
1 T	soy sauce or more
1 t	sugar
1-2 t	sesame oil
¼ t	Sichuan peppercorn powder for dipping (page 314)

Method:

1. Cut the chicken into 3/4" pieces. Mix the chicken with the next 3 ingredients. Add cornstarch and mix well.

2. Heat oil; sauté hot pepper, garlic and ginger root. Add chicken and stir until chicken turns color (about 2-4 minutes).

3. Add the last 7 ingredients, stir and cook until well blended (about 1-2 minutes). Serve hot.

Calories:	1382	Iron:	19mg
Carbohydrates:	26gm	Vit. B1:	0.74mg
Protein:	171gm	Vit. B2:	3.5mg
Fat:	60 gm	Vit. A:	9571IU
Cholesterol:	716mg	Vit. C:	53mg
Calcium:	162mg	Fiber:	1gm

LOTUS LEAF
WRAPPED STEAMED CHICKEN
(Ho Ye Zheng Ji)

Ingredients:

1	chicken, whole, about 2-3 pounds
2-3	lotus leaves, fresh or dried
2 T	cornstarch
3	green onions, minced
2 t	minced ginger root
1 T	sherry
¼ t	pepper
4 T	soy sauce
1 T	sugar

Method:

1. Bone the chicken, leaving the skin on. Cut into 1" bite-size pieces. Marinate chicken with the last 6 ingredients for an hour or more. Mix with 1 T cornstarch.

2. Soak the lotus leaves in warm water (if using dried leaves) until softened. Wash and dry. If fresh leaves are used, wash and dry them.

3. Divide the chicken into 2-3 portions (depending on the size of the leaves). Wrap one portion of chicken in each leaf. Repeat.

4. Place the wrapped chicken in a dish and steam in a boiling steamer for 30-40 minutes.

5. Unwrap the chicken and arrange on a plate with its juice. (Thicken juice with a little blended cornstarch if desired.) Serve hot.

Makes 4-6 servings.

Calories:	1260	Iron:	20mg
Carbohydrates:	28gm	Vit. B1:	0.65mg
Protein:	170gm	Vit. B2:	3.5mg
Fat:	45gm	Vit. A:	7141IU
Cholesterol:	716mg	Vit. C:	9mg
Calcium:	172mg	Fiber:	0

雞絲豆芽　CHICKEN SHREDS WITH BEAN SPROUTS
(Ji Si Dou Ya)

Ingredients:

- ½ lb chicken breast, boned and shredded
- ½ t salt
- ¼ t pepper
- 1 t sherry
- ⅛ t MSG (optional)
- 1 t cornstarch
- 2 t cornstarch blended with 2 T water
- 1 t sesame oil or more
- 3 T oil
- 1 C shredded bamboo shoots, or shredded fresh mushrooms, or both
- ½ lb fresh bean sprouts
- 4 green onions, shredded
- 2 T soy sauce
- ½ t sugar
- ¼ t pepper

Methods:

1. Mix the first 6 ingredients together in a bowl. Set aside.
2. Heat oil in a pan or wok; stir-fry the chicken until the color turns. Transfer to a dish.
3. Add the last 6 ingredients; stir and cook for 2 minutes.
4. Add blended cornstarch, chicken, sesame oil and mix well. Serve immediately.

Makes 4-6 servings.

Calories: 820
Carbohydrates: 24gm
Protein: 54gm
Fat: 57gm
Cholesterol: 147mg
Calcium: 104mg

Iron: 6mg
Vit. B1: 045mg
Vit. B2: 0.66mg
Vit. A: 1136IU
Vit. C: 35mg
Fiber: 2gm

**CHICKEN DICES
WITH PEAS AND CARROTS
(Wan Dou Ji Ding)**

Ingredients:

¾ lb	chicken breast, diced
3 T	soy sauce
¼ t	pepper
¼ t	onion powder
1 t	sesame oil (optional)
1 t	sherry
1 T	cornstarch
3 T	oil
1	onion, diced
2-3	slices of ginger root
1	box (10oz) of frozen peas and carrots, thawed
¼-½ C	toasted nuts of your choice (optional)
1 T	soy sauce or to taste
⅛ t	pepper
1 T	sesame oil
1 t	cornstarch blended with 1 T water
½ C	water

Method:

1. Mix the chicken with the next 6 ingredients. Set aside.
2. Heat oil in a pan or wok; saute' onion and ginger root. Add chicken and stir-fry until color turns (about 2 minutes). Remove.
3. Add the last 7 ingredients and bring to a boil. Add cooked chicken, mix well. Serve hot.

Makes 4-6 servings.

Calories:	1160	Iron:	10mg
Carbohydrates:	50gm	Vit. B1:	0.75mg
Protein:	80gm	Vit. B2:	0.90mg
Fat:	71gm	Vit. A:	26499IU
Cholesterol:	221mg	Vit. C:	33mg
Calcium:	174mg	Fiber:	4gm

棒々鶏

BON BON CHICKEN SHREDS
(Bang Bang Ji)

Ingredients:

1	chicken breast
4-6	green onions
1 T	sesame paste (page 315)
2	cloves of garlic, crushed and minced
⅛-1 t	Sichuan peppercorn powder for seasoning (page 314)
2 t	sugar
2 t	sesame oil
½-2 t	red hot pepper oil, (recipe on page 313)
2 T	vinegar
3 T	soy sauce
¼ t	pepper
1 T	oil
1 t	finely shredded ginger root
¼ t	MSG (optional)*

Method:

1. Place the chicken in a sauce pan; add enough water to cover half the chicken. Cover pan and bring to a boil. Reduce to medium heat and cook for 5 minutes. Turn the chicken over and cook for another 5 minutes. Transfer the chicken to a plate and allow to cool.

2. Bone the chicken and tear the meat into 2"x1/6" shreds or as the Chinese say, "four tooth picks piled together."

3. Wash the green onions; discard the green parts and roots; finely shred the white parts of the onion. Put shredded onion and chicken on a serving dish.

4. Mix the last 12 ingredients in a small bowl. Pour this mixture over the chicken. Mix well before serving. Serve cold.

Sliced and peeled cucumber and shredded carrot can be added to this dish. Put the cucumber and carrot on the plate first, then lay the chicken and onion over the cucumber; add sauce and serve.

*For discussion of MSG, see *Nutrition and Diet with Chinese Cooking*, pages 7-9.

Calories: 870	Carbohydrates: 12gm
Protein: 80gm	Fat: 52gm

CHICKEN LIVERS WITH SICHUAN PEPPERCORN POWDER
(Jiao Ma Feng Fan)

Ingredients:

- ½ lb chicken livers
- 1 T oyster or soy sauce
- ¼ t pepper
- ½ t onion or garlic powder
- 1 t minced ginger root
- 2 t sherry
- 2 T flour for coating the liver
  Oil for deep-frying
  Sichuan powder for dipping (page 314)

Method:

1. Wash and dry the chicken livers. Cut into 1/3" slices.

2. Mix the livers with the next 5 ingredients. Let stand for 30 minutes. Add flour to livers. Mix to coat.

3. Heat oil in a pan or wok. Deep-fry the chicken livers one by one until brown. Serve with a small dish of Sichuan peppercorn powder for dipping.

Makes 4 servings.

Calories: 677	Cholesterol: 1430 mg	Vit. B2: 4 mg
Carbohydrates: 16 gm	Calcium: 57 mg	Vit. A: 27104 IU
Protein: 58 gm	Iron: 21 mg	Vit. C: 36 mg
Fat: 40 gm	Vit. B1: .5 mg	Fiber: 1 gm

Calculated with 2 T oil for deep-frying

With the exception of the newly added Rice Noodle section, the nutritional calculations of all the recipes in this book are for **the whole recipe,** not per serving. 1 or 2 tablespoons of oil can be reduced from each recipe if desired. A reduction of 1 tablespoon of oil will reduce the calories of the recipe by 120, and the fat by 14 grams.

Ingredients:

1	chicken, about 2-3 pounds
3 t	instant chicken bouillon
1	medium onion, chopped
4	slices of ginger root
2	cloves of star anise
1 t	Sichuan peppercorns
1 T	sherry
1 t	sugar
¼ t	pepper
	Water to cover the chicken
1	envelope of unflavored gelatin (¼ oz)
	Vegetable of your choice (optional), such as:
½ C	chopped celery
½ C	frozen peas and carrots, thawed and drained
½ C	chopped green pepper
½ C	chopped nuts
½ C	chopped parsley or coriander

Method:

1. Put the chicken and the next 9 ingredients into a deep sauce pan; cover and bring to a boil.

2. Lower to medium heat and cook until the liquid is reduced to 2½ C. Turn the chicken 2-3 times while cooking.

3. Transfer the chicken to a dish. Bone the chicken and cut into 1" pieces (the skin can be left on, if preferred).

4. Mix the chicken pieces with the vegetables of your choice in a bowl or deep serving dish.

5. Pour the chicken broth through a strainer into a sauce pan. Sprinkle the unflavored gelatin on the chicken broth and cook over medium heat until the gelatin dissolves.

6. Pour the chicken broth over the chicken and vegetables; chill in the refrigerator until firm.

7. Before serving: Dip the bottom and sides of the bowl in hot water for a few seconds. Cover the bowl with a serving dish. Turn upside down and remove bowl from the jellied chicken. Serve cold

as is, or with a small bowl of soy sauce, vinegar, and sesame oil mixture for dipping.

Makes 4-6 servings.

Calories: 1605	Iron: 22mg
Carbohydrates: 32gm	Vit. B1: 1.01mg
Protein: 185gm	Vit. B2: 3.67mg
Fat: 78gm	Vit. A: 2057IU
Cholesterol: 716mg	Vit. C: 81mg
Calcium: 274mg	Fiber: 4gm

EGG SHEETS
(Dan Si)

蛋 絲

Ingredients:

2	eggs	
¼ t	salt	
¼ t	onion powder or garlic powder	
¼ t	pepper	
½ t	oil	

Method:

1. Beat the eggs with the next 3 ingredients.
2. Spread ¼ t oil evenly in a non-stick 9″ skillet with a small piece of paper towel.
3. Heat pan, pour half of the eggs in the pan and tip the pan so that a thin layer of egg covers the pan.
4. Cook over medium heat until the surface is dried. Turn and cook for a few seconds. Remove. Cook the other portion of the egg in the same manner.

The egg sheets can be used for wrapping meat balls (page 136). They can also be used in many dishes as part of the ingredients, garnishing or flavoring when cut into shreds, rectangular, diamond shape etc.

Calories: 181	Carbohydrates: none
Protein: 12gm	Fat: 14gm

CRISP AND TENDER DUCK
(Xiang Cui Ya)

Ingredients:

	1	ready to cook duck, fresh or frozen (thawed), about 4-6 pounds
{	2 T	sherry
	3-4 T	Sichuan peppercorn powder for dipping (page 314)
	1 t	onion or garlic powder
	1	inch of ginger root, crushed
	2-3 T	or more cornstarch
		Sichuan peppercorn powder for dipping (page 314)

Method:

1. Wash and dry the duck. Cut the back of the duck open.

2. Flatten the duck and spread the next 4 ingredients evenly on both sides of the duck. Let set for 4-5 hours or overnight in refrigerator.

3. Place the duck in a boiling steamer and steam for 1 hour or until it is tender. Cool.

4. Spread cornstarch on the steamed duck; pat so that the cornstarch sticks on the duck.

5. Turn the oven on broil. Place a rack on a shallow tray. Place the duck on the rack. Broil, 6 inches away from the heat, for a few minutes or until the duck skin is crisp. Turn, and broil the other side the same way.

6. Cut the duck into 2-inch pieces and arrange neatly on a platter. Serve hot with a small dish of Sichuan peppercorn powder for dipping.

The nutritional value for 1 pound of duck:

Calories: 1210	Iron: 6 mg
Carbohydrates: none	Vit. A 0
Protein: 60gm	Vit. B1: 0.29 mg
Fat: 106 gm	Vit. B2: 0.71 mg
Cholesterol: 336 mg	Vit. C: 0
Calcium. 37 mg	Fiber: 0

With the exception of the newly added Rice Noodle section, the nutritional calculations of all the recipes in this book are for **the whole recipe,** not per serving.

红 烧 鸭

SIMMERED DUCK
(Hung Shao Ya)

Ingredients:

1	ready to cook duck, about 3-5 pounds
6	slices of ginger root
1	medium onion, diced
2	or more, whole star anise
½ C	soy sauce
1 T	sherry
1 T	brown sugar
4-6	dried mushrooms, soaked and quartered
	Water
¼ lb	pork, thinly sliced
2 t	soy sauce
⅛ t	pepper
⅛ t	onion powder
1 t	cornstarch
1 T	oil
1-3	green onions, minced
1 t	minced ginger root

Method:

1. Place the duck, with the next 7 ingredients, in a deep sauce pan; add enough water to cover the duck. Cover pan and bring to a boil.

2. Turn to low heat; Simmer for 2-3 hours or until the duck becomes tender and the liquid reduced to 1/3 C. Place the duck in a serving dish (breast up). Keep hot.

3. Mix the pork slices with the next 4 ingredients.

4. Heat oil in a pan or wok; sauté onion and ginger root. Add pork and stir-fry until the pork is cooked (about 1½ minutes). Place the cooked pork on the duck and serve hot.

Makes 6-8 servings.

Calories: 6100	Iron: 28mg
Carbohydrates: 20gm	Vit. B1: 1.1mg
Protein: 294gm	Vit. B2: 2.9mg
Fat: 527gm	Vit. A: 220mg
Cholesterol: 1008mg	Vit. C: 8mg
Calcium: 260	Fiber: 0

Calculated with 3 pounds of duck (domestic, cooked with skin).

PRESSED DUCK IN ALMOND SAUCE
(Xing Ren Ya)

杏 仁 鴨

Ingredients:

½	ready to cook duck, about 2½ pounds
1 T	salt
¼ t	pepper
½ t	onion or garlic powder
4	slices of ginger root
¼ C	flour
¼ C	cornstarch
½	green pepper or more, diced
1½ T	cornstarch blended with 2 T water
	Oil for deep-frying, about 1-2 cups
1/3 C	almond slices or slivers
½ C	onion, chopped
4	cloves of garlic, crushed
4	slices of ginger root
1½ C	liquid (reserved from steaming duck plus water)
1 t	instant chicken bouillon
1 T	soy sauce
1/3 C	sugar
1/3 C	vinegar
¼ t	salt
¼ t	pepper
1 C	pineapple tidbits
½ C	sliced carrot
1 T	almond extract
½ t	sesame oil

Method:

1. Clean and dry the duck. Mix the next 4 ingredients together; rub the mixture evenly on the duck inside and out. Keep in refrigerator, covered, overnight or longer.

2. Place the duck in a heat-proof dish and steam in a covered, boiling steamer for 1½ hours. Bone (leave the skin on) without disturbing the meat. Transfer the duck to a board. Press the duck to a 1″ thickness.

3. Mix the flour and cornstarch in a small bowl. Sprinkle the mixture generously on the duck. Pat to make sure the flour mixture

sticks on the duck. Shake off the excess flour-cornstarch mixture.

4. Heat oil in a pan or wok; fry the duck until both sides brown and crisp. Remove.

5. Cut the duck into 1" sections. Arrange the duck neatly on a platter. Keep hot.

6. Mix the last 11 ingrdients in a bowl. Set aside.

7. Pour off the oil until 1 T remains. Heat the oil and brown the almonds for a few seconds. Remove.

8. Saute onion, garlic and ginger root in the remaining oil. Add the sauce mixture from Step 6; bring to a boil.

9. Add blended cornstarch and green pepper; bring to a boil. Stir while cooking. Pour the sauce over the duck. Serve hot.

Makes 6 servings.

Calories: 6448	Iron: 23mg
Carbohydrates: 202gm	Vit. B1: 1.3mg
Protein: 254gm	Vit. B2: 2.7mg
Fat: 511gm	Vit. A: 5832IU
Cholesterol: 840mg	Vit. C: 83mg
Calcium: 307mg	Fiber: 3gm

Calculated with 4 1/8 T oil

SALTED STEAMED DUCK
(Zheng Ya)

Ingredients:

- 2 T   Sichuan peppercorn powder for dipping
- 1 T   salt
- ¼ t   pepper
- ¼ t   onion powder
- ¼ t   ground thyme
- 4   slices of ginger root
- 1 T   sherry
- 1 ready to cook whole duck (about 3-5 pounds)
- Few coriander leaves for garnishing

Method:

1. Wash and dry the duck.

2. Mix the first 7 ingredients in a small bowl. Rub the mixture evenly on the duck inside and out. Keep the duck refrigerated in a plastic bag overnight or longer.

3. Steam the duck in a boiling steamer for 1¼ hours. Do not open the steamer during steaming. Let cool.

4. Brush off all the solids, then cut the duck into 2" pieces. Arrange the duck on a platter and garnish with coriander. Serve hot, warm, or cold.

Makes 6-8 servings.

Calories: 5869	Iron: 21mg
Carbohydrates: 2gm	Vit. B1: 1mg
Protein: 286gm	Vit. B2: 2.5mg
Fat: 512gm	Vit. A: 0
Cholesterol: 1008mg	Vit. C: 0
Calcium: 134	Fiber: 0

Calculated with 3 pounds of duck (domestic, cooked with skin).

SMOKED DUCK
(Xuan Ya)

Ingredients:

¼ t   pepper
1 t   onion or garlic powder
1 t   minced ginger root
2 T   sherry
2 T   Sichuan peppercorn powder for dipping (page 314)
1 t   salt
1   ready to cook duck, about 3-6 pounds
       Parsley or coriander leaves for garnishing
¼ C   sugar
¼ C   black tea leaves
¼ C   flour
3-4 C dried pine needles

Method:

1. Mix the first 6 ingredients in a small bowl.

2. Dry the duck inside and out. Rub the mixture from Step 1 evenly on the duck. Keep the duck, covered in plastic wrap, in the refrigerator overnight or longer.

3. Steam the duck in a covered boiling steamer, on high heat, for 1¼ hours. Let it cool to room temperature.

4. Place a layer or two of aluminum foil on the bottom of a large deep sauce pan. Spread the last 4 ingredients on the foil. Put a rack over the mixture. Place the duck on the rack.

5. Cover the pan and smoke the duck over low heat for 10 minutes. Turn the duck and smoke for 10 more minutes. Do not open the lid during smoking process.

6. Chop the duck into 1"x2" pieces and neatly arrange on a platter. Garnish with parsley and serve hot or cold.

Camphor wood chips can be used instead of pine needles to smoke the duck. If camphor is used, the duck is then called "Camphor-smoked duck." The duck can also be deep-fried after the smoking process.

Makes 4-6 servings.

Nutritional value for 1 pound of duck:

Calories: 1210
Carbohydrates: none
Protein: 60gm
Fat: 106 gm
Cholesterol: 336 mg
Calcium 37 mg

Iron: 6 mg
Vit. A 0
Vit. B1: 0.29 mg
Vit. B2: 0.71 mg
Vit. C: 0
Fiber: 0

With the exception of the newly added Rice Noodle section, the nutritional calculations of all the recipes in this book are for the **whole recipe,** not per serving.

EIGHT-TREASURES
SICHUAN DUCK
(Ba Bao Nuo Mi Ya)

Ingredients:

- 3 T Sichuan peppercorn powder for dipping (page 314)
- ½ t onion powder
- ½ t pepper
- 1 ready to cook duck, fresh or frozen (thawed), about 4-6 pounds
  Sichuan peppercorn powder and cornstarch for coating
- 1-2 T oil
- 2 green onions, minced
- 1 T finely minced ginger root
- 1 ½ C water
- ¾ C glutinous rice, also called sweet rice; soaked and drained
- 3-4 Chinese dried mushrooms, soaked and diced
- 2 T dried shrimp, soaked and chopped
- ¼ C dried lotus seeds, soaked and drained
- ¼ C bamboo shoots, diced
- 1 oz old fashioned country-style ham, diced
- 3 T soy sauce
- ¼ t pepper
- ½ t sugar
- 1 T sherry

Method:

Prepare ahead:

Soak glutinous rice, dried mushrooms, dried shrimp and dried lotus seeds separately in cold water for 1 hour, then prepare as the recipe requires.

For the duck:

Mix the first 3 ingredients together. Rub the mixture on duck inside and out. Place the duck in a plastic bag and keep it in refrigerator overnight or longer.

For the stuffing:

Heat 1 T oil in a nonstick sauce pan; sauté green onions and ginger root. Add the last 11 ingredients; stir to mix. Cover pan and bring to a boil. Remove lid and continue boiling until water has evaporated. Cover pan and simmer over lowest heat for 15 minutes. Cool. The stuffing is now ready to use.

Rice can also be cooked in a microwave oven. Just place all the ingredients in a container suitable for microwave cooking and cook on full power WITHOUT covering for 10 minutes. Cover the container with plastic wrap and cook on low power for 15 minutes. Cool.

Rice can also be steamed. Place all the ingredients, except water, in a bowl and steam in a boiling steamer for 30-40 minutes. Cool.

Cooking and serving:

Stuff the cooked rice into the duck cavity. Place the duck in a large deep dish and steam in a boiling steamer for 1½ hours or until duck is tender. Remove the steamed whole duck to a serving platter. Skim off fat from the juice, then pour juice over the duck and serve. Diners serve themselves by picking up a portion of duck meat with a pair of chopsticks and taking a portion of stuffing with a spoon.

The nutritional value for 1 pound of duck:

Calories: 1210	Iron: 6 mg
Carbohydrates: none	Vit. A: 0
Protein: 60gm	Vit. B1: 0.29 mg
Fat: 106 gm	Vit. B2: 0.71 mg
Cholesterol: 336 mg	Vit. C: 0
Calcium: 37 mg	Fiber: 0

PEKING (BEIJING) DUCK
(Baijing Ya)

This duck will be eaten with Chinese (or Mandarin) pancakes, sauce and green onions. Recipes on following pages. In Beijing, the duck is also eaten with "Bing." Recipe on page 76. The pancakes, sauce and onions may be prepared a day or two before roasting duck.

Ingredients for duck:

1	duck, fresh or frozen, 4-6 pounds
½ C	sherry
3 T	honey

Method:

1. In a large mixing bowl, combine the sherry and honey together.
2. Wash and dry the duck inside and out. Remove the excess fat from the duck.
3. Baste the duck with sherry mixture and then marinate it in the same mixture for a few hours; turn several times during the marinating process.
4. Place the duck, breast up and uncovered, on a roasting rack in a shallow pan. Keep it in the refrigerator at least 24 hours or until the skin of the duck dries.
5. Roast duck in oven at 350° for 30 minutes. Reduce to 250° and continue to roast for 1½ hours. Increase temperature to 375° and roast for 10 more minutes, or until the duck turns golden brown; turn once while roasting for crispness on both sides.

To serve: Slice the duck skin into 1"x2" pieces, then slice the meat in the same way. Arrange the skin, crisp side up, in the center of a platter and place the meat slices neatly around the skin. Serve hot with Chinese pancakes, sauce and onions.

To eat: Place a warm pancake on a plate. With a piece of green onion, spread a thin layer of sauce on the pancake. Put the onion in the middle of the pancake, place one or two pieces each of the skin and meat on the pancake. Roll the pancake into a cylindrical roll. Hold the roll with fingers and eat or place the duck and sauce on a sesame seed Shao Bing (page 76) and eat in the same manner.

Drying the duck's skin in the refrigerator is more hygenic than at room temperature. Bacteria will grow within a few hours at room temperature and some can produce toxin. Food poisoning can result by eating this kind of meat. The skin of the duck will be very crisp after roasting; the drying process contributes to the end result of Peking duck. I am very proud of having developed this method of skin drying.

The nutrition information of one pound ready to cook duck:

Calories: 1213	Iron: 6mg
Carbohydrates: 0	Vit. B1: 0.2mg
Protein: 60gm	Vit. B2: 0.7mg
Fat: 106gm	Vit. A: 0
Cholesterol: 336mg	Vit. C: 0
Calcium: 37mg	Fiber: 0

Sauce for Peking Duck:

Mix 6 T soy sauce, 6 T Hoisin sauce, 3 T sugar and 1 T sesame oil together. Place the sauce in small sauce dish and put the dish in the center of a plate.

Onions for Peking Duck:

Use 20 white parts of the green onions. Make slits lengthwise about ½" on each end of the onions. Place the onions in a bowl of ice cold water and keep in refrigerator for 1-2 hours or until the cut parts open up like a flower. Arrange the onions on a platter around the sauce dish. Serve with duck.

CHINESE (OR MANDARIN) PANCAKES
(Dan Bing)

Ingredients:

- 2 C   all purpose flour
- 1 C   boiling water
-       Oil for brushing

Method:

1. Pour boiling water slowly onto the flour in a mixing bowl. Mix water and flour with a wooden spoon or a pair of chopsticks into a warm dough.
2. Knead the dough for 5 minutes.
3. Form the dough into a cylindrical roll about 1" in diameter.
4. Cut the roll evenly into 1" pieces. Flatten them with the palm of your hand into 2" diameter round cakes.
5. Brush a thin layer of oil on one piece of flattened cake and lay another piece (without oil) over it.
6. Roll the two cakes into a flat, thin round sheet about 5" in diameter.
7. Heat an ungreased skillet over low heat. Cook the rolled cakes until they bubble slightly; turn, and cook the other side for a few seconds.
8. While the cakes are still warm, pull apart into two thin cakes. Pile all the cooked cakes together to prevent dryness. Serve warm. If the cakes become too cold, steam the pile of cakes for 10 minutes. The cakes should remain stacked while steaming, or, fold each pancake in thirds and arrange on a tier of the steamer and steam for one minute. Serve immediately with Peking duck or other dishes.

Calories: 934		Iron: 2mg	
Carbohydrates: 170gm		Vit. B1: 1.3mg	
Protein: 23gm		Vit. B2: 1.1mg	
Fat: 16 gm		Vit. A: 0	
Cholesterol: 0		Vit. C: 0	
Calcium: 35mg		Fiber: 0	

1. *Beijing duck farm.*

2. *Drying the ducks before roasting.*

210

3. Roasted ducks.

4. *Beijing duck served with seseme seeds Shao Bing.*

seafood

SQUIRREL FISH
(Song Shu Yu)

Ingredients:

- 1¼ t salt
- ½ t pepper
- 1 t onion or garlic powder
- 1 lb or more whole fish (pike, bass, etc.)
- ¼-½ C flour or more
- Oil for deep-frying
- 1 onion, minced
- 2-4 cloves of garlic, crushed
- 1 t finely minced ginger root
- 1 T cornstarch
- 1 T soy sauce
- 1 T sherry
- ¼ C vinegar
- 1/3 C sugar
- 1/3 C catsup
- 1 T sesame oil
- 3 Chinese dried mushrooms, soaked and diced into the size of frozen carrots
- ¼ C frozen peas and carrots, thawed
- ¼ C water chestnuts, diced into the size of frozen carrots
- 1 t chicken bouillon cube dissolved in 1 C water

Method:

1. Wash and dry the fish. Remove the head and reserve.

2. Split the fish lengthwise in half. Remove the back and side bones but retain the tail intact on the fillets.

3. Score the meat side of the fish in crisscross cuts, ½" apart, almost down to the skin but do not cut through the skin.

4. Combine the first 3 ingredients together. Sprinkle the mixture evenly on the fish. Let set 10 minutes or more.

5. Place the flour in a plate. Dip the fish in the flour until a layer of flour coats the fish all over. Shake off the excess flour.

6. Arrange the fish fillets, meat sides out, in a parallel position. Turn the fish tail in between the fillets in a vertical position.

7. Mix the last 11 ingredients in a bowl. Set aside.

8. Heat oil in a wok. Carefully place the fish in a large, round, Chinese slotted frying spoon. Fry the fish until brown. Place the fried fish on a platter. Coat the fish head in a layer of flour and fry until brown. Place the head in front of the fried fish.

9. Pour off all the oil but 1 T from the wok. Sauté onion, ginger root garlic. Add the sauce mixture from Step 7. Cook and stir until sauce thickens. Pour over the fish and serve hot.

Makes 4-6 servings.

Calories: 1869	Iron:	3mg
Carbohydrates: 187gm	Vit. B1:	0.32mg
Protein: 94gm	Vit. B2:	0.30mg
Fat: 96gm	Vit. A:	7670IU
Cholesterol: 265mg	Vit. C:	25mg
Calcium: 77mg	Fiber:	2gm

Calculated with 5 T oil for deep-frying.

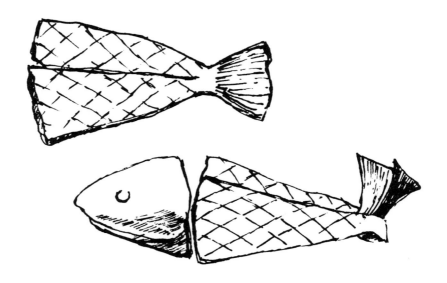

216

FRIED WHOLE FISH
(Gan Jain Yu)

Ingredients:

- 1 lb   ready to cook fish (pike, bass, red snapper, etc.)
- 1 t   salt or Sichuan peppercorn powder for dipping (page 314)
- ½ t   onion powder
- ¼ t   pepper
- 1 t   sherry
- Flour, about 2-3 T
- Oil for deep-frying
- 1 t   finely shredded ginger
- 2 T   soy sauce
- 2 T   vinegar
- 1 t   sesame oil
- 1 t   hot pepper oil (page 313) (optional)

Method:

1. Score the fish, crosswise, diagonally 3-4 times on both sides, about ½" deep and 1" apart.

2. Mix the next 4 ingredients together. Rub the mixture on the fish and in between the scores.

3. Spread a layer of flour on the fish. Pat on flour to make sure it sticks on the fish. Shake off excess flour.

4. Mix the last 5 ingredients in a small dish. Set aside.

5. Heat oil in a pan or wok; fry the fish until golden brown and crisp. Transfer the fish to a serving plate and serve with the sauce mixture from Step 4 for dipping.

Makes 4-6 servings.

Calories: 1047		Iron: 0.8mg	
Carbohydrates: 13gm		Vit. B1: 0.11mg	
Protein: 83gm		Vit. B2: 0.44mg	
Fat: 71gm		Vit. A: 0	
Cholesterol: 265mg		Vit. C: 0	
Calcium: 14mg		Fiber: 0	

Calculated with 4 T oil for deep-frying.

葱 燴 魚

BRAISED FISH WITH GREEN ONIONS
(Cong Hui Yu)

Ingredients:

1	lb	ready to cook whole fish (pike, bass, red snapper, trout, etc.)
½	t	salt
½	t	pepper
1	t	onion or garlic powder
		Flour for coating (about 2 T)
10-15		green onions, washed and cut into 1" sections
2	t	or more sesame oil
2-3	T	oil
4		slices of ginger root
1	C	water
1	T	sugar
3-4	T	soy sauce
¼	t	pepper
1	T	sherry

Method:

1. Score the fish, crosswise, diagonally, 3-4 times on both sides (about ½" deep and 1" apart).

2. Mix the next 3 ingredients together. Rub the mixture evenly in between the scores and on the fish.

3. Sprinkle a layer of flour on the fish. Pat the fish so that the flour sticks to the fish. Shake off the excess flour.

4. Heat oil in a non-stick pan or wok; sauté ginger root. Add fish and fry until brown. Turn and fry in the same manner.

5. Add the last 5 ingredients; cover and cook for 5 minutes. Turn and cook another 5 minutes.

6. Add green onions and cook until the onion is wilted and the liquid is reduced to ½ C. Add sesame oil and mix well. Serve hot.

Makes 4-6 servings.

Calories: 960	Cholesterol: 265 mg	Vit. B2: 0.25 mg
Carbohydrates: 47 gm	Calcium: 153 mg	Vit. A: 400 IU
Protein: 88 gm	Iron: 5 mg	Vit. C: 64 mg
Fat: 44 gm	Vit. B1 0.12 mg	Fiber: 2 gm

BRAISED FISH IN BROWN SAUCE
(Hung Shao Yu)

Ingredients:

1-2 lb	whole fish (pike, bass, trout etc.)
½ t	salt
½ t	pepper
½ t	onion powder
	Flour for coating the fish (about 2 T)
1 T	sesame oil
4-5 T	oil
3-4	green onions, cut into 2-inch sections
3-4	slices of ginger root
4 T	soy sauce
1 T	sherry
3	Chinese dried mushrooms soaked and shredded or ten fresh mushrooms, sliced
1 C	sliced bamboo shoots (about 1-8 oz can, drained)
1 T	brown sugar
1 C	water

Method:

1. Wash and dry the fish. Score the fish diagonally 3-4 times, about ½-inch deep and 1-inch apart on both sides.

2. Combine salt, pepper, and onion powder; rub the mixture evenly on the fish and in between the scores.

3. Coat the fish with a layer of flour. Pat so that the flour sticks to the fish.

4. Heat oil in a pan or wok; add fish and fry until brown. Turn and fry in the same manner.

5. Add the last 8 ingredients; cover and bring to a boil. Reduce to medium heat and cook until the sauce is reduced to ½ C. Add sesame oil and mix. Serve hot.

Calories:	910	Carbohydrates:	20gm
Protein:	46gm	Fat:	72gm

Calculated with 1 pound whole pike.

荷 包 魚

MEAT STUFFED FISH
(He Bao Yu)

Ingredients:

1-1½ lb ready to cook whole fish of your choice (pike, bass, white fish, etc.)

⎧ ½ C   ground pork, about ¼ pound
⎪ 1   green onion, minced
⎪ ¼ t   minced ginger root
⎨ ⅛ t   pepper
⎪ 1 T   sherry
⎪ 1 T   soy sauce
⎪ 1 t   sesame oil
⎩ 1 t   cornstarch

1 T   cornstarch for coating fish
4 T   oil

⎧ 3-4   green onions, shredded
⎪ 4-6   slices of ginger root
⎪ 4 T   soy sauce
⎨ 1 T   sherry
⎪ 1 T   sugar
⎪ 1 T   vinegar
⎩ 1½ C   water

Method:

1. Wash and dry the fish. Spread a thin layer (about 2 t) of cornstarch inside the fish cavity.

2. Mix the next 8 ingredients together thoroughly. Stuff this mixture in the fish cavity.

3. Coat outside of fish with 1 T cornstarch. Heat oil in a non-stick pan; fry the fish until both sides brown. Cover pan while frying to prevent spattering.

4. Add the last 7 ingredients; cover and cook for 10 minutes or until the juice is reduced to ¼ C. Turn once while cooking. Serve hot.

Makes 4-6 servings.

Calories: 1324	Cholesterol: 265mg	Vit. B2: 0.45mg
Carbohydrates: 34gm	Calcium: 94mg	Vit. A: 800IU
Protein: 106gm	Iron: 7mg	Vit. C: 12mg
Fat: 81gm	Vit. B1: 1mg	Fiber: 0.5gm

SWEET AND SOUR FISH
(Tan Cu Yu)

糖 醋 鱼

Ingredients:

1	whole fish, about 1 pound (pike, red snapper, bass, etc.)
1¼ t	salt
¼ t	pepper
½ t	onion powder
1 t	sherry
	Flour for coating (2 T)
2	green onions, minced, for garnishing
4 T	oil
2 T	shredded ginger root
2-4	cloves of garlic, crushed
½ C	sugar
1 T	cornstarch
¼ C	catsup
¼ C	vinegar
1 C	water
1 T	soy sauce
½ C	sliced carrots
1 C	sliced bamboo shoots (optional)

Method:

1. Wash and dry the fish. Make a few slashes, diagonally, on both sides of the fish down to the bone.

2. Mix the next 4 ingredients together. Rub the mixture evenly in between the slashes and over the whole fish.

3. Coat the fish with a layer of flour (making sure to coat in between the slashes), patting the fish so that the flour adheres. Shake off excess flour.

4. Heat oil in a non-stick pan or wok; fry the fish until both sides turn brown. Transfer to a serving platter and keep hot.

5. In a bowl, thoroughly mix together the last 8 ingredients.

6. Sauté ginger and garlic in the remaining oil; add the sauce mixture (Step 5) and cook until the sauce thickens. Pour the sauce over the fish. Sprinkle with minced onion and serve immediately.

Calories: 1617
Carbohydrates: 169gm
Protein: 84gm
Fat: 67gm
Cholesterol: 265mg
Calcium: 48mg

Iron: 2mg
Vit. B1: 0.68mg
Vit. B2: 0.85mg
Vit. A: 5900IU
Vit. C: 11mg
Fiber: 1gm

HOT BEAN SAUCE FISH
(Dou Ban Yu)

Ingredients:

1 lb	fish (pike, bass or trout)
1-2 T	sherry
1-2 T	cornstarch, or more for coating
1 C	or more oil for deep-frying
3-4	cloves of garlic, minced
4-5	green onions, minced
½ in	ginger root, finely minced
2 T	hot (Sichuan) bean sauce
1 T	cornstarch blended with 2-4 T water
3-4	Chinese dried mushrooms, soaked and diced
¼ C	water chestnuts or bamboo shoots, diced
2 T	soy sauce
2 T	sherry
2 t	brown sugar
½ t	pepper
1 T	red oil (page 313)
1 T	vinegar
1 T	sesame oil
3/4 C	water

Method:

1. Clean and dry the fish. Score the fish, about ½" deep and 1" apart crosswise and diagonally on both sides.

2. Sprinkle 1-2 T sherry on the fish (to remove or cover up the fishy smell). Coat the fish with a thin layer of cornstarch. (The cornstarch will prevent sticking and spattering while frying).

3. Heat oil in pan or wok; fry fish until light brown. Transfer to a dish.

4. Pour all but 1 T oil from pan. Heat the oil; add garlic, green onions, ginger root and sauté for 1 minute. Add hot bean sauce and stir for ½ minute.

5. Add the last 10 ingredients together with the fish; cover and bring to a boil. Reduce to low heat and simmer for 15 minutes. Turn once during simmering time.

6. Add blended cornstarch and cook until the sauce thickens. (If the sauce is already reduced to a few tablespoons, do not use the blended cornstarch to thicken the sauce any more.) Transfer the fish with the sauce to a serving dish and serve hot.

Makes 4-6 servings.

Calories: 1129	Cholesterol: 218 mg	Vit. B2: .7 mg
Carbohydrates: 55 gm	Calcium: 131 mg	Vit. C: 27 mg
Protein: 51 gm	Iron: 21 mg	Fiber: 8 gm
Fat: 75 gm	Vit. B1: .4 mg	

Calculated with 1 pound whole white fish and 1 T oil for deep-frying.

BOILED FISH
(Xi Hu Yu)

Ingredients:

1-1½ lb	ready to cook fresh fish (white, pike, etc.)
	Water
4-6	slices of ginger root
3	green onions, cut into 3″ sections
1 T	sherry
3	green onions, shredded
1½ T	cornstarch blended with 3 T water
3 T	oil
1 T	(or more) shredded ginger root
½ C	minced coriander
1 t	instant chicken bouillon
1½ C	water
3 T	soy sauce
1 T	vinegar
1 T	sugar
1 T	sherry
¼ t	pepper

223

Method:

1. Mix the last 7 ingredients in a bowl. Set aside. Split the fish lengthwise in half (if possible, do not cut through the back but leave the two halves connected.)

2. Put 2-3 cups of water in a large sauce pan; add ginger root slices and onion sections. Cover the pan and bring to a boil. Turn to low heat and cook for 5 minutes.

3. Add fish and cook on high heat for 5-7 minutes, or until the fish is cooked. Carefully remove the fish to a long serving plate. Keep warm.

4. Heat oil in a pan or wok, sauté shredded ginger root; add the sauce mixture from Step 1 and bring to a boil. Add blended cornstarch and cook until the sauce thickens.

5. Add green onion shreds; mix well. Pour over the fish; garnish with coriander and serve immediately.

Makes 4-6 servings.

Calories: 973	Iron: 2 mg
Carbohydrates: 33 gm	Vit. B1: 0.24 mg
Protein: 84 gm	Vit. B2: 0.12
Fat: 53 gm	Vit. A: 600IU
Cholesterol: 265 mg	Vit. C: 9 mg
Calcium: 52 mg	Fiber: 0

SHARK'S FIN
WITH ASSORTED SHREDS
(Ji Si Yu Chi Gen)

Ingredients:

1 C	dried shark's fin
¼ lb	chicken breast, shredded
¼ t	salt
1 t	cornstarch
3 T	cornstarch blended with ¼ C of water
2	green onions, finely shredded
2 t	sesame oil
1 T	vinegar
	Coriander leaves for garnishing
½ C	shredded bamboo shoot
2 oz	shredded old-fashioned, country style ham
15-20	dried lily buds, soaked and washed
3-4	dried mushrooms, soaked and shredded
	Egg shreds (page 197) (optional)
1 t	finely shredded ginger root
3 C	water
3 t	instant chicken bouillon
½ t	pepper
1 T	sherry

Method:

1. Soak the dried shark's fin in water overnight. Wash and drain.

2. Place the soaked shark's fin in a sauce pan; fill with water 3″ above the fin; cover and bring to a boil. Reduce to low heat and cook for 2 hours or until it becomes tender. Rinse and drain.

3. Mix the chicken shreds with ¼ t salt and 1 t cornstarch. Set aside.

4. Place the shark's fin and the last 10 ingredients in a large sauce pan; cover and bring to a boil.

5. Add chicken shreds a few at a time and cook for 1 minute.

6. Add blended cornstarch and cook until the sauce thickens. Add sesame oil, green onion and vinegar; mix well. Pour into a tureen; garnish with coriander. Serve hot.

Makes 4-6 servings.

Calories: 561	Cholesterol: 158mg	Vit. B2: 0.33mg
Carbohydrates: 31mg	Calcium: 35mg	Vit. A: 512IU
Protein: 38gm	Iron: 2mg	Vit. C: 6mg
Fat: 30gm	Vit. B1: 0.19mg	Fiber: 1gm

Shark's fin is not included in this calculation (see page 10).

STEAMED FISH WITH FERMENTED BEANS (HOT)
(Dou Shi Yu)

Ingredients:

1 lb	ready to cook whole fish (pike, white, bass, etc.)
1 t	cornstarch blended with 1 T water
3 T	or more fermented black beans, minced
2-4	cloves of garlic, minced
2-4	slices of ginger root, shredded
2-4	green onions, shredded
½ t	pepper
4-6	hot pepper, shredded
1 oz	shredded old fashioned, country-style ham
2	dried mushrooms, soaked and shredded
⅛ t	MSG (optional)
2 T	oil
1 T	soy sauce
1 t	sugar

Method:

1. Score the fish, diagonally, 3-4 times on both sides, about ½" deep and 1" apart.

2. Place the fish in a shallow heat-proof dish. Mix the last 12 ingredients and spread on the fish evenly.

3. Set the dish in a boiling steamer and steam for 20 minutes.

4. Pour the liquid into a small sauce pan without disturbing the fish.

5. Bring the liquid to a boil and thicken with 1 t blended cornstarch. Pour the sauce over the fish and serve hot.

Makes 4-6 servings.

Calories: 857
Cholesterol: 276 mg
Vit. B2: 0.17 mg
Carbohydrates: 17 gm
Calcium: 34 mg
Vit. A: 3425IU
Protein: 89 gm
Iron: 2 mg
Vit. C: 59 mg
Fat: 46 gm
Vit. B1: 0.97 mg
Fiber: 2 gm

SMOKED FISH
(Xun Yu)

Ingredients:

5 T	soy sauce
4	slices of ginger root
3	green onions, cut into 2-inch lengths
2 T	sherry
¼ t	pepper
1-2 lb	fish, whole or fillets (pike, bass, white, flounder etc.)
1-2 C	oil for deep-frying
1 C	water
1 t	five-spice powder
4 T	brown sugar
1 T	sesame oil
2	slices of ginger root

Method:

1. If a whole fish is used, cut it crosswise into ¾" thick pieces. If fish fillets are used, cut them into 1½" wide sections.

2. Mix the first 5 ingredients in a bowl. Marinate the fish with the soy sauce mixture for several hours at room temperature or in refrigerator overnight. Turn fish occasionally for even flavor.

3. Boil the last 5 ingredients for 1 minute. Transfer to a dish.

4. Heat oil in a non-stick pan; drop fish pieces one by one into the oil. Fry until dark brown. Cover pan while frying to prevent splashing and splattering.

5. Soak the fried fish in the boiled sugar-spice mixture for 3-4 minutes. Transfer the soaked fish to a plate. Serve cold.

Calories: 850
Carbohydrates: 46 gm
Protein: 38 gm
Fat: 58 gm

Calculated with 4 T oil for deep-frying.

红 烧 鱼 块

BRAISED FISH SECTION
(Hong Shao Yu Kuai)

Ingredients:

1 lb	middle section of a large fish (carp, pike, white etc.)
	Flour for coating
2-3 T	Sichuan hot bean sauce
2-4	green onions, minced
1 T	minced ginger root
4-5	cloves of garlic, minced
	Oil for deep-frying
¼ C	minced Sichuan pickle
¼ C	minced pork about 1 ounce
2 T	sherry
2 T	soy sauce or to taste
2 T	brown sugar
1 T	vinegar
1 C	chicken broth or water

Method:

1. Make deep, crisscross scores, about 1-inch apart on both sides of the fish section. Coat the fish with a layer of flour. Shake off excess flour. Set aside.

2. Heat oil in a pan or wok, deep-fry the fish until light brown on both sides. Remove

3. Pour off all oil except 2 T. Add Sichuan hot bean sauce to the oil and stir for few seconds. Add minced onion, ginger, and garlic; stir for 1 minute.

4. Add the last 7 ingredients and the fish; cover and bring to a boil. Turn to low heat and simmer until the cooking liquid is reduced to ¼ cup; turn once during cooking.

5. Transfer the fish to a serving plate. Add the cooking juice to the fish and serve hot.

Calories: 1080	Cholesterol: 285 mg	Vit. B1: 0.95 mg
Carbohydrate: 25 gm	Calcium: 25 mg	Vit. B2: 0.49
Protein: 59 gm	Iron: 2.5 mg	Vit. C: trace
Fat: 83 gm	Vit. A: 8IU	Fiber: 1 gm

Calculated with whole pike and 5 T oil

FISH FILLET IN CLEAR SAUCE
(Chao Yu Pian)

Ingredients:

- 1 T   sherry
- 1 t   salt
- ½ t   onion powder
- 1   egg white
- 1 lb   fish fillet
- 2 T   cornstarch
- 1 C   sliced bamboo shoots (1 8 oz can)
  Oil for deep-frying
- 4-5   slices of ginger root
- 3-4   cloves of garlic, crushed
- 1   chicken bouillon cube dissolved in ½ C water
- 3   white part of green onions, minced
- 1 t   cornstarch blended with 2 T water
  Parsley for garnishing

Method:

1. Mix the first 4 ingredients in a bowl, set aside.
2. Slant slice the fish fillet into 1½ x ¼" slices. Transfer the fish fillet to the egg-white mixture and mix gently. Let it set for 1 hour or more. Coat the fish slices one by one with a layer of cornstarch before cooking.
3. Heat oil in wok until lukewarm. Arrange the fish pieces one by one on a shallow, round, slotted spatula. Place the spatula holding the fish in the oil and fry for 1 minute or until the fish pieces turn white. Drain.
4. Pour off all but 2 T oil. Saute ginger root and garlic until dark. Discard the ginger root and garlic.
5. Add bamboo shoots and stir for a few seconds. Add the last 3 ingredients; cook until the sauce thickens.
6. All 1 T oil and the cooked fish; mix well. Transfer the fish to a serving dish or plate, garnish with parsley and serve hot.

Calories: 1145	Cholesterol: 320 mg	Vit. B1: 2.03 mg
Carbohydrate: 21 gm	Calcium: 2 mg	Vit. B2: 1.24 mg
Protein: 91gm	Iron: 2 mg	Vit. C: 5 mg
Fat: 76 gm	Vit. A: 20IU	Fiber: 1.5 gm

Calculated with Walleye pike fillet and 5 T oil for deep-frying.

芝麻鱼片

Ingredients:

        1   egg
      ½ t   onion powder
      ¼ t   pepper
      1 t   sherry
      ¾ t   salt
      1 T   cornstarch
      1 t   minced ginger root
      ⅛ t   MSG (optional)
      1 lb   fish fillet of your choice, fresh or frozen
      2 T   cornstarch
              Oil for deep-frying
      ¼ C   cornstarch
      ½ C   flour
      ½ t   salt
      1 t   sugar
      ½ t   onion powder
      ¼ t   pepper
    3-4 T   sesame seeds
      1 t   baking powder
    ½ C+2 T   water

Method:

1. Mix the first 8 ingredients in a bowl.

2. Dry the fish and cut it into 1" wide pieces. Put the fish in the egg mixture and let it stand for 1 hour or more.

3. Mix the last 9 ingredients in a bowl to form a batter.

4. Sprinkle a layer of cornstarch on the fish.

5. Heat oil. Coat the fish with a layer of batter. Deep-fry the fish until golden brown. Transfer to a serving plate. Serve hot with the sauces of your choice. See below:

Brown Sauce:

1½ C water, 1 t instant chicken bouillon, 1 T soy sauce, ⅛ t pepper, 1½ T cornstarch. Mix all the ingredients in a small sauce pan and bring to a boil. Pour over the fish and garnish with green onions.

Sweet and Sour Sauce:

Bring to a boil a mixture of ¼ C catsup, ¼ C sugar, ¼ C vinegar, ¼ C water and 1 t cornstarch. Pour over the fried fish and serve.
  Makes 4-6 servings.

Calories: 1638	Cholesterol: 554mg	Vit. B2: 0.55mg
Carbohydrates: 103gm	Calcium: 406mg	Vit. A: 598IU
Protein: 96gm	Iron: 6mg	Vit. C: 9mg
Fat: 91gm	Vit. B1: 0.63mg	Fiber: 2mg

Calculated with 5 T oil for deep-frying.

FISH FILLET IN BROWN SAUCE
(Hui Yu Kuai)

熗 魚 塊

Ingredients:

1 lb	fish fillet
½ t	onion or garlic powder
¾ t	salt
1	egg white
1 T	sherry
¼ t	pepper
1 t	minced ginger root
⅛ t	MSG (optional)
1 T	or more cornstarch for coating
4-5 T	oil
1	green pepper, diced
½ C	carrot slices
1	onion, diced
2-4	slices of ginger root
1 C	water
1 t	instant chicken bouillon
¼ t	pepper
2 T	soy sauce
2 T	brown sugar
1 T	sesame oil
1 T	cornstarch blended with 2 T water

Method:

1. Dry and cut the fish fillet into 2" long sections. Marinate the fish with the next 7 ingredients; let stand for 1 hour or more. Turn occasionally for even flavor. Coat with a layer of cornstarch before frying.

2. Mix the last 7 ingredients in a small bowl. Set aside.

3. Heat oil in a pan or wok; fry the fish pieces until both sides are brown and crisp. Transfer to a serving plate. Keep warm.

4. Sauté onion and ginger root in the remaining oil; add green pepper and carrots and stir for 1 minute. Add the sauce mixture from Step 2; bring to a boil. Pour the sauce over the fish and serve hot.

Makes 4-6 servings.

Calories: 1344		Iron: 6mg	
Carbohydrates: 63gm		Vit. B1: 0.39mg	
Protein: 105gm		Vit. B2: 1mg	
Fat: 72gm		Vit. A: 5901IU	
Cholesterol: 227gm		Vit. C: 134mg	
Calcium: 154mg		Fiber: 2gm	

SIMMERED FISH TAILS
(Hong Shao Hua Shui)

Ingredients:

1 lb	fresh fish tail (carp or pike, etc.)
	Cornstarch for coating (about 2 T)
2 t	cornstarch blended with 2 T water
1	leek, about ½ pound, shredded
½ C	water
4 T	oil
4	cloves of garlic, sliced
4	slices of ginger root

3	green onions, shredded
2-4	slices of ginger root
4 T	soy sauce
1 T	sherry
1 T	brown sugar
½ t	pepper
2 t	sesame oil

Method:

1. Split the fish tail in half. Discard the big bones. Cut the fish tail, lengthwise, into 1" wide strips.

2. Mix the last 7 ingredients in a bowl. Marinate the fish in this mixture for 1 hour or more.

3. Coat the fish with a layer of cornstarch (save the marinade).

4. Heat oil in a pan or wok; saute' garlic and ginger root until black. Discard.

5. Add fish and fry 1 minute on both sides.

6. Add marinade and cook for 1 minute.

7. Add shredded leeks and cook for 2 minutes.

8. Add blended cornstarch, water and cook until sauce thickens (salt and pepper to taste). Serve hot.

Makes 4-6 servings.

Calories: 1333	Cholesterol: 265mg	Vit. B2: 0.31mg
Carbohydrates: 67gm	Calcium: 19mg	Vit. A: 689IU
Protein: 90gm	Iron: 6mg	Vit. C: 49mg
Fat: 76gm	Vit. B1: 0.3mg	Fiber: 3gm

红燴蝦

RED BRAISED SHRIMP (PRAWNS)
(Hong Hui Xia)

Ingredients:

1 lb	large shrimp in the shell
3 T	oil
1 T	sherry
3-4	green onions
4-5	thin slices of ginger root
2 T	sugar
¾ t	salt
1 T	soy sauce
½ t	chicken bouillon dissolved in ½ C water
1-2	drops of red food coloring (optional)

Method:

1. Wash and dry the shrimp and remove the legs. Devein by cutting the back open but do not shell the shrimp.

2. Discard the roots and green parts of the green onions. Shred the white parts of the onions and ginger slices into fine shreds.

3. Heat 2 T oil in a pan or wok; add shrimp and fry for 1-2 minutes; turn and fry in the same manner.

4. Add the last 8 ingredients; bring to a boil. Turn to low heat and simmer for few minutes or until the liquid reduces to 3-4 T. Turn once during cooking.

5. Remove the shrimp to a serving plate. Add 1 T oil to the cooking liquid and mix well. Spread the liquid on the shrimp and serve hot.

Calories: 760		Iron: 5 mg	
Carbohydrate: 32 gm		Vit. A: 100IU	
Protein: 57 gm		Vit. B1: 0.08 mg	
Fat: 45 gm		Vit. B2: 0.11 mg	
Cholesterol: 390 mg		Vit. C: 12 mg	
Calcium: 220 mg		Fiber: 0.5 gm	

BUTTERFLY SHRIMP
(Mian Bao Zha Xia)

Ingredients:

- 1 t   salt
- 1 t   onion or garlic powder
- ¼   pepper
- 1 t   finely minced ginger root
- 1 T   sherry
- 1 lb   large shrimp in the shell
- 1   egg, beaten
- ½ C   breadcrumbs or more
  - Oil for deep-frying
  - Sichuan peppercorn powder for dipping

Method:

1. Shell the shrimp but leave the shell of the tail on.

2. Cut the shrimp lengthwise from the back in half (cut down but do not cut through, so that the two halves remain attached).

3. Flatten the shrimp; spread the first 5 ingredients evenly on the shrimp. Let set for 1 hour or more.

4. Coat the shrimp with egg first then coat with a layer of breadcrumbs. Press the shrimp and shake off the excess breadcrumbs before frying.

5. Heat oil in a pan; fry the shrimp until light brown. Arrange the fried shrimp on a platter. Serve hot with a small dish of Sichuan peppercorn powder for dipping. Dip with Sichuan peppercorn powder before eating.

Calories:	1045	Iron:	3.3 mg
Carbohydrate:	41gm	Vit. A:	600IU
Protein:	68 gm	Vit. B1:	22mg
Fat:	68 gm	Vit. B2:	0.39 mg
Cholesterol:	640 mg	Vit. C:	0
Calcium:	285 mg	Fiber:	0

桃花泛

Ingredients:

½ lb	shelled shrimp, fresh or frozen
½ t	salt
1 T	sherry
¼ t	onion powder
⅛ t	pepper
1 T	cornstarch
2 C	cooked rice (medium grain)
	Oil for deep-frying
2-3	cloves of garlic, crushed
½ C	chopped onion
3	slices of ginger root
½ C	sugar
1½ T	cornstarch
½ C	vinegar
2/3 C	water
½ C	catsup
2/3 t	salt
2 T	soy sauce
1 T	sesame oil
½ C	water chestnuts, sliced
½ C	frozen peas
⅛ lb	fresh mushrooms, diced

Method:

1. Split the shrimp into half lengthwise. Mix the shrimp with the next 5 ingredients. Set aside.

2. Press (or roll) the cooked rice on a lightly greased cookie sheet into a ¼" thickness.   Dry the rice in a 300° oven for 1-2 hours or until the rice is completly dried. Break the dried rice into 2" squares. Set aside.

3. Heat oil for deep-frying in a wok or pan; fry the rice until light brown. Remove.

4. Combine the last 11 ingredients in a bowl. Set aside.

5. Heat 2 T oil in a pan; sauté minced onion, garlic and ginger root. Add shrimp and stir for 1-2 minutes. Remove.

6. Add the sauce mixture from Step 4 to the pan. (At the same time, heat the oil for deep-frying and fry the rice once more until dark brown; remove to a serving dish and keep hot.) Stir and cook until the sauce thickens. Add the cooked shrimp and mix well.

7. Transfer the sauce to a bowl, and pour the sauce on the rice immediately. There should be a sizzling sound when the hot sauce is poured on the hot rice.

In China the rice is dried in the sun or at room temperature. This method takes a much longer time- from one to two days.

Calories: 2000	Iron: 10 mg
Carbohydrate: 280 mg	Vit. A: 2000IU
Protein: 50 gm	Vit. B1: 1 mg
Fat: 80 gm	Vit. B2: 0.3 mg
Cholesterol: 195 mg	Vit. C: 30 mg
Calcium: 204 mg	Fiber: 2.5 gm

Calculated with 5 T oil

芥菜花炒蝦仁 SHRIMP WITH BROCCOLI
(Jie Cai Hua Chao Xia Ren)

Ingredients:

2/3 lb	shelled shrimp, fresh or frozen
½ t	salt
¼ t	pepper
½ t	onion powder
1 t	sherry
1 t	minced ginger root
2 t	cornstarch
1 T	soy sauce
4 T	oil
2	green onions, minced
1 t	sesame oil
1	large stalk or broccoli
1/3 t	salt
1 t	sherry
1 t	sugar
1 t	sesame oil

Method:

1. Cut a slit along the back line about half the depth of the shrimp. Mix the shrimp with the next 7 ingredients. Set aside.

2. Wash the broccoli, then cut the flowerlets into 1" long pieces.

3. Heat 1 T oil in a pan or wok; sauté onion. Add the last 5 ingredients, stir and cook for 2 minutes. Transfer to a serving plate.

4. Add 3 T oil; stir-fry shrimp until color turns (about 1-1½ minutes). Add 1 t sesame oil; mix well. Place the cooked shrimp over the cooked broccoli. Serve immediately.

Makes 4-6 servings.

Calories:	1000	Iron:	7mg
Carbohydrates:	26gm	Vit. B1:	0.24mg
Protein:	67gm	Vit. B2:	0.49mg
Fat:	68gm	Vit. A:	4525IU
Cholesterol:	453mg	Vit. C:	192mg
Calcium:	392mg	Fiber:	3gm

STIR-FRY SHRIMP, CHONG-QING STYLE
(Ma La Xia Ren)

Ingredients:

- ¾ lb   shelled shrimp, fresh or frozen
- 1½ t   Sichuan peppercorn powder for dipping
- 1 t   sherry
- ¼ t   pepper
- ⅛ t   MSG (optional)
- 2 t   cornstarch
- 3 T   oil
- 1 t   Sichuan peppercorns
- 2-4   green onions, minced
- 1 t   minced ginger root
- 3-4   hot peppers, minced
- 1   tomato, diced
- ¼ t   Sichuan peppercorn powder for seasoning
- 1/3 C   water
- 1 t   cornstarch
- 1 T   soy sauce
- 1 t   sherry
- ⅛ t   pepper
- 1 t   sugar
- 1 T   sesame oil

Method:

1. Make a slit along the back of each shrimp. Mix the shrimp with the next 5 ingredients.

2. Combine the last 7 ingredients in a small bowl. Set aside.

3. Heat 2 T oil in a pan or wok; add shrimp and stir-fry until color turns (about 1½-2 minutes). Remove.

4. Add 1 T oil, saute Sichuan peppercorns until black. Discard.

5. Add minced onion and ginger root, hot pepper and the sauce mixture from Step 2. Cook until the sauce thickens.

6. Add shrimp and tomato; mix well. Transfer to a serving dish. Sprinkle with Sichuan peppercorn powder for seasoning and serve hot.

Makes 4-6 servings.

Calories: 900
Carbohydrates: 23 gm
Protein: 63 gm
Fat: 60 gm

Cholesterol: 510 mg
Calcium: 239 mg
Iron: 6 mg
Vit. B1: 0.11 mg

Vit. B2: 0.19 mg
Vit. A: 3424IU
Vit. C: 58 mg
Fiber: 2 gm

豆瓣蝦

SHRIMP WITH HOT BEAN SAUCE
(Dou Ban Xia)

Ingredients:

1 lb	shrimp in the shell
3	cloves of garlic or more, minced
1 t	minced ginger root
1 T	hot bean sauce or more
1 T	cornstarch
3 T	oil
1 t	sugar
1 T	soy sauce or more
¼ t	pepper
1 T	sherry
1 t	vinegar
2 t	sesame oil

Method:

1. Remove the legs of the shrimp with a pair of scissors. Cut the back open and devein (do not shell shrimp). Wash and drain. Mix with 1 T cornstarch.

2. Heat oil in a pan or wok; add shrimp and stir for 1 minute.

3. Add garlic, ginger root, and hot bean sauce; stir for 1-2 minutes. Add last 6 ingredients and mix well. Serve hot.

Makes 4-6 servings.

Calories: 800
Carbohydrates: 24gm
Protein: 58gm
Fat: 50gm
Cholesterol: 680mg
Calcium: 215mg

Iron: 6mg
Vit. B1: 0.13mg
Vit. B2: 0.15mg
Vit. A: 6IU
Vit. C: 0
Fiber: 0

PALACE SHRIMP (HOT)
(Gong Bao Xia Ren)

宫保蝦仁

Ingredients:

- 1 lb shelled shrimp, fresh or frozen
- 1 T sherry
- ½ t onion powder
- ¼ t pepper
- 1 t salt
- ⅛ t MSG (optional)
- 1 T cornstarch
- 1 onion, chopped
- ½ C frozen peas and carrots, thawed, or sliced bamboo shoots
- 4 T oil
- 5-6 dried or fresh hot peppers, diced
- 4 slices of ginger root
- 2 cloves of garlic, crushed
- lemon, tomato or parsley for garnishing
- ½ C water
- 1 t instant chicken bouillon
- 1 t cornstarch
- ½ t sugar
- 1 t vinegar
- 1 t sherry
- 1 T sesame oil
- ⅛ t pepper
- 2 t soysauce (or to taste)

Method:

1. Mix the shrimp with the next 6 ingredients. Set aside.
2. Combine the last 9 ingredients in a small bowl. Set aside.
3. Heat oil in a pan or wok; sauté hot pepper, ginger, and garlic; add shrimp; stir-fry until color turns (about 1½-2 minutes). Remove.
4. Add onion to the remaining oil; stir for 1 minute.
5. Add peas and carrots; mix well.
6. Add the sauce mixture from Step 2; bring to a boil.
7. Add cooked shrimp; mix well. Garnish with lemon slices, tomato slices, or parsley before serving. Serve hot.

241

Makes 4-6 servings.

Calories: 1140
Carbohydrates: 35gm
Protein: 85gm
Fat: 75gm

Cholesterol: 680mg
Calcium: 328mg
Iron: 9mg
Vit. B1: 0.3mg

Vit. B2: 0.3mg
Vit. A: 9742IU
Vit. C: 64mg
Fiber: 3gm

彩虹蚵仁

RAINBOW SHRIMP
(Cai Hong Xia Ren)

Ingredients:

½ lb shelled shrimp, fresh or frozen
½ t onion powder
⅛ t pepper
1 T sherry
1/3 t salt
1 t minced ginger root
2 t cornstarch
4 T oil
2 cloves of garlic, minced
2 slices of ginger root
2 green onions, minced
1 firm tomato, diced
1 t sesame oil or more
1 t vinegar
½ green pepper diced
½ C carrots, sliced
½ C diced bamboo shoots or water chestnuts
½ C roasted almonds or other nuts
½ C water
1½ t instant chicken bouillon
½ t sugar
⅛ t pepper
1 t sherry
1 t cornstarch blended with 1 T water

Method:

1. Mix the shrimp with the next 6 ingredients.
2. Combine the last 6 ingredients in a small bowl.
3. Heat oil in a pan or wok; sauté garlic and ginger root. Add shrimp; stir-fry until color turns (about 1½-2 minutes). Remove.
4. Add green pepper, carrot, bamboo shoots and almonds; stir for 1 minute. Add the sauce mixture from Step 2; stir for 1 minute.
5. Add green onion, tomato, sesame oil, vinegar and cooked shrimp; mix well and serve.

Makes 4-6 servings.

Calories: 1341	Cholesterol: 340 mg	Vit. B2: 1 mg
Carbohydrates: 53 gm	Calcium: 383 mg	Vit. A: 8097IU
Protein: 61 gm	Iron: 9 mg	Vit. C: 174 mg
Fat: 101 gm	Vit. B1: 0.6 mg	Fiber: 5 gm

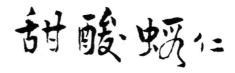

SWEET AND SOUR SHRIMP
(Tian Suan Xia Ren)

Ingredients:

1 lb	shelled shrimp, fresh or frozen
1 T	sherry
½ t	onion powder
¼ t	pepper
1½ t	salt
1 t	minced ginger root
⅛ t	MSG
	Oil for deep-frying
1/3 C	flour
1/3 C	cornstarch
1	egg
3-4 T	water
½ t	baking powder
¼ t	baking soda

Method:

1. Pat the shrimp dry and mix with the next 6 ingredients. Let stand for 30 minutes or more.

2. Combine the last 6 ingredients together to form a smooth batter. Use 3 T of water first; if it is too thick, add more water.

3. Put the shrimp in the batter; mix well

4. Heat oil in a pan or wok; deep-fry the shrimp one by one until golden brown. Keep the shrimp warm in the oven while preparing the sauce (see below). Serve with sauce.

Sweet and Sour Sauce:

¼ C   catsup
½ C   sugar
2 T   cornstarch
¼ C   vinegar
1 C   pineapple tidbits in heavy syrup (or 1 C canned litchi)
1 C   pineapple syrup from the can (or 1 C canned litchi syrup)
1 T   soy sauce
  ½   green pepper, diced
  1   firm tomato, diced or cut into wedges (optional)

Put all the ingredients, except the green pepper and tomato, in a sauce pan; mix well. Bring the sauce to a boil. Stir while cooking. Add the green pepper and tomato; pour the sauce over the cooked shrimp. Serve hot.

Makes 4-6 servings.

Calories: 2300	Iron: 13 mg
Carbohydrates: 297 gm	Vit. B1: 0.74 mg
Protein: 98 gm	Vit. B2: 0.63 mg
Fat: 82 gm	Vit. A: 3807IU
Cholesterol: 914 mg	Vit. C: 9 mg
Calcium: 458 mg	Fiber: 3 gm

Calculated with 1 T oil for deep-frying.

SHRIMP WITH CASHEW NUTS
(Yao Guo Xia Qiu)

腰果蝦球

Ingredients:

2/3 lb	shelled shrimp, fresh or frozen
½ t	onion or garlic powder
1 t	minced ginger root
1 t	salt
¼ t	pepper
1 t	sherry
1 T	cornstarch
¼ C	or more cashews , pecans, or almonds
½ C	diced bamboo shoot
½ C	frozen peas, thawed
4 T	oil
½	onion, chopped
3	slices of ginger root
½ C	water
1 t	instant chicken bouillon
⅛ t	pepper
1 t	sesame oil
1 t	vinegar
1 t	cornstarch

Method:

1. Score the shrimp, lengthwise, along the back line to 2/3 depth of the shrimp. Mix the shrimp with the next 5 ingredients. Let set for 20 minutes or more. Mix with 1 T cornstarch. Set aside.

2. Combine the last 6 ingredients in a small bowl. Set aside.

3. Heat oil in a pan or wok; fry the nuts for 1 minute. Remove.

4. Add shrimp in the remaining oil and stir-fry until color turns (about 2 minutes). Remove.

5. Saute onion and ginger root. Add green peas and bamboo shoot and stir for 1 minute.

6. Add the sauce mixture from Step 2; stir for 1 minute. Add cooked shrimp and cashews, mix well. Serve hot.

Makes 4-6 servings.

Calories: 1062
Carbohydrates: 29gm
Protein: 61gm
Fat: 78gm

Cholesterol: 370mg
Calcium: 209mg
Iron: 6mg
Vit. B1: 0.2mg

Vit. B2: 0.2 mg
Vit. A: 451IU
Vit. C: 3mg
Fiber: 1gm

椒盐蝦

SICHUAN PEPPERCORN SHRIMP
(Jiao Yan Xia)

Ingredients:

2/3 lb	shelled shrimp, fresh or frozen
1 t	minced ginger root
1 t	sherry
¼ t	onion powder
⅛ t	pepper
1 t	Sichuan peppercorn powder for dipping (page 314)
1 t	sesame oil
1	small egg
4 T	glutinous rice powder (see page 44)
1 T	Sichuan peppercorn powder for dipping
	Parsley leaves and lemon slices for garnish
	Oil for deep-frying

Method:

1. Dry the shrimp with paper towel. Mix the shrimp with the next 7 ingredients. Add rice powder and mix well.

2. Heat oil in a pan or in a wok. Drop the shrimp one by one into the oil. Fry until light brown. Remove to a serving plate. Surround the shrimp with parsley and lemon slices.

3. Serve hot with a small dish of Sichuan peppercorn powder for dipping.

Makes 4-6 servings.

Calories: 1209
Carbohydrates: 48 gm
Protein: 70 gm
Fat: 79 gm

Cholesterol: 687 mg
Calcium: 257 mg
Iron: 7 mg
Vit. B1: 0.15 mg

Vit. B2: 0.27 mg
Vit. A: 590IU
Vit. C: 1 mg
Fiber: 0

Calculated with 5 T oil for deep-frying.

SHRIMP WITH TOMATO SAUCE
(Qie Zhi Xia Ren)

茄 汁 蝦 仁

Ingredients:

- 1 t salt
- ¼ t pepper
- 1 T sherry
- ½ t onion powder
- 1 t sesame oil
- ⅛ t MSG (optional)
- 2 t cornstarch
- 1 lb shelled shrimp, fresh or frozen
- 3-4 T oil
- 1 onion, minced
- 2-3 slices of ginger root, minced
- ¼ C catsup
- 2 t cornstarch
- 2 T sugar
- ⅛ t pepper
- 1 t sesame oil
- 2 T soy sauce
- ¼ C water
- 1 T vinegar

Method:

1. Pat the shrimp dry and mix with the first 7 ingredients.
2. Mix the last 8 ingredients in a small bowl. Set aside.
3. Heat 3 T oil in a pan or wok; add shrimp; stir-fry until color turns (about 1½ minutes). Remove.
4. Add 1 T oil; sauté onion and ginger root. Add the sauce mixture from Step 2; stir and bring to a boil.
5. Add shrimp and mix well. Serve hot.
Makes 4-6 servings.

Calories: 1090		Iron: 9 mg	
Carbohydrates: 65 gm		Vit. B1: 0.2 mg	
Protein: 85 gm		Vit. B2: 0.3 mg	
Fat: 53 gm		Vit. A: 975IU	
Cholesterol: 453 mg		Vit. C: 16 mg	
Calcium: 335 mg		Fiber: 1 gm	

Ingredients:

1 lb	large or medium shrimp in the shell
4 T	oil
1 t	Sichuan peppercorn powder for seasoning (page 314) or to taste
2-4	hot pepper, fresh or dried, diced
2 t	sherry
2-4	green onions, minced
2 t	minced ginger root
1 t	sugar

Method:

1. Wash and remove the legs of the shrimp with a pair of scissors. Devein by cutting the back open. If using large shrimp, cut into 2-3 sections.

2. Heat oil in a pan or wok. Add Sichuan peppercorn powder, hot pepper, and shrimp; stir-fry for 3 minutes.

3. Add the last 3 ingredients; stir for 1 minute.

4. Add sherry and mix well. Serve hot.

Makes 4-6 servings.

Calories: 817		Iron: 5mg	
Carbohydrates: 14gm		Vit. B1: 0.1mg	
Protein: 55gm		Vit. B2: 0.15mg	
Fat: 59gm		Vit. A: 3424IU	
Cholesterol: 453mg		Vit. C: 58mg	
Calcium: 203mg		Fiber: 1.5gm	

DRY COOKED SHRIMP SHANGHAI STYLE
(Gan Bian Xia)

Ingredients:

1 lb	shrimps (small, unshelled)
3 T	oil
4	slices of ginger root
3 T	soy sauce
2 T	sherry
3 T	tomato catsup
1 T	water
1 t	onion powder
¼ t	pepper
1 t	sesame oil
1 T	brown sugar

Method:

1. Wash the shrimp; cut off the legs, feelers, appendages, and swimmerets. Do not remove the head and shell.

2. Combine the last 8 ingredients in a small bowl; set aside.

3. Heat oil in a pan or wok; sauté ginger root. Add shrimp and stir for 1 minute.

4. Add the sauce mixture from Step 2; stir and cook until the liquid evaporates.

Serve hot as a main dish or cold as appetizer. Discard the ginger root before serving.

Calories: 760   Carbohydrates: 16gm
Protein: 58gm   Fat: 48gm

豌豆蝦仁　STIR-FRY SHRIMP WITH GREEN PEAS
(Wan Dou Xia Ren)

Ingredients:

1 lb shelled shrimp, fresh or frozen (thawed)
1 t salt
¼ t pepper
1 T sherry
½ t onion powder
1 t sesame oil
1 T cornstarch
1 C soaked, ready to use wood ears, broken into 1" pieces
1 C frozen peas, thawed
1 fresh tomato, diced
2-3 T oil
2 green onions, minced
1 t minced ginger root
¼ C water
½ t cornstarch
1 t sesame oil
1 T soy sauce
⅛ t pepper
½ t sugar

Method:

1. Pat the shrimp dry, then mix with the next 6 ingredients.

2. Combine the last 6 ingredients in a small bowl. Set aside.

3. Heat oil in a non-stick pan or wok. Add shrimp; stir-fry on high heat for 1½ - 2 minutes. Transfer to a dish.

4. Sauté onion and ginger root in the remaining oil. Add wood ears and peas. Mix well.

5. Add the sauce mixture from Step 2. Cook until the sauce thickens. Add shrimp and tomatoes. Mix well and serve hot.

Calories: 913	Cholesterol: 680 mg	Vit. B2: 0.3 mg
Carbohydrates: 40 gm	Calcium: 324 mg	Vit. A: 1488 IU
Protein: 90 gm	Iron: 10 mg	Vit. C: 36 gm
Fat: 41 gm	Vit. Ba: 0.61 mg	Fiber: 3 gm

DRIED SHRIMP
WITH WINTER MELON
(Xia Mi Hui Dong Gua)

Ingredients:

1 lb	winter melon
3 T	oil
½	medium onion, chopped
3	slices of ginger root
2 oz	dried shrimp, soaked
	Coriander or minced green onion for garnishing
¼ t	salt or to taste
¼ t	pepper
1 t	sherry
1½ C	water reserved from soaking the shrimp

Method:

1. Remove the skin and seeds from the winter melon and cut into ½" slices. (Whole winter melon looks like a long watermelon. It is sold by sections.)

2. Soak the dried shrimp in 2 C hot water for 30 minutes. Wash, drain, and reserve the water.

3. Heat oil in a pan or wok; saute onion, ginger root, and shrimp. Add winter melon and the last 4 ingredients; cover and cook over medium heat until the melon is tender and the liquid is reduced to ¼ C.

4. Transfer to a serving dish; garnish with greens. Serve hot.
Makes 4-6 servings.

Calories: 542	Iron: 3mg
Carbohydrates: 6gm	Vit. B1: 0.42mg
Protein: 31gm	Vit. B2: 0.61mg
Fat: 43gm	Vit. A: 11IU
Cholesterol: 255mg	Vit. C: 3mg
Calcium: 113mg	Fiber: 0

Winter melon is not included in this calculation. See page 10

SPICY QUICK STIR-FRIED SHRIMP
(Zha Xia)

Ingredients:

1 lb	large shrimp in the shell
5-6	cloves of garlic, or more finely minced
1 T	minced ginger root
1 t	salt or to taste
¼ t	pepper
1 T	sherry
1 T	cornstarch
4 T	oil
	Lemon slices and parsley for garnishing

Method:

1. Cut off the legs of the shrimp; devein by cutting the back open; wash and drain (do not shell).
2. Mix the shrimp with the next 5 ingredients.
3. Mix the shrimp with 1 T cornstarch.
4. Heat oil in a pan or wok. Fry the shrimp quickly until the shell turns pink (takes about 3-5 minutes). Remove to a serving dish. Garnish with lemon slices and parsley. Serve immediately.

Makes 4-6 servings.

Calories: 824		Iron: 5mg	
Carbohydrates: 16gm		Vit. B1: 1mg	
Protein: 55gm		Vit. B2: 0.1mg	
Fat: 58gm		Vit. A: 0	
Cholesterol: 453mg		Vit. C: 2mg	
Calcium: 193mg		Fiber: 0.3gm	

Calculated with shrimp in shell

BRAISED SHRIMP OR LOBSTER
(Hong Shao Xia)

Ingredients:

1 lb	large shrimp in the shell or lobster tails
2-3 T	oil
2-4	cloves of garlic, minced
2-4	green onions, minced
1 T	minced ginger root
4 T	soy sauce
2-3	dried mushrooms, soaked and shredded
1/4 t	pepper
1 T	vinegar
1 T	sugar
1 T	sherry
1 T	sesame oil

Method:

1. Wash and remove the legs of the shrimp with a pair of scissors. Cut backs open and devein (do not shell). Cut the shrimp or lobster into 1" sections.

2. Heat oil, sauté garlic, green onions and ginger root until brown. Add shrimp or lobster and stir-fry for 5 minutes.

3. Add the last 7 ingredients; stir and cook until the liquid evaporates. Serve hot.

Makes 4-6 servings.

Calories: 897	Iron: 8 mg
Carbohydrates: 28 gm	Vit. B1: 0.99 mg
Protein: 58 gm	Vit. B2: 0.25 mg
Fat: 59 gm	Vit. A: 400 IU
Cholesterol: 453 mg	Vit. C: 7 mg
Calcium: 250 mg	Fiber: 0

With the exception of the newly added Rice Noodle section, the nutritional calculations of all the recipes in this book are for **the whole recipe,** not per serving. 1-2 tablespoons of oil can be reduced from each recipe if desired. A reduction of 1 tablespoon of oil will reduce the calories of the recipe by 120, and the fat by 14 grams.

水晶蝦餅

Ingredients:

⅔ lb	shelled shrimp, fresh or frozen
1	strip of bacon, cut into ½" pieces
2	slices of ginger root
½	small onion
	Fresh watercress or spinach, and 1 T toasted black sesame seeds for garnishing
2-3 T	oil
8	water chestnuts, coarsely chopped
½ t	salt
¼ t	pepper
1 t	sherry
1	egg white
1-2 t	sesame oil
2 T	cornstarch

Method:

1. Dry the shrimp and mince with the next 3 ingredients into a paste.

2. Add the last 7 ingredients to the shrimp paste and mix well.

3. Heat oil in a non-stick pan. Drop a teaspoonful of shrimp paste into the oil. Flatten the paste into the size of a dollar coin. Brown both sides over medium heat. Repeat until the paste is used up.

4. Arrange the cooked shrimp patties on a plate. Garnish with fresh watercress or spinach and sprinkle with toasted black sesame seeds. Serve hot.

Makes 4-6 servings.

Calories: 789	Cholesterol: 384 mg	Vit. B2: 0.26 mg
Carbohydrates: 27 gm	Calcium: 213 mg	Vit.A: 200IU
Protein: 61 gm	Iron: 6 mg	Vit. C: 6 mg
Fat: 47 gm	Vit. B1: 0.15 mg	Fiber: 1 gm

With the exception of the newly added Rice Noodle section, the nutritional calculations of all the recipes in this book are for **the whole recipe,** not per serving.

BREADED SHRIMP BALLS
(Mian Bao Xia Qiu)

Ingredients:

- ½ lb   shelled shrimp, fresh or frozen
- 1   strip of bacon
- ½   onion, chopped
- 2   slices of ginger root
- 5   water chestnuts, coarsely minced
- 5-6   slices day old white or whole wheat bread
  Oil for deep-frying (about 4 T)
- ½ t   salt
- ¼ t   pepper
- 1 t   sherry
- 1   small egg
- 1 T   cornstarch
- ⅛ t   MSG (optional)

Method:

1. Mince the first 4 ingredients together into a paste. Add water chestnuts and the last 6 ingredients; mix well.

2. Trim off and discard the bread crusts. Dice the bread into ¼" cubes. Dry the bread cubes in a preheated 350° oven for 5 minutes. Cool.

3. Form the shrimp paste in ¾" balls. Roll the shrimp balls in the bread cubes until they are covered with a layer of bread. Press gently to make sure the bread sticks on the shrimp paste.

4. Heat oil in a pan or wok; deep-fry the shrimp balls until brown. Remove with a slotted spoon. Drain and serve hot.

The shrimp balls can be reheated in a 300° oven for 10 minutes or kept warm in a low heat oven until time to serve. They can be served as a main dish, appetizer or hors d'oeuvres.

Makes 10-15 shrimp balls.

Calories:	1317	Iron:	8mg
Carbohydrates:	79gm	Vit. B1:	0.33mg
Protein:	59gm	Vit. B2:	0.37mg
Fat:	83gm	Vit. A:	544IU
Cholesterol:	603mg	Vit. C:	3mg
Calcium:	272mg	Fiber:	0.5gm

蝦 球

"RACING" SHRIMP BALLS
(Xia Qiu)

The shrimp balls should be served "racing" from the kitchen to the dinner table and eaten immediately. If not served right away, the shrimp balls shrink.

Ingredients:

1 lb	shelled shrimp, fresh or frozen
2 oz	pork fat, finely minced
	Sichuan peppercorn powder for dipping (page 314)
	Oil for deep-frying
1 T	sherry
1½	onion powder
1 t	finely minced ginger root
1 t	salt
¼ t	sugar
¼ t	pepper
1	egg white
1 t	baking powder
2 T	cornstarch

Method:

1. Place the shrimp and minced fat on a chopping board. Cut (pound, mash, etc.) the shrimp into a paste with the back of a cleaver.

2. Transfer the paste to a mixing bowl. Add the last 9 ingredients to the paste and mix well.

3. Heat oil in a pan or wok over medium heat. When oil is warm, gently drop rounded heaping teaspoonfuls of the shrimp paste into the oil.

4. Repeat the process until the paste is used up. Continue to heat the oil on medium heat and cook until the shrimp balls float on the oil. Turn the shrimp balls with a slotted spoon while frying for even cooking.

5. Transfer the shrimp balls to a serving dish and serve immediately with a dish of Sichuan peppercorn powder. Dip the shrimp balls in the peppercorn powder first before eating.

Calories: 1360   Carbohydrates: 21gm
Protein: 86gm   Fat: 102gm
Calculated with 3 T oil for deep-frying.

DRIED SHRIMP ANN WEI EGGS
(An Wei Dan)

Ingredients:

1 oz	dried shrimp
4	eggs, beaten
2	green onions, minced
1 t	minced ginger root
1 t	sherry
1 C	frozen peas and carrots, thawed
½ t	salt
½ t	pepper
2 t	cornstarch blended with 1 T water
1 C	chicken broth, canned, or 1 t instant chicken bouillon dissolved in 1 C of water
3 T	oil
1 T	sesame oil
	Coriander or parsley for garnishing

Method:

1. Soak the dried shrimp in hot water for 1 hour; drain and mince.

2. Beat eggs; combine minced dried shrimp; add the next 7 ingredients and mix well. Add ½ C chicken broth. Mix well.

3. Heat oil in a non-stick pan or wok; add egg mixture and cook over medium heat until the egg is almost dry.

4. Add ½ C chicken broth around edges of the pan; cover and cook over medium heat for 1-2 minutes.

5. Turn to other side; add 1 T sesame oil and cook for 1 minute.

6. Transfer to a serving dish. Cut into squares; garnish with coriander or other greens. Serve hot.

Makes 4-6 servings.

Calories:	1015	Iron:	8mg
Carbohydrates:	25gm	Vit. B1:	0.53mg
Protein:	47gm	Vit. B2:	0.73mg
Fat:	80gm	Vit. A:	16152IU
Cholesterol:	1063mg	Vit. C:	20mg
Calcium:	209mg	Fiber:	2gm

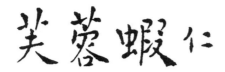

Ingredients:

- ¼ lb   shrimp, shelled (fresh or frozen)
- 1 t   sherry
- ⅛ t   pepper
- ¼ t   onion powder
- ¼ t   salt
- 1 t   minced ginger root
- 2 t   cornstarch
- 4 T   oil
-         Coriander leaves for garnishing
- 4   eggs, beaten with ¾ t salt
- 4   green onions, shredded
- ½ C   shredded bamboo shoot
- ½ C   shredded asparagus or celery cabbage
- 2 oz   fresh mushrooms, shredded
- ½   small carrot, finely shredded
- ⅛ t   pepper

Method:

1. Mix the first 7 ingredients together. Set aside.
2. Combine the last 7 ingredients in a bowl.
3. Heat oil in a pan or wok; stir-fry shrimp until color turns (about 1-2 minutes).
4. Add the egg mixture (Step 2); stir and cook over medium heat until the egg is cooked. Garnish with chopped coriander. Serve hot.

Makes 4-6 servings.

Calories: 1023		Iron: 8mg	
Carbohydrates: 23gm		Vit. B1: 0.54	
Protein: 51gm		Vit. B2: 1mg	
Fat: 80gm		Vit. A: 9177IU	
Cholesterol: 1106mg		Vit. C: 35mg	
Calcium: 241mg		Fiber: 2gm	

SNOW WHITE SHRIMP FOO YOUNG
(Xue Bai Fu Rong)

Ingredients:

½ lb	shelled shrimp, fresh or frozen
⅛ t	white pepper
¼ t	onion powder
1 t	sherry
½ t	salt
⅛ t	MSG (optional)
2 t	cornstarch
3-4 T	oil
6	egg whites, beaten with ¼ t salt
1 oz	minced ham
¼ C	minced coriander or minced green onion

Method:

1. Mix the shrimp with the next 6 ingredients in a small bowl.

2. Heat oil in a pan or wok; stir-fry shrimp until color turns (about 2 minutes). Separate the shrimp while stirring.

3. Add egg whites; stir gently until it dries.

4. Transfer the shrimp Foo Young to a serving dish. Place the minced ham in the center of the dish and surround with minced coriander. Serve hot.

Makes 4-6 servings.

Calories: 776		Iron: 10mg	
Carbohydrates: 13gm		Vit. B1: 0.01mg	
Protein: 72gm		Vit. B2: 0.86mg	
Fat: 47gm		Vit. A: 3350IU	
Cholesterol: 351mg		Vit. C: 6mg	
Calcium: 289mg		Fiber: 0.2gm	

炒鱿魚巻

Ingredients:

¼ lb	dried squid, (about 2-4 squid)
	Water
4-5 T	baking soda
1 T	cornstarch
2-4	red hot pepper (fresh or dried), diced
2-4	cloves of garlic, sliced
1 t	minced ginger root
4 T	oil
2	green onions, minced
½ C	water
1 t	instant chicken bouillon
1 T	soy sauce
½ t	sugar
1 t	sherry
1 t	vinegar
¼ t	pepper
1 t	sesame oil
2 t	cornstarch

Method:

1. Place the dried squid in a pan or in a container; add enough water to cover the squid. Add baking soda and stir until the soda dissolves. Let stand overnight or until the squid softens.

2. Discard the soda water. Immerse the squid in fresh cold water for a few hours. Change water several times in order to get rid of the soda, otherwise it will give the squid a bitter taste.

3. Wash the squid; remove the skin and membrane from both sides of the body and arms (head).

4. Score in crisscross pattern inside the squid body almost down to the back (⅛" apart). Cut the squid into 1½"x1" pieces. Cut the arms into 1½" sections.

5. Scald the squid in boiling water for 2 seconds. Rinse and drain. Pat dry and mix with 1 T cornstarch.

6. Heat oil in a pan or wok. When the oil is very hot; stir-fry the squid quickly for 1 minute. Remove.

7. Combine the last 9 ingredients in a small bowl. Saute hot pepper, garlic and ginger root. Add the water mixture and bring to a boil. Add cooked squid and green onions; mix well. Serve immediately.

Makes 4-6 servings.

Calories: 1020	Cholesterol: No information	Vit. B2: 0.6mg
Carbohydrates: 30gm	Calcium: 71mg	Vit. A: 3424IU
Protein: 75gm	Iron: 3mg	Vit. C: 58mg
Fat: 62gm	Vit. B1: 0.14mg	Fiber: 2gm

No cholesterol information on squid is available. See page 10.

DRIED SQUID WITH MEAT
(You Yu Rou Si)

魷魚炒肉絲

Ingredients:

1-2	dried squid (¼ lb)
4 T	baking soda
¼ lb	pork, shredded
1 T	soy sauce
½ t	sherry
1 t	cornstarch
½ C	shredded bamboo shoots
½ C	shredded carrots
4	green onions, shredded
3 T	oil
1 t	shredded ginger root
2-4	cloves of garlic, sliced
2 T	soy sauce or to taste
½ t	brown sugar
1 t	sherry
1 T	sesame oil
1 T	vinegar
1 T	water
¼ t	pepper
½ t	cornstarch blended with 1 T water

Method:

1. Place the dried squid and soda in a pan or container. Add water until it covers the squid. Stir until the soda dissolves. Let stand overnight or until the squid has expanded and is soft.

2. Wash squid; remove the skin and membrane from both sides of the body and arms (head).

3. Cut the squid into 2" long shreds, then immerse the shreds in fresh, cold water for a few hours. Change water several times in order to get rid of the soda.

4. Combine the last 8 ingredients in a small bowl. Set aside.

5. Mix the pork with the next 3 ingredients. Set aside.

6. Heat oil in a pan or wok; sauté squid for 1 minute. Remove.

7. Saute ginger root and garlic in the remaining oil; add pork and stir for 1 minute. Add bamboo shoots, carrots and stir for 1 minute.

8. Add the sauce mixture from Step 4 and cook for 1 minute. Add green onions and cooked squid; mix well. Serve hot.

Makes 4-6 servings.

Calories: 1179		Iron: 8mg	
Carbohydrates: 31gm		Vit. B1: 1.2mg	
Protein: 100gm		Vit. B2: 0.98mg	
Fat: 72gm		Vit. A: 631IU	
Cholesterol: 71mg		Vit. C: 20mg	
Calcium: 151mg		Fiber: 2gm	

No cholesterol information on squid is available. See page 10.

FRESH SQUID WITH VEGETABLES
(Sun Chao Xian You)

Ingredients:

2/3 lb	cleaned squid, fresh or frozen
3	cloves of garlic, minced or ½ t garlic powder
1 t	minced ginger root
1 t	sesame oil
¼ t	pepper
1 T	sherry
1 t	vinegar
½ t	salt
1 t	soy sauce
1 t	sugar
⅛ t	MSG (optional)
2 t	cornstarch
4 T	oil
1	onion, diced
4	slices of ginger root
1	green pepper, diced
½ C	thinly sliced carrots
½ C	sliced bamboo shoots (optional)
1 T	soy sauce
¼ t	salt
⅛ t	MSG (optional)
2 t	sesame oil

Method:

1. Wash squid. Cut the body open with a pair of scissors. Discard the head, tentacles, and intestine. Pull the skin and membrane off both sides of the body.

2. Score inside of the squid (almost through to the back) in a crisscross pattern ⅛" apart. Cut the squid into 1½" x 1" pieces. Pat dry.

3. Mix the squid with the next 10 ingredients; let stand for half an hour then mix with the cornstarch.

4. Heat 3 T oil in a pan or wok. Stir-fry squid until curls up (about ½-1 minute). Transfer to a dish.

5. Add 1 T oil; sauté onion and ginger root. Add green pepper, carrots, bamboo shoots, and the last 4 ingredients; stir-fry for 1½ minutes.

6. Add cooked squid; mix well. Serve hot.

Makes 4-6 servings.

Calories: 1000		Iron: 3mg	
Carbohydrates: 33gm		Vit. B1: 0.2mg	
Protein: 52gm		Vit. B2: 0.5mg	
Fat: 70gm		Vit. A: 3166IU	
Cholesterol: No information		Vit. C: 128mg	
Calcium: 90mg		Fiber: 2mg	

No cholesterol information on squid is available.

SQUID WITH MUSTARD GREENS
(Jie Cai Xian Tou)

Ingredients:

1 lb	squid, fresh or frozen
½ t	salt
½ t	garlic powder or onion powder
⅛ t	pepper
1 t	minced ginger root
1 t	sherry
⅛ t	MSG
1 T	soy sauce
2 t	cornstarch
4 T	oil
1 C	minced pickled mustard greens (page 310) or ½ C shredded Sichuan pickle
2	green onions, minced
3	slices of ginger root
1 t	sugar
2 t	sherry

Method:

1. Wash squid; discard the head, tentacles, and intestines. Cut the body open with a pair of scissors. Pull off the skin and membrane from both sides of the body.

2. Score inside of the squid (almost through to the back) in a crisscross pattern ⅛" apart. Cut the squid into 1½" x 1" pieces.

3. Mix the squid with the next 8 ingredients.

4. Heat oil in a pan or wok; stir-fry squid until it curls up (about ½-1 minute). Remove.

5. Saute ginger root in the remaining oil. Add mustard green; stir and mix well.

6. Add 1 t sugar, 2 t sherry, and cooked squid and mix well. Transfer to a serving plate; sprinkle the minced onions over the squid. Serve hot.

Approximately 2½ pounds of squid make 1 pound of cleaned squid.

Makes 4-6 servings.

Calories:	935	Iron:	3mg
Carbohydrates:	18gm	Vit. B1:	0.11mg
Protein:	74gm	Vit. B2:	0.59mg
Fat:	60gm	Vit. A:	8600IU
Cholesterol:	No information	Vit. C:	23mg
Calcium:	98mg	Fiber:	3gm

No cholesterol information on squid is available. See page 10.

葱炒鲜鱿

FRESH SQUID WITH GREEN ONIONS
(Cong Chao Xian You)

Ingredients:

1 lb	cleaned squid, fresh or frozen

1 T	soy sauce
½ t	salt
½ t	onion powder
¼ t	pepper
1 t	minced ginger root
1 t	sherry
⅛ t	MSG (optional)
2 t	cornstarch

2	bunches of green onions, shredded
1 t	sesame oil
5 T	oil
2-4	slices of ginger root

½ C	water
1 T	soy sauce
¼ t	salt
1 t	sherry
1 t	sugar
⅛ t	MSG (optional)
1 t	cornstarch

Method:

1. Wash squid. Cut the body open with a pair of scissors. Discard the head, tentacles, and intestines. Pull off the skin and membrane from both sides of the body.

2. Score inside of the squid (almost through to the back) in a diamond pattern ⅛" apart. Cut the squid into 1½" x 1 " pieces. Wash and pat dry.

3. Mix the squid with the next 8 ingredients.

4. Combine the last 7 ingredients in a small bowl. Set aside.

5. Heat 4 T oil in a pan or wok; stir-fry the squid until curled (about ½-1 minute). Remove to a dish.

6. Add 1 T oil; sauté ginger root. Add onion shreds and mix well.

7. Add the sauce mixture Step 4; bring to a boil. Add squid and 1 t sesame oil; mix well. Serve hot.

Makes 4-6 servings.

Calories: 1137
Carbohydrates: 27gm
Protein: 76gm
Fat: 79gm
Cholesterol: No information
Calcium: 118mg

Iron: 4mg
Vit. B1: 0.14mg
Vit. B2: 0.63mg
Vit. A: 2000IU
Vit. C: 32mg
Fiber: 1gm

No cholesterol information on squid is available.

FRESH SCALLOPS WITH MUSHROOMS
(Xian Bei Chao Xiang Gu)

Ingredients:

1 T   sherry
1 t   salt
½ t   onion powder
¼ t   pepper
1 t   minced ginger root
⅛ t   MSG (optional)
2 t   cornstarch or more
1 lb   scallops, fresh or frozen
1 T   sesame oil
1   green onion, minced
2 t   cornstarch blended in 1 T water
4 T   oil
2   slices of ginger root
1 t   chicken bouillon dissolved in ½ C of water
4   dried mushrooms, soaked and quartered or ¼ lb fresh
       mushrooms, sliced
½ C   sliced bamboo shoots or ¼ lb snow pea pods, washed and
       cleaned
1 T   soy sauce
½ t   sugar

Method:

1. Wash the scallops and pat dry with a towel. Cut the scallops in half horizontally.

2. Mix the scallops with the first 7 ingredients.

3. Heat oil in a pan or wok; add scallops and stir-fry for 1 minute. Remove.

4. Saute ginger root slices in the remaining oil; add the last 5 ingredients. Bring to a boil.

5. Add blended cornstarch; cook until sauce thickens.

6. Add cooked scallops, minced onion, and 1 T sesame oil; mix well. Serve hot.

Makes 4 servings.

Calories: 1055	Iron: 9mg
Carbohydrates: 37gm	Vit. B1: 0.12mg
Protein: 72gm	Vit. B2: 0.42mg
Fat: 70gm	Vit. A: 217IU
Cholesterol: 159mg	Vit. C: 7mg
Calcium: 143mg	Fiber: 1gm

DRIED SCALLOPS WITH BEAN SPROUTS
(Gan Bei Dou Ya SI)

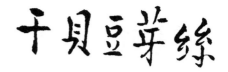

Ingredients:

2 oz	dried scallops
2 C	water
2-3	green onions, shredded
1 t	sesame oil
1 t	cornstarch blended with 1 T water
3 T	oil
1 t	minced ginger root
1	carrot, shredded (optional)
1 lb	fresh bean sprouts, washed and cleaned
¾ t	salt or to taste
¼ t	pepper
1 t	vinegar
½ t	sugar
1 t	sherry
⅛ t	MSG
1 C	shredded bamboo shoots (optional)

Method:

1. Wash the dried scallops and place in a small sauce pan. Add water and bring to a boil. Reduce to low heat and simmer for 1 hour or until the scallops become tender.

2. Tear the scallops into fine shreds. Set aside.

3. Heat oil in a pan or wok; saute ginger root, carrots, and scallop shreds for one minute. Add the last 8 ingredients and stir until the bean sprouts are wilted.

4. Add the green onions, 1 t blended cornstarch, and sesame oil; mix well. Serve hot.

Makes 4-6 servings.

Calories: 476		Iron: 9mg	
Carbohydrates: 78gm		Vit. B1: 0.59mg	
Protein: 43gm		Vit. B2: 0.69mg	
Fat: 1gm		Vit. A: 489IU	
Cholesterol: 59mg		Vit. C: 91mg	
Calcium: 139mg		Fiber: 3gm	

干貝蘿蔔球　DRIED SCALLOPS WITH RADISH BALLS
(Gan Bei Luo Bo Qiu)

Ingredients:

3 oz	dried scallops
2 C	hot water
1-2	green onions, minced
1 T	sesame oil
½ t	sugar
1 lb	radishes, peeled and diced
	Soy sauce to taste
3 T	oil
1 t	instant chicken bouillon
¼ t	pepper
1 t	sherry

Method:

1. Wash the dried scallops, then soak in hot water for 2 hours or until softened. Drain, but reserve the water.

2. Tear the scallops into fine shreds by hand.

3. Place the scallop shreds in a sauce pan and add reserved water. Cover and bring to a boil. Reduce to low heat and simmer for 30 minutes.

4. Heat oil in a pan or wok; sauté ginger root. Add radishes and the last 3 ingredients; stir and mix for 1 minute.

5. Add scallops with liquid to the radishes; cover and bring to a boil. Turn to medium heat and cook until the radishes become tender and the liquid is reduced to ¼ C.

6. Add 1 T sesame oil ½ t sugar, soy sauce to taste, and mix well. Transfer to a serving dish. Garnish with minced onion. serve hot.

Makes 4-6 servings.

Calories:	690	Iron:	7mg
Carbohydrates:	28gm	Vit. B1:	0.13mg
Protein:	42gm	Vit. B2:	0.24mg
Fat:	45gm	Vit. A:	245IU
Cholesterol:	89mg	Vit. C:	146mg
Calcium:	227mg	Fiber:	3gm

DEEP-FRIED OYSTERS
(Sheng Jian Su Hao)

生煎酥蠔

Ingredients:

½ lb oysters
½ t salt
Oil for deep-frying (about one cup)
Sichuan peppercorn powder for dipping (page 314)
Few lettuce leaves
4 T flour
2 T cornstarch
¼ t pepper
½ t onion or garlic powder
1 t minced ginger
1 T soy sauce
⅛ t salt
¼ t baking powder
¼ t baking soda
3 T water or less

Method:

1. Wash the oysters; drain. Mix with ½ t salt; let stand for 20 minutes.

2. Blanch the oysters in 3 cups of boiling water for few seconds. Rinse, drain, and pat dry.

3. Mix the last 10 ingredients in a bowl to form a smooth batter. Add the oysters to the batter; mix gently.

4. Heat oil in a pan or wok; deep-fry the oysters one by one until brown. Arrange on a lettuce lined serving plate; serve the oysters hot with a small dish of Sichuan peppercorn powder for dipping.

Makes 4 servings.

Calories: 829		Iron: 14mg	
Carbohydrates: 45gm		Vit. B1: 0.4mg	
Protein: 25gm		Vit. B2: 0.5	
Fat: 61gm		Vit. A: 769IU	
Cholesterol: 114mg		Vit. C: 0	
Calcium: 250mg		Fiber: 0	

Calculated with 4 T oil for deep-frying.

271

醃蠔燒肉

PRESERVED OYSTERS AND PORK
(Yan Hao Shao Rou)

Ingredients:

¼ lb	dried preserved oysters or mussels, about ½ C
2 lb	pork (butt, fresh ham, etc.)
1 T	sugar
2 C	water
4 T	soy sauce
1	onion, diced
4	slices of ginger root
2-4	cloves of garlic, sliced

Method:

1. Soak the oysters in warm water for 4 hours or until soft. Wash and drain.

2. Cut the pork into 1½" cubes.

3. Place the pork in a medium sauce pan; add the last 4 ingredients. Cook and stir over high heat until liquid evaporates.

4. Add water and oysters; cover and bring to a boil. Reduce to medium heat; cook until the meat is tender and the liquid is reduced to ½ C.

5. Add sugar and cook for 2 more minutes. Serve hot. Add ½-1 C water if the liquid evaporates before the meat becomes tender.

If too much liquid remains after the meat becomes tender, increase to high heat without covering and cook until the liquid is reduced to ½ C.

Makes 5-6 servings.

Calories:	2012	Iron:	60mg
Carbohydrates:	54gm	Vit. B1:	8.72mg
Protein:	219gm	Vit. B2:	2.14mg
Fat:	96gm	Vit. A:	22IU
Cholesterol:	790mg	Vit. C:	6mg
Calcium:	540mg	Fiber:	0

ABALONE WITH CHICKEN BREAST
(Bao Yu Ji Pain)

Ingredients:

1	16 oz can of abalone
1/3 lb	chicken breast, skinned and boned

⎰ 1/3 t salt
⎱ ⅛ t pepper
  ¼ t onion powder
  1 t sherry
  1 t cornstarch

1 T   minced ham
       Few coriander leaves
1 T   cornstarch blended with 2 T water
3 T   oil
¼ C   minced onion
1 t   minced ginger root

1 C   water
1 t   instant chicken bouillon
½ C   sliced bamboo shoots or more
1 T   soy sauce
½ t   sugar
1 t   vinegar
⅛ t   MSG (optional)
1 T   sesame oil

Method:

1. Cut the abalone into 2"x1"x1/6" slices. Cut chicken into the same size as abalone.
2. Mix the chicken with the next 5 ingredients.
3. Heat oil in a pan or wok; sauté onion and ginger root. Add chicken; stir-fry until color turns (about 1-2 minutes). Remove.
4. Add abalone and the last 8 ingredients; bring to a boil.
5. Add cooked chicken and blended cornstarch; bring to a boil.

Transfer to a serving platter; garnish with ham and coriander. Serve hot.

Makes 4-6 servings.

Calories:	1166	Iron:	3mg
Carbohydrates:	29gm	Vit. B1:	0.73mg
Protein:	108gm	Vit. B2:	0.38mg
Fat:	67gm	Vit. A:	207IU
Cholesterol:	104mg	Vit. C:	3mg
Calcium:	101mg	Fiber:	1gm

Cholesterol of abalone is not included.

ONION FLAVORED SEA CUCUMBER
(Cong Bao Hai Sen)

Ingredients:

1 lb	soaked ready-to-cook sea cucumber strips
6-10	green onions
4-6	slices of ginger root
4-5	cloves of garlic, crushed
4 T	oil
1 T	sugar
2 t	cornstarch blended with 2 T water
1 T	sherry
½	salt
1 T	soy sauce
½ t	chicken bouillon
½ C	water

Method:

1. Boil 3 cups of water in a sauce pan; blanch the sea cucumber in the boiling water for 1 minute. Drain.

2. Remove the roots and green parts of the onions. Cut the white parts of the onions into 2" sections.

3. Heat oil in a pan or wok, add onion whites, ginger root and garlic and fry. Remove the onion whites to a small dish when they turn to light brown and save. Continue frying until the ginger and garlic turn to dark. Discard ginger and garlic. Pour the flavored oil into a small bowl.

4. Add 2 T flavored oil in the pan with 1 T of sugar; stir and cook until the sugar turns light brown.

5. Add sea cucumbers; stir and cook for 1 minute. Add the last 5 ingredients; stir and cook for 3 minutes.

6. Add onion whites, the rest of the flavored oil, and the blended cornstarch; stir and cook until the sauce thickens. Transfer to a serving dish and serve hot.

If the soaked ready-to-cook sea cucumbers are not available, dried sea cucumbers can be used. To prepare dried sea cucumbers, see page 54.

No nutrition information is available for sea cucumber, so the calculations are omitted.

葱薑焗蟹

Ingredients:

    1 lb   crab legs and claws in the shell
    2 T   soy sauce
    ½ t   pepper
    1 T   sherry
    1 t   sesame oil
    ⅛ t   MSG (optional)
    3-5   green onions, shredded
    ¼ t   salt
    1 t   sugar
    3 T   oil
    1 T   minced garlic
    1 T   minced ginger root
    1 T   cornstarch
    1 T   sesame oil

Method:

1. Cut the legs through the joints. Crack the crab lightly. Mix the crab with the next 5 ingredients. Let stand for 1 hour.

2. Coat the crab with 1 T cornstarch.

3. Heat oil in a sauce pan or wok (do not use a teflon pan); sauté garlic and ginger root. Add crab; stir and cook for 5-8 minutes.

4. Add green onions, ¼ t salt, and ½ t sugar; stir and cook for 2 minutes. Add 1 T sesame oil and serve immediately.

Makes 4-6 servings.

Calories:	840	Iron:	7.3mg
Carbohydrates:	19gm	Vit. B1:	0.4mg
Protein:	39gm	Vit. B2:	0.25mg
Fat:	65gm	Vit. A:	5110IU
Cholesterol:	218mg	Vit. C:	14mg
Calcium:	134mg	Fiber:	0

STEAMED LAKE CRABS
(Qing Zheng Xie)

Ingredients:

    6   live crabs, about 2 pounds
  ⎧ 2 T   soy sauce
  ⎪ 3 T   vinegar
  ⎨ 1 T   finely shredded ginger
  ⎪ 2 t   sugar
  ⎩ 1 t   sherry

Method:

1. Wash the crabs. Place the crabs on a tier of a steamer and steam over boiling water for 15 minutes.

2. Combine the last 5 ingredients together and place the sauce in a small sauce dish.

3. Place the steamed crabs on a platter and serve with the sauce

The best season for lake crab in the Shanghai area is October when they are at their plumpest and most flavorful. Crab meat can be cooked with eggs or as part of Wontons, stuffed buns, meat dumplings, fillings, or cooked with bean curd. See *Nutrition and Diet with Chinese Cooking* for recipes.

Calories: 430   Carbohydrates: 10gm
Protein: 76gm   Fat: 9gm

蟹肉芥菜花

CRAB MEAT WITH BROCCOLI
(Xie Rou Jie Cai Hua)

Ingredients:

2	stalks of broccoli
¼ t	salt
4 T	oil
¼	onion, minced
1 t	minced ginger root
	Minced green onion or coriander for garnishing
1	egg white, beaten
1 T	cornstarch blended with 2 T water
1	can of crab meat, flaked (about 6 oz)
2 t	instant chicken bouillon
2 C	milk
1 t	sherry
¼ t	white pepper
½ t	sugar
½-1 t	sesame oil

Method:

1. Wash and break the broccoli flowerets into 1" small pieces.

2. Heat 2 T oil in a pan or wok; add broccoli and salt; stir-fry for 2 minutes. Transfer to a serving dish.

3. Add 2 T oil; sauté onion and ginger root. Add the last 7 ingredients; bring to a boil.

4. Stir in egg white and blended cornstarch; bring to a boil. Pour over the broccoli and serve hot.

Makes 4-6 servings.

Calories: 1168
Carbohydrates: 55gm
Protein: 79gm
Fat: 72gm
Cholesterol: 227mg
Calcium:

Iron: 5mg
Vit. B1: 0.59mg
Vit. B2: 2.1mg
Vit. A: 8057IU
Vit. C: 354mg
Fiber: 5gm

HOISIN SAUCE CRAB
(Tain Jiang Xie)

甜 醬 蟹

Ingredients:

1½ lb	crab legs and claws in the shell, fresh or frozen
4-5 T	Hoisin sauce
4 T	water
1 t	sesame oil
3 T	oil
4	green onions, minced
1 T	minced ginger root
2 t	cornstarch blended with 2 T water
1 T	soy sauce
1 t	brown sugar
½ t	pepper
2 T	sherry

Method:

1. Crack the claws and legs slightly. Pat dry set aside.
2. Mix the next 3 ingredients in a small bowl. Set aside.
3. Heat oil in a pan or wok (do not use teflon pan); sauté onion and ginger root. Add crab and the sauce mixture from Step 2; stir for 3 minutes.
4. Add the last 4 ingredients; stir and cook for 3 minutes.
5. Add blended cornstarch; stir and cook for 1 minute. Serve hot.
Makes 4-6 servings.

Calories:	1012	Iron:	7mg
Carbohydrates:	30gm	Vit. B1:	0.93mg
Protein:	87gm	Vit. B2:	0.48
Fat:	56gm	Vit. A:	10530IU
Cholesterol:	452mg	Vit. C:	22mg
Calcium:	280mg	Fiber:	1gm

vegetables

乾煸四季豆

DEEP-FRIED FRESH STRING BEANS
(Gan Bian Se Chi Dou)

Ingredients:

1-1½ lb	fresh string beans
2 T	dried shrimp soaked and minced, or minced ham
2 T	minced Sichuan pickles
2	green onions, minced
1 t	sesame oil
1 t	minced ginger root
	Oil for deep-frying (about 1 cup)
¾ t	salt
¾ t	sugar
¼ t	pepper
1 t	sherry

Method:

1. Wash and dry the string beans. Snap off both ends of the beans.

2. Heat oil in a pan or wok. Deep-fry the string beans until the skins are wrinkled. Remove.

3. Pour off all the oil except 1 T. Add Sichuan pickles, shrimp and the last 4 ingredients; stir and cook for 1 minute.

4. Add fried beans, minced green onions and sesame oil. Mix well. Serve hot or cold.

If you invite friends, this is a good dish that you can prepare in advance.

Makes 4-6 servings.

Calories: 763	Iron: 5mg
Carbohydrates: 44gm	Vit. B1: 0.62mg
Protein: 24gm	Vit. B2: 0.85mg
Fat: 58gm	Vit. A: 3088IU
Cholesterol: 127mg	Vit. C: 91mg
Calcium: 313mg	Fiber: 5gm

Calculated with 4 T oil for deep-frying and cooking.

PICKLES WITH BABY LIMA BEANS
(Zha Cai Chao Bian Dou)

Ingredients:

- ½ lb pork (butt, loin, or fresh ham, etc.), diced
- 1 T soy sauce
- ½ T cornstarch
- 1 t sherry
- ½ C minced Sichuan pickles (mustard pickles)
- 1-2 green onions, minced
- 2 T oil
- ½ onion, minced
- 1 10 oz package frozen baby lima beans, thawed
- ¼ t pepper
- 1 T soy sauce (or to taste)
- ½ t salt
- ⅛ C water
- ⅛ t MSG (optional)

Method:

1. Mix the first 4 ingredients together in a small bowl.

2. Heat oil in a pan or wok; sauté onion; add pork. Stir and mix the pork for 2 minutes.

3. Add the last 6 ingredients and cook for 3-4 minutes.

4. Add Sichuan pickles and minced green onions; mix well. Serve hot.

Makes 4-6 servings.

Calories: 1052	Iron: 16mg
Carbohydrates: 72gm	Vit. B1: 2.4mg
Protein: 66gm	Vit. B2: 0.8mg
Fat: 56gm	Vit. A: 855IU
Cholesterol: 0	Vit. C: 54mg
Calcium: 156mg	Fiber: 5gm

花椒扁豆

BABY LIMA BEANS, SICHUAN STYLE
(Hua Jiao Bian Dou)

Ingredients:

1	10 oz package frozen baby lima beans, thawed
2 T	oil
2	green onions, minced
1 t	minced ginger root
1 t	Sichuan peppercorn powder for dipping
1-2	hot peppers, minced (optional)
¼ C	water
½ t	sugar
¼ lb	fresh mushrooms, washed and diced
½ T	soy sauce (or to taste)
⅛ t	MSG (optional)
1 T	sesame oil

Method:

1. Heat oil in a pan or wok; sauté onion and ginger root.
2. Add lima beans; stir and cook for 1 minute.
3. Add the last 8 ingredients; stir and cook for 2-3 minutes. Serve hot.

Makes 4-6 servings.

Calories:	700	Iron:	6mg
Carbohydrates:	61gm	Vit. B1:	0.3mg
Protein:	20gm	Vit. B2:	0.7mg
Fat:	43gm	Vit. A:	744IU
Cholesterol:	0	Vit. C:	53mg
Calcium:	72mg	Fiber:	5gm

STIR-FRY ASPARAGUS
(Chao Lu Sun)

Ingredients:

    1 lb   fresh asparagus
    3 T   oil
    2   green onions, shredded or garlic, crushed
    2   slices of ginger root
    ½ t   salt or more
    ¼ t   pepper
    2 T   water

Method:

1. Cut off the butt ends of the asparagus. Clean and wash.
2. Slant slice or rolling-cut the asparagus if the stalks are very large. Cut them into 1½" sections if they are small.
3. Heat oil in a pan or wok; saute onions (or garlic) and ginger root.
4. Add asparagus and the last 3 ingredients; stir-fry until the asparagus is cooked but still crunchy (about 2-3 minutes; the rolling-cut pieces may take a little longer). Serve hot.

Makes 4 servings.

Calories: 448	Iron:	2mg
Carbohydrates: 15gm	Vit. B1:	0.5mg
Protein: 6gm	Vit. B2:	0.5mg
Fat: 43gm	Vit. A:	2290IU
Cholesterol: 0	Vit. C:	88mg
Calcium: 63mg	Fiber:	3gm

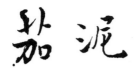

Ingredients:

- 1 lb eggplant
- ¼ t salt
- 1 T soy sauce
- 2 t sesame oil
- 1 T oil
- 1 T vinegar
- ¼ t pepper
- 2-4 cloves of garlic, minced
- 1 t minced ginger root
- ⅛ t MSG (optional)
-      Minced coriander for garnishing

Method:

1. Wash the eggplant, remove the stem, and peel. Cut the eggplant into ½" wide strips.

2. Place the eggplant in a heat-proof bowl and steam in a boiling steamer for 30 minutes, or until soft and tender.

3. Add the next 9 ingredients to the eggplant. Mash the eggplant with a pair of chopsticks or with a fork.

4. Transfer the mashed eggplant to a serving plate. Garnish with the minced coriander. Serve hot or cold.

Makes 4-6 servings.

Calories: 318	Cholesterol: 0	Vit. B2: 0.3mg
Carbohydrates: 29gm	Calcium: 68mg	Vit. A: 45IU
Protein: 7gm	Iron: 4mg	Vit. C: 23mg
Fat: 22gm	Vit. B1: 0.2mg	Fiber: 4gm

MEAT STUFFED EGGPLANT
(Sui Rou Niang Qie Zi)

碎肉釀茄子

Ingredients:

- ½ lb   ground pork or beef
- 2   green onions, minced
- 1 t   minced ginger root
- ½ t   pepper
- 1 t   sherry
- 2 T   soy sauce
- 2 oz   shelled shrimp, fresh or frozen, minced
- 2 t   sesame oil
- 2 t   cornstarch
- 1 lb   eggplant
- 1 T   Sichuan peppercorn powder for dipping (page 314)
-    Parsley or coriander for garnishing
-    Oil for deep-frying
- ¾ C   flour
- ¼ C   cornstarch
- 2   eggs
- ½ C   water or more
- ½ t   salt
- ¼ t   pepper

Method:

1. Mix the first 9 ingredients in a bowl thoroughly. Set aside.

2. Wash the eggplant and remove the stem (do not peel). Cut the eggplant crosswise into ⅛″ slices. (If the eggplant is small in diameter, slice it lengthwise.)

3. Spread a layer of meat in between two slices of eggplant. Repeat the process until all the eggplant slices and meat are used up.

4. Blend the last 6 ingredients in a bowl into a smooth batter.

5. Heat oil in a pan or wok.

6. Dip the meat-stuffed eggplant in the batter until a thin layer of the batter covers the eggplant.

7. Deep-fry the stuffed eggplant over medium heat until light brown and crisp. Drain on a paper towel, then arrange the cooked eggplant on a platter. Garnish with parsley or coriander. Serve hot with a small dish of Sichuan peppercorn powder for dipping.

Makes 4-6 servings.

Calories: 1821	Cholesterol: 689mg	Vit. B2: 1.2mg
Carbohydrates: 135gm	Calcium: 251mg	Vit. A: 3017IU
Protein: 82gm	Iron: 15mg	Vit. C: 51mg
Fat: 105gm	Vit. B1: 2.4mg	Fiber: 5gm

Calculated with 4 T oil for deep-frying.

加喱茄子

EGGPLANT WITH CURRY
(Ka Li Qie Zi)

Ingredients:

1 lb	eggplant
½ C	chopped coriander
3 T	oil
5	cloves of garlic, crushed
1 T	curry powder blended with 2 or more T water
2 T	soy sauce or to taste
1 t	sugar
½ t	pepper
1½ C	water

Method:

1. Wash the eggplant and remove the stem (do not peel). Rolling cut the eggplant into 1½" pieces.

2. Heat oil in a pan or wok; brown garlic. Add eggplant and blended curry powder; stir and cook for 2 minutes.

3. Add the last 4 ingredients; cover and cook for 4-5 minutes or until the eggplant becomes tender and the cooking liquid is reduced to 2 T. Transfer to a plate, and garnish with minced coriander. Serve hot.

Makes 4-6 servings.

Calories: 539	Cholesterol: 0	Vit. B2: 0.3mg
Carbohydrates: 36gm	Calcium: 83mg	Vit. A: 45IU
Protein: 8gm	Iron: 5mg	Vit. C: 24mg
Fat: 43gm	Vit. B1: 0.3mg	Fiber: 4gm

EGGPLANT WITH VEGETABLES
(Shao Qie Zi)

Ingredients:

1 lb	eggplant
1-2 C	oil for deep-frying
4	cloves of garlic, crushed
3	slices of ginger root
1 T	cornstarch blended with 2 T water
1 T	sesame oil
½ C	sliced bamboo shoots
½ C	sliced mushrooms
3 T	soy sauce
1 t	brown sugar
1 T	sherry
¼ t	pepper
½ C	water
½ C	young, green soybeans or frozen peas (optional)

Method:

1. Peel the eggplant and cut into 2"x½" strips.
2. Heat oil in a pan or wok; deep-fry the eggplant until soft. Drain.
3. Pour off all but 2 T of the oil. Sauté garlic and ginger root; add eggplant and the last 8 ingredients.
4. Cover pan and cook the eggplant for 4 minutes; stir several times while cooking.
5. Add blended cornstarch; cook until the sauce thickens. Transfer to a serving dish; add sesame oil and serve hot.

Calories: 890	Carbohydrates: 30gm
Protein: 5gm	Fat: 85gm

Calculated with 4 T oil for deep-frying.

麻辣黄瓜

HOT AND SPICY CUCUMBERS
(Ma La Huang Gua)

Ingredients:

1 lb	baby or regular cucumbers
1 t	salt
2-4	cloves of garlic, minced
1 T	vinegar
1 t	sugar
1 T	sesame oil
1 t	(or more) hot pepper oil or sauce
¼ t	pepper
1 T	soy sauce
1 T	oil
½ t	Sichuan peppercorn powder for seasoning (page 314) or more

Method:

1. Wash and cut off both ends of the baby cucumbers. Quarter the cucumbers lengthwise, then cut into 2" sections. (If using regular cucumbers, split in half, lengthwise; remove the seeds and cut into 2" sections; then cut into ¼" strips.)

2. Mix the cucumbers with 1 t salt. Let stand for 20 minutes or more. Stir occasionally for even flavor. Drain.

3. Add the last 9 ingredients to the cucumbers. Mix and chill. Serve cold.

Makes 4-6 servings.

Calories: 349	Cholesterol: 0	Vit. B2: 0.2mg
Carbohydrates: 23gm	Calcium: 126mg	Vit. A: 1120IU
Protein: 5gm	Iron: 6gm	Vit. C: 50mg
Fat: 29gm	Vit. B1: 0.2mg	Fiber: 3gm

CUCUMBER WITH GELATIN
(Fen Pi Ban Huang Gua)

粉皮拌黄瓜

Ingredients:

- ½ lb   baby or regular cucumbers
- 1 T   unflavored gelatin (one envelope)
- 1½ C   milk
- ¼ t   salt
- 2 T   sesame paste
- 1 T   oil
- 1 T   sesame oil
- 1 t   sugar
- 1 t   or more hot pepper oil or paste (optional)
- 1½ T   vinegar
- 3 T   soy sauce
- ¼ t   pepper
- 3-6   cloves of garlic, minced
- 1 T   water

Method:

1. Soften the gelatin in 1 C of milk. Heat the milk over medium heat and stir until the gelatin dissolves. Add ½ C cold milk and mix well. Pour the milk into a small mold. Chill until the gelatin is firm. (This step can be done a day ahead of time).

2. Wash, dry and remove the ends of the cucumbers.

3. Quarter the cucumbers lengthwise (if you use the baby ones.), then cut into 2" sections. Mix the cucumbers with ¼ t salt. Set aside.

4. Cut the gelatin into ½"x½"x2" strips and place on a serving platter.

5. Drain the cucumber strips, then place on the gelatin.

6. Mix the last 10 ingredients together into a smooth paste. Pour this mixture over the cucumbers; mix well before eating. Serve chilled.

The unflavored gelatin in this recipe takes the place of the gelatin that is made from green-bean flour. The color and texture of unflavored gelatin closely resembles the green-bean gelatin. If you have the chance, get the green-bean gelatin and use it. It will be more authentic.

Makes 4-6 servings.

Calories: 550	Cholesterol: 32mg	Vit. B2: 0.8mg
Carbohydrates: 41gm	Calcium: 517mg	Vit. A: 1644IU
Protein: 29gm	Iron: 7mg	Vit. C: 53mg
Fat: 32gm	Vit. B1: 0.3mg	Fiber: 3gm

芝麻醬拌黃瓜

**CUCUMBERS WITH
SESAME PASTE (HOT)**
(Zi Ma Jiang Bam Huang Gua)

Ingredients:

1	small cucumber
1 T	sesame paste (recipe on page 315)
2 t	oil
2 t	sesame oil
½ t	sugar
1 t	(or more) hot oil or hot pepper paste
1 T	vinegar
1½ T	soy sauce
¼ t	pepper
1 T	water
2	cloves of garlic, minced

Method:

1. Wash, dry and remove both ends of the cucumber. Split the cucumber into halves, lengthwise, remove seeds. Cut the cucumber into 2" sections.

2. Slice the cucumber lengthwise, into ⅛" slices.

3. Mix the last 10 ingredients in a small bowl into a smooth paste.

4. Place the cucumber slices on a serving dish. Pour the sesame paste mixture over the cucumber. Mix well before eating. Serve cold.

Makes 4-6 servings.

Calories: 317	Iron: 4mg
Carbohydrates: 15gm	Vit. B1: 0.2mg
Protein: 5gm	Vit. B2: 0.2mg
Fat: 28gm	Vit. A: 520IU
Cholesterol: 0	Vit. C: 24mg
Calcium: 176mg	Fiber: 2gm

BRAISED MUSHROOM BALLS
(Hung Shao Xiang Gu Qiu)

红烧香菇球

Ingredients:

½ lb	ground pork or beef
1 T	soy sauce
⅛ t	salt
¼ t	pepper
½ t	onion powder
½ t	minced ginger root
2 t	sherry
2 t	cornstarch
1 lb	fresh mushrooms, large and firm
2 T	cornstarch to powder the mushrooms
2 T	oil
2	green onions, shredded
2	slices of ginger root
½ lb	spinach (or other green-colored vegetables)
¼ t	salt
2 T	soy sauce
1 t	brown sugar
¾ C	water

Method:

1. Mix the first 8 ingredients together thoroughly in a bowl.

2. Wash and dry mushrooms. Use a sharp paring knife to remove the stem and make a concave space (gill side) for stuffing the meat.

3. Sprinkle a layer of cornstarch on the concave side of the mushrooms, and spread about 1 t meat on this side of each mushroom.

4. Put a pair of meat-stuffed mushrooms together (meat side to meat side). Press gently to form a ball. Secure the ball with a toothpick. Repeat with remainder of mushrooms.

5. Put the mushroom balls in a pan. Add the last three ingredients; cover and bring to a boil. Turn to medium heat and cook until the liquid is reduced to ¼ C. Transfer to a serving platter.

6. Heat oil in a pan or wok. Saute onion and ginger root; add spinach and ½ t salt. Stir and mix until the spinach is wilted. On the platter surround the mushroom balls with the cooked spinach (or

other cooked green vegetables of your choice). Serve hot. Remove toothpicks before serving.

Calories: 929	Cholesterol: 142mg	Vit. B2: 3.1mg
Carbohydrates: 57gm	Calcium: 311mg	Vit. A: 18544IU
Protein: 64gm	Iron: 19mg	Vit. C: 134mg
Fat: 51gm	Vit. B1: 2.7mg	Fiber: 5gm

冬菇炒筍片

**DRIED MUSHROOMS
WITH BAMBOO SHOOTS**
(Dong Gu Chao Sun Pian)

Ingredients:

20	dried, medium sized mushrooms
1 C	(or more) sliced bamboo shoots
2 T	oil
2 t	sesame oil
2	green onions, shredded
2	slices of ginger root
4 T	soy sauce
1 T	brown sugar
¼ t	pepper
1 t	sherry
2 C	water

Method:

1. Soak the mushrooms in hot water for 1 hour. Squeeze out the excess water and cut off the stems of the mushrooms.

2. Heat oil in a pan or wok. Sauté onion and ginger root. Add mushrooms and stir for 1 minute.

3. Add the last 5 ingredients; cook for 2 minutes.

4. Add bamboo slices; cover and cook until the liquid almost dries. Stir several times while cooking for even flavor.

5. Add sesame oil and mix well. Serve hot or cold.

Makes 2 servings.

Calories: 509	Cholesterol: 0	Vit. B2: 0.4mg
Carbohydrates: 36gm	Calcium: 101mg	Vit. A: 0
Protein: 9gm	Iron: 5mg	Vit. C: 0
Fat: 39gm	Vit. B1: 0.3mg	Fiber: 1gm

MUSHROOMS WITH OYSTER SAUCE
(Hao You Xiang Gu)

Ingredients:

```
1 lb   fresh mushrooms
 3 T   oil
   2   green onions, minced
 1 t   minced ginger root
 1 t   cornstarch blended with 2 t water
 2 T   oyster sauce
 ⅛ t   salt or to taste
 ¼ t   pepper
 1 t   sherry
 ½ t   sugar
 2 t   sesame oil
```

Method:

1. Wash the mushrooms. Cut the larger mushrooms into 2-3 slices.

2. Heat oil; sauté onion and ginger root.

3. Add mushrooms and the last 6 ingredients; stir-fry for 2 minutes.

4. Add the blended cornstarch and mix well. Serve hot.

Makes 4-6 servings.

Calories: 580	Iron: 3mg
Carbohydrates: 20gm	Vit. B1: 0.2mg
Protein: 8gm	Vit. B2: 1.1mg
Fat: 50gm	Vit. A: 400IU
Cholesterol: 0	Vit. C: 13mg
Calcium: 49mg	Fiber: 2gm

FRESH MUSHROOMS WITH VEGETABLES
(Xiang Gu Qing Cai)

Ingredients:

½ lb	fresh mushrooms
1	10 oz package of frozen peas and carrots, thawed
½ C	bamboo shoots, diced
3 T	oil
1-3	green onions, minced
1 t	minced ginger root
2 T	soy sauce (or to taste)
⅛ t	salt
⅛ t	pepper
½ t	sugar
1 t	sesame oil

Method:

1. Wash and dry the mushrooms. Cut the mushrooms into halves or quaters.

2. Heat oil in a pan or wok; sauté onion and ginger root.

3. Add mushrooms, peas and carrots, bamboo shoots; stir and mix for 1 minute.

4. Add the last 5 ingredients; stir and cook for 1-2 minutes. Transfer to a serving dish and serve immediately.

Makes 4-6 servings.

Calories:	619	Iron:	7mg
Carbohydrates:	45gm	Vit. B1:	0.8mg
Protein:	17gm	Vit. B2:	1.3mg
Fat:	44gm	Vit. A:	26240IU
Cholesterol:	0	Vit. C:	37mg
Calcium:	116mg	Fiber:	6gm

STIR-FRY ZUCCHINI
(Chao Nen Gua)

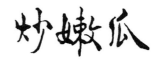

Ingredients:

1 lb	zucchini
3 T	oil
2	green onions, minced
1 t	minced ginger root
¾ t	salt or to taste
¼ t	pepper
⅛ t	MSG (optional)

Method:

1. Rolling-cut or slice the zucchini into a 1/6″ slices.
2. Heat oil in a pan or wok; saute onion and ginger root.
3. Add zucchini, salt and pepper, (MSG); stir-fry for 3 minutes (if rolling cut, cook 1 minute longer). Serve hot or cold.
Makes 4-6 servings.

Calories: 464		Iron: 2 mg	
Carbohydrate: 20 gm		Vit. B1: 0.2 mg	
Protein: 5 gm		Vit. B2: 0.4 mg	
Fat: 42 gm		Vit. A: 2237 IU	
Cholesterol: 0		Vit. C: 105 mg	
Calcium: 136 mg		Fiber: 3 gm	

297

辣白菜

HOT AND SPICY CABBAGE
(La Bai Cai)

Ingredients:

1½ lb	cabbage
¾ t	salt
1 T	sugar
3 T	vinegar
3 T	oil
1 t	Sichuan peppercorns
2-4	hot peppers, diced
¼ C	water

Method:

1. Cut the cabbage into 1½" square pieces.
2. Put the next 3 ingredients in a small bowl. Set aside.
3. Heat oil in a pan or wok. Fry the Sichuan peppercorns until black. Discard the peppercorns.
4. Add hot pepper and cabbage; stir and mix for ½ minute. Add water, cover, and cook until the cabbage is wilted.
5. Add the vinegar mixture from Step 2 and mix well. Serve hot or cold.

Makes 4-6 servings.

Calories: 594
Carbohydrates: 52gm
Protein: 9gm
Fat: 43gm
Cholesterol: 0
Calcium: 334mg

Iron: 3mg
Vit. B1: 0.4mg
Vit. B2: 0.4mg
Vit. A: 3469IU
Vit. C: 367mg
Fiber: 7gm

**CELERY CABBAGE
WITH GREEN PEPPER**
(Jing Jiao Chao Bai Cai)

青椒炒白菜

Ingredients:

1 lb	celery cabbage, shredded
1	large green pepper, shredded
1 C	shredded carrots
2-3 T	oil
1	onion, shredded
1-2	slices of ginger root, shredded
¼ t	salt
2 T	soy sauce (or to taste)
1 t	sugar
⅛ t	MSG (optional)
1 T	sesame oil

Method:

1. Wash all the vegetables and cut into shreds.

2. Heat oil in a pan or wok; sauté onion and ginger root.

3. Add celery cabbage, green pepper, carrot shreds and the last 5 ingredients. Stir and cook until the vegetables are wilted. Serve hot.

The vegetables in this dish can also be sliced rather than shredded.

Makes 4-6 servings.

Calories: 408
Carbohydrates: 34gm
Protein: 10gm
Fat: 29gm
Cholesterol: 0
Calcium: 259mg

Iron: 5mg
Vit. B1: 0.3mg
Vit. B2: 0.4mg
Vit. A: 6569IU
Vit. C: 190mg
Fiber: 5gm

翡 翠 糕

STEAMED SPINACH
(Fei Cui Gao)

Ingredients:

2	10 oz packages of frozen chopped spinach, thawed and drained
3	eggs
1	medium onion, minced
1 t	cornstarch, blended with 1 t water
1 t	minced ginger root
1 t	sherry
½ t	pepper
1¼ t	salt
½ C	minced ham, regular or country style
2 T	oil
1 T	sesame oil
⅛ t	MSG (optional)

Method:

1. Beat the eggs in a mixing bowl until fluffy.
2. Add the next 10 ingredients to the egg and mix well.
3. Add spinach to the egg mixture and mix well.
4. Put the spinach in a well-greased bowl and steam in a boiling covered steamer for 30 minutes.
5. Remove the bowl from the steamer. Use a small knife to loosen the spinach from the sides of the bowl.
6. Place a serving dish over the spinach bowl. Turn upside down and remove the bowl. Cut the steamed spinach into smaller pieces without disturbing its basic shape. Serve hot as is or with white gravy (see below).

Gravy:

Put 1 t instant chicken bouillon and ¾ C of milk in a sauce pan and bring to a boil. Add 2 t blended cornstarch and ¼ t sesame oil: cook until the sauce thickens. Pour over the spinach before serving.

Makes 4-6 servings.

Calories: 1192	Cholesterol: 826mg	Vit. B2: 1.6mg
Carbohydrates: 31gm	Calcium: 740mg	Vit. A: 46031IU
Protein: 58gm	Iron: 19mg	Vit. C: 167mg
Fat: 95gm	Vit. B1: 1.5mg	Fiber: 5gm

Gravy is not included in this calculation.

FRESH SPINACH SALAD, CHINESE STYLE
(Liang Ban Bo Cai)

凉拌菠菜

Ingredients:

- 5 oz   (or more) ready-to-cook fresh spinach
- ½ C   (or more) thinly sliced water chestnuts
- ¼ C   (or more) toasted slivered almonds
- ¼ C   bacon bits (optional)
- 4 T   sesame paste (recipe on page 315)
- 2 T   oil
- 1 T   sesame oil
- 1 t   sugar
- 2 T   vinegar
- 3 T   soy sauce
- ¼ t   pepper
- 2   (or more) cloves of garlic, minced, or 1 minced green onion

Method:

1. Put the first 4 ingredients into a large salad bowl.
2. In a small bowl thoroughly mix the last 8 ingredients, then pour the mixture over the spinach. Toss before serving.

Calories: 930	Cholesterol: 0	Vit. B2: 0.9mg
Carbohydrates: 41gm	Calcium: 696mg	Vit. A: 11351IU
Protein: 22gm	Iron: 12mg	Vit. C: 74mg
Fat: 81gm	Vit. B1: 0.7mg	Fiber: 5gm

炒豆芽

STIR-FRY BEAN SPROUTS
(Chao Dou Ya)

Ingredients:

1 lb   fresh bean sprouts
2 T   oil
3   green onions, shredded
2   slices of ginger root (optional)
{ ¼ t   pepper
{ 2 T   soy sauce (or to taste)

Method:

1. Wash bean sprouts and drain.
2. Heat oil in a pan or wok, sauté onions and ginger root.
3. Add bean sprouts and the last 2 ingredients; stir and turn for 2-3 minutes. Serve hot.

Makes 4 servings.

Calories: 420   Iron: 6mg
Carbohydrates: 32gm   Vit. B1: 0.60mg
Protein: 17gm   Vit. B2: 0.61
Fat: 28gm   Vit. A: 90IU
Cholesterol: 0   Vit. C: 92mg
Calcium: 96mg   Fiber: 3gm

BEAN SPROUTS AND GREEN PEPPER
(Su Za Jin)

Ingredients:

½ lb	fresh bean sprouts
1	large green pepper, shredded
4	green onions, shredded
1 C	carrots, finely shredded (optional)
2 T	oil
1 t	shredded ginger root
1	onion, shredded
1 T	sesame oil
2 T	soy sauce
¼ t	salt
½ t	sugar
⅛ t	MSG (optional)

Method:

1. Wash the bean sprouts and drain.
2. Wash the green pepper and remove the seeds; cut into 2″ long shreds.
3. Heat oil in a pan or wok; sauté ginger root and onion.
4. Add bean sprouts, green pepper shreds, green onions, carrots, and the last 4 ingredients. Stir and cook for 2-3 minutes. Add 1 T sesame oil and mix well. Serve hot.

Makes 4 servings.

Calories: 580	Iron: 5mg
Carbohydrates: 44gm	Vit. B1: 0.4mg
Protein: 14gm	Vit. B2: 0.5mg
Fat: 44gm	Vit. A: 5985IU
Cholesterol: 0	Vit. C: 178mg
Calcium: 138mg	Fiber: 3gm

三色菜球

COLORFUL VEGETABLE BALLS
(Cai Hong Cai Qiu)

Ingredients:

- 1 C   cucumber or Chinese radish balls
- 1 C   carrot balls
- 1 C   canned mushrooms, drained or 100 gm medium size fresh mushrooms, washed.
- 1   chicken bouillon cube
- 1 C   water
- 1 T   sesame oil
- 1 T   oil
- ¼ t   salt or to taste
- 2 t   cornstarch blended with 1T water

Method:

1. Peel and trim the cucumber (or radish) into ¾'' diameter balls. Trim the carrots in the same manner. (about 100 gm each)

2. Place the cucumber, carrot, chicken bouillon and water in a pan or wok; cover and bring to a boil. Reduce to medium heat and cook for 3 minutes.

3. Add mushrooms, and last 4 ingredients; cook until the sauce thickens. Serve hot

Calories: 360		Iron: 2 mg	
Carbohydrate: 22 gm		Vit. A: 11000IU	
Protein: 5 gm		Vit. B1: 0.19 mg	
Fat: 29 gm		Vit. B2: 0.55 mg	
Cholesterol: 0		Vit. C: 22 mg	
Calcium: 60 mg		Fiber: 2 gm	

Han-San-Si temple of Suzhou, an ancient city near Shanghai.

甜醬胡桃

BEAN-PASTED NUTS
(Tain Jiang Hu Tao)

Ingredients:

½ lb	walnuts (or peanuts or almonds)
½ C	Hoisin sauce
1 T	sugar
4 T	water
	Oil for deep-frying

Method:

1. Heat oil in a pan or a wok; add nuts; deep-fry (takes less than 1 minute) until they turn light brown. Remove from heat and drain. Add 1 T oil to the pan.

2. Add Hoisin sauce, sugar, and water. Cook over medium heat until the sugar is melted and the sauce thickens.

3. Add nuts and mix well. Serve cold or hot.
Authentically the nuts should be blanched before frying. The skin of the nuts is high in fiber. If you don't mind the roughness, don't blanch them. You save time and get more nutrients.

To blanch the nuts:

Soak the nuts in hot water for half an hour. Drain and remove the skin by hand.

Makes 4-6 servings.

Calories: 1622	Iron: 11mg
Carbohydrates: 61gm	Vit. B1: 1.1mg
Protein: 50gm	Vit. B2: 0.4mg
Fat: 143gm	Vit. A: 82IU
Cholesterol: 0	Vit. C: 4mg
Calcium: 317mg	Fiber: 6gm

Oil for deep-frying is not included in this calculation.

CHINESE TEMPURA BATTER
(You Zha Fen)

油 炸 粉

Ingredients:

½ C	flour
½ C	cornstarch
½ t	onion powder or garlic powder
3/4 t	baking powder
3/4 t	baking soda
1 t	salt
¼ t	pepper
9-10 T	water
1 t	instant chicken bouillon (optional)

Method:

Mix all the ingredients together into a smooth batter. It is ready to use for your favorite vegetables. (Cut the vegetables such as carrots, onions, eggplant, potato, asparagus, green pepper, mushrooms, etc. into pieces, coat them with batter and deep-fry in hot oil and serve.)

Calories: 437
Carbohydrates: 98gm
Protein: 6gm
Fat: 0.6gm
Cholesterol: 0
Calcium: 9mg

Iron: 0.4mg
Vit. B1: 0.3mg
Vit. B2: 0.3mg
Vit. A: 0
Vit. C: 0
Fiber: 0.3gm

燴 麵 筋

BRASED STEAMED GLUTEN
(Hui Mian Jing)

Ingredients:

5 C	flour
2 C	water
2 t	salt
3 T	oil
1 t	sesame oil
2	green onions, shredded
3 T	soy sauce
1 T	brown sugar
¼ t	onion powder
2 t	instant chicken bouillon
¼ t	pepper
3	slices of ginger root
1 t	sherry
4	cloves of star anise (optional)
6	dried mushrooms, soaked and quartered
2 C	water

Method:

1. Place the first 3 ingredients in a mixing bowl; mix to form a dough. Knead the dough on a lightly floured board for 10 minutes. Return the dough to the mixing bowl; cover with a dampened cloth and keep in the refrigerator for 6 hours or overnight.

2. Rinse the dough under a light stream of cold water (a strong force of water will wash away the gluten). Use your hands to rub and squeeze the dough gently. After a little while you will feel and see a sticky substance (gluten) left on the dough while the white starch is being washed away. Continue the process until all the white starch is washed away; meanwhile, carefully try to gather and keep the gluten.

3. Put the gluten in a heat-proof plate and steam in a boiling and covered steamer for 40 minutes. Cut the gluten into 1½"x1"x¼" pieces.

4. Mix the last 10 ingredients in a small bowl. Set aside.

5. Heat oil in a non-stick pan or wok; brown the gluten on both sides.

6. Add the sauce mixture from Step 4; cover and bring to a boil. Turn to low heat and simmer until the liquid reduced to a few tablespoons.

7. Add sesame oil and green onions, mix well. Serve hot or cold. Makes 4 servings.

This is a basic gluten dish made from the protein of wheat flour. It is a good vegetable protein with no cholesterol and is low in fat. The gluten can be deep-fried and cooked with meat and vegetables. Recipes in *Nutrition and Diet with Chinese Cooking*, pages 66 and 186-189.

Calories: 750	Cholesterol: 0	Vit. B2: 0.4mg
Carbohydrates: 6gm	Calcium: 130mg	Vit. A: 400IU
Protein: 62gm	Iron: 5mg	Vit. C: 7mg
Fat: 53gm	Vit. B1: 0.2mg	Fiber: 2gm

CRISP RICE
(Guo Ba)

Ingredients:

1 C   medium grain rice, enriched
2 C   water
½ t   salt

Method:

1. Cook the rice as the directions indicate. (page 368)

2. Put the cooked rice on a greased cookie sheet or cake pan. Press the rice into a ¼" thickness.

3. Dry the rice in a 375° oven until light brown and crisp (about 1-2 hours). For sizzling rice, deep-fry before using.

Makes two portions.

Calories: 670	Cholesterol: 0	Vit. B2: 0.06mg
Carbohydrates: 149gm	Calcium: 44mg	Vit. A: 0
Protein: 12gm	Iron: 5mg	Vit. C: 0
Fat: 1gm	Vit. B1: 0.8mg	Fiber: 0

雪裡紅

MUSTARD GREENS, PICKLED
(Xue Li Hung)

Ingredients:

1 lb   mustard greens
1 T   salt

Method:

1. Wash mustard greens and drain.
2. Put the mustard greens in a mixing bowl; sprinkle evenly with salt.
3. With your hands, mix and squeeze the greens until they are wilted. Squeeze off liquid before using.

To keep: Pack tightly in a glass jar and keep in refrigerator. It can be kept for a few days.

Pickled mustard greens can be stir-fried with a little oil and served as a vegetable dish. For uses in other recipes, see *Nutrition and Diet with Chinese Cooking,* pages 27, 76, 198, and 209.

Calories: 98
Protein: 9gm
Carbohydrates: 17gm
Fat: 2gm
Cholesterol: 0
Calcium: 580mg

Iron: 9mg
Vit. B1: 0.3mg
Vit. B2: 0.7mg
Vit. A: 22,220IU
Vit. C: 308mg
Fiber: 4gm

SPICY RICE POWDER
(Wu Xiang Mi Fen)

五香米粉

Ingredients:

1 C	long grain rice
2 T	five-spice powder
2 t	salt
2 t	onion or garlic powder
½ t	pepper

Method:

1. Put all the ingredients in a dry wok or pan. Stir the mixture over medium heat for 10 minutes or until the rice turns light brown. Remove and cool.

2. Roll the rice with a rolling pin on a hard surface into a coarse powder, or chop the rice in a blender for ½ minute. Keep the rice powder in a clean covered jar. It is ready for your favorite recipes.

Calories: 697	Iron: 6mg
Carbohydrates: 154gm	Vit. B1: 0.8mg
Protein: 13gm	Vit. B2: 0.8mg
Fat: 0.8gm	Vit. A: 0
Cholesterol: 0	Vit. C: 0
Calcium: 46mg	Fiber: 0.6gm

辣椒醬

HOT PEPPER PASTE OR SAUCE
(La Jiao Jiang)

Ingredients:

- 1 lb — fresh hot peppers, green or red
- 1 C — oil
- 1 oz — garlic (about 1 whole bulb) or more
- 4 — slices of ginger root
- 2-4 T — or more fermented black beans (optional)
- 1 T — salt
- 4-6 — dried mushrooms, soaked and coarsely minced or ¼ lb fresh mushrooms (optional)
- ¼ C — dried shrimp, soaked and minced (optional)

Method:

1. Wash the hot peppers and discard the stems.
2. Cut the peppers in half, crosswise. Remove skin from garlic.
3. Place the first 6 ingredients in a blender and blend for 2 minutes
4. Pour the pepper mixture into a deep sauce pan (add mushrooms and shrimp); cover and bring to a boil. Reduce to low heat and simmer for ½ hour. Stir occasionally while cooking.
5. Transfer the cooked pepper paste to a clean jar and keep refrigerated. It is ready to use for your favorite recipes or as a dip with daily meals.

The pepper paste can be frozen for 6 months. Thaw before using.

Calories: 2435		Iron: 5mg	
Carbohydrates: 49gm		Vit. B1: 1mg	
Protein: 18gm		Vit. B2: 1.6mg	
Fat: 234gm		Vit. A: 96768IU	
Cholesterol: 0		Vit. C: 1657mg	
Calcium: 138mg		Fiber: 40gm	

RED HOT PEPPER OIL
(La Jiao You)

Place ¼ C of hot red ground pepper, pepper flakes or cayenne powder, 1 T Sichuan peppercorn and 1 t salt in a bowl. Heat 1 C oil in a pan or wok. Add a 1-inch piece of green onion and cook until the green part of the onion turns light brown.* Pour the hot oil over the pepper and stir with a pair of chopsticks. Cover the bowl and let steep for 1 hour. The oil will turn red and have a Sichuan peppercorn aroma. This red oil is ready for use in your favorite dishes. It can be kept at room temperature for weeks.

*In China, this method is used to test the temperature of the oil. When the onion browns, it is an indication that the temperature is right.

花椒麺

**SICHUAN PEPPERCORN
POWDER FOR DIPPING**
(Hua Jiao Mian)

Heat a medium sauce pan or wok over medium heat. Add ½ C Sichuan peppercorns; stir and turn for 2 minutes. Add 1/3 C salt; stir and turn for 2 more minutes. Let cool. Place the cold, roasted peppercorns in a blender; cover and blend into a fine powder. Or crush the peppercorns with a mortar and pestle. Transfer the powder to a clean jar and keep at room temperature. The powder can be kept for months.

花椒粉

**SICHUAN PEPPERCORN
POWDER FOR SEASONING**
(Hua Jiao Fan)

Place ½ C Sichuan peppercorn in a blender. Cover the blender and blend for a few minutes, or until the peppercorns are reduced to a powder. Let stand in the blender for a few minutes, then transfer the powder to a container. The powder is now ready to use in your favorite dishes. This unroasted peppercorn powder gives the food not only a spicy flavor but also a "Ma" (numb) feeling to the tongue. The powder can be kept at room temperature for months.

SESAME PASTE
(Zi Ma Jiang)

Ingredients:

   1 C   sesame seeds
   ¼ C   Oil

Method:

   Spread 1 C sesame seeds in a tray. Roast the seeds in a preheated 300° oven for 12-15 minutes or until light brown. Or stir the sesame seeds in a wok over high heat until light brown. Allow the sesame seeds to cool. Place seeds in a blender; add ¼ C of oil; cover and blend seeds into a paste. Transfer the paste to a container and keep it in the refrigerator. The sesame paste is ready for use in your favorite dishes.

   Sesame seeds can also be ground with a mortar and pestle.

Calories:	1346	Iron:	16mg
Carbohydrates:	33gm	Vit. B1:	1.4mg
Protein:	28gm	Vit. B2:	0.7mg
Fat:	129gm	Vit. A:	46IU
Cholesterol:	0	Vit. C:	0
Calcium:	1763	Fiber:	10gm

bean curd

豆腐做法

Ingredients:

    1 C   soybeans
           Coagulants:
    ½ t   calcium sulfate for soft bean curd or
    ½ t   calcium chloride for firmer bean curd

Method:

1. Soak soybeans in cold water overnight. It will yield 3 cups of soaked soybeans.

2. Put a layer of clean cloth in a colander. Set the colander in a large pan. Set aside.

3. Blend one cup of soaked soybeans with 2-3 cups of water in a blender (covered) for two minutes.

4. Pour the blended soybeans into the colander. Squeeze the soy milk (the liquid) into the pan and discard the solids. Repeat until the three cups of soaked soybeans are used up.

5. Boil the soy milk in the pan (I will call this pan, "pan A"). Stir the soy milk while cooking to prevent scorching. Keep boiling on low heat for 1 minute.

6. Put the coagulant in another large pan and add 1/3 C of hot water; stir to dissolve. (I will call this pan, "pan B").

7. Pour the boiling soy milk from pan A to pan B. Pour the soy milk back and forth between the two pans 4-5 times. Let it set for a few minutes. The soy milk will coagulate gradually.

8. Line a colander with 2-3 layers of cheese cloth. (A square wooden case can also be used). Pour the coagulated soybean milk into the colander. The coagulated bean curd will remain on the cloth while the whey will be strained away.

9. Gently press out the excess water from the bean curd. Cool before using.

Makes about ¾ pound of bean curd.

If the soy milk does not coagulate (after step 7), cook over medium heat until it coagulates, stir while cooking.

Bean curd can be obtained in some supermarkets in the produce section. It is very convenient to be able to buy ready-made bean curd. Firmer bean curd is good for fried and dried bean curd.

One pound of bean curd:
- Calories: 327
- Carbohydrates: 11gm
- Protein: 35gm
- Fat: 19gm
- Cholesterol: 0
- Calcium: 481mg
- Iron: 8.6mg
- Vit. B1: 0.3mg
- Vit. B2: 0.1mg
- Vit. A: 0
- Vit. C: 0
- Fiber: 0

MEATLESS BEAN CURD
(Su Dou Fu)

素豆腐

Ingredients:

1 lb	bean curd, diced
1 t	sesame oil
1	green onion, minced
3 T	oil
2	cloves of garlic, minced
2 t	minced ginger root
2 t	chicken bouillon dissolved in 1 C water
¼ t	pepper
1 t	cornstarch blended with 1 T water

Method:

1. Heat oil in a pan or wok; saute garlic and ginger root.

2. Add bean curd; cook for 1 minute. Stir gently while cooking.

3. Add dissolved bouillon and ¼ t pepper; bring to a boil. Reduce heat and cook for 5 minutes.

4. Add blended cornstarch and mix well. Transfer to a serving dish. Garnish with sesame oil and minced green onions. Serve hot.

Makes 4-6 servings.

- Calories: 766
- Carbohydrates: 16gm
- Protein: 36gm
- Fat: 65gm
- Cholesterol: 0
- Calcium: 581mg
- Iron: 8mg
- Vit. B1: 0.29mg
- Vit. B2: 0.14mg
- Vit. A: 200IU
- Vit. C: 4mg
- Fiber: 1mg

鍋貼豆腐

Ingredients:

1 lb	bean curd
¾ t	salt mixed with a pinch of pepper and onion powder
2-3 T	flour
1	egg, beaten
1 t	sesame oil
4-5 T	oil
2	green onions, minced
1 t	minced ginger root
1½ C	water
1 t	chicken bouillon
¼ t	pepper
1 t	sugar
1 T	soy sauce

Method:

1. Cut the bean curd into 1″x1″x1/3″ pieces and pat dry. Sprinkle the salt mixture evenly over the bean curd. Let stand for a few minutes or longer.

2. Roll the bean curd in the flour. Dip the bean curd pieces, one at a time, in the beaten egg.

3. Heat oil in a pan or wok; fry the bean curd until light brown on both sides. Transfer to a dish.

4. Sauté onion and ginger root. Add the last 5 ingredients and the fried bean curd; bring to a boil.

5. Reduce to medium heat and cook until the liquid is reduced to ¼ C. Add sesame oil and mix gently. Serve hot.

Makes 4-6 servings.

Calories: 987		Iron: 9mg	
Carbohydrates: 28gm		Vit. B1: 0.3mg	
Protein: 44gm		Vit. B2: 0.2mg	
Fat: 81gm		Vit. A: 990IU	
Cholesterol: 275mg		Vit. C: 6mg	
Calcium: 625mg		Fiber: .8gm	

HONEY COMB BEAN CURD
(Fong Chao Dou Fu)

蜂 巢 豆 腐

Ingredients:

1 lb	bean curd, frozen
½ lb	chicken breast
1 t	salt
¼ t	pepper
½ t	onion powder
1 t	sherry
2 t	cornstarch
1 T	cornstarch blended with 1 T water
1 T	sesame oil
3 T	chopped coriander for garnishing
3 T	oil
2	green onions, shredded
3	slices of ginger root
⅛ lb	fresh mushrooms, washed and sliced
⅛ lb	snow pea pods, washed and cleaned
1 C	water or more
2 t	instant chicken bouillon
1 T	soy sauce
¼ t	salt
1 oz	sliced ham (optional)

Method:

1. Pat the bean curd dry. Keep it in the freezer overnight or longer. Thaw completely and cut into 2"x1"x½" pieces before using.

2. Slice the chicken then mix with the next 5 ingredients.

3. Heat oil in a pan or wok; sauté onion and ginger root. Add chicken and stir for 1 minute.

4. Add bean curd and the last 5 ingredients; bring to a boil.

5. Add mushrooms, and pea pods; bring to a boil.

6. Add blended cornstarch and cook until the sauce thickens. Transfer to a serving dish. Garnish with sesame oil and chopped coriander. Serve hot.

After fresh bean curd has been frozen, holes appear which gives it the appearance of honey comb. The spongy character soaks up flavor easily. It is also the best way to use up any surplus fresh bean curd.

Makes 4-6 servings.

Calories: 1220	Cholesterol: 200mg	Vit. B2: 1.1mg
Carbohydrates: 39gm	Calcium: 674	Vit. A: 960IU
Protein: 89gm	Iron: 14mg	Vit. C: 21gm
Fat: 80mg	Vit. B1: 0.6mg	Fiber: 2gm

SEASONED CUSTARD BEAN CURD
(Dou Fu Nao)

Ingredients:

1 C   coagulated soy milk (Step 7 of the bean curd recipe on page 318, sodium sulfate is used as coagulant)

1 T   minced Sichuan pickle
1 T   soy sauce
1 T   soaked and minced dried shrimp or minced ham
1 T   minced green onion
1 t   sesame oil
1/8 t MSG
1 t   hot pepper oil
       Pinch of pepper

Method:

1. Place 1 C coagulated soy milk in a Chinese rice bowl or soup bowl.
2. Add the last 8 ingredients. Serve hot. Mix before eating.

Makes 1 serving.

Calories: 238	Cholesterol: 35mg	Vit. B2: 0.2mg
Carbohydrates: 12gm	Calcium: 140mg	Vit. A: 116IU
Protein: 26gm	Iron: 5mg	Vit. C: 3mg
Fat: 10gm	Vit. B1: 0.2mg	Fiber: 0.1gm

BEAR'S PALM BEAN CURD
(Xiong Zhang Dou Fu)

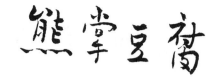

Ingredients:

- 1 T soy sauce
- ¼ t pepper
- ¼ t onion powder
- 1 t sherry
- 2 t cornstarch
- ½ lb chicken breast or pork
- 1 lb bean curd, cut into 1½"x1"x½" slices
- 1 T cornstarch blended with 2 T water
- 1 t sesame oil or more
- 3 T oil
- 2 green onions, shredded
- 2 slices of ginger root
- 1 T dried black wood ears, soaked and cleaned
- 1-1½ C water
- 1 chicken bouillon cube
- 2 T soy sauce
- ½ C bamboo shoots, sliced
- ½ t sugar
- ¼ t pepper

Method:

1. Slice the meat and mix with the first 5 ingredients.
2. Cut the bean curd.
3. Heat oil in a non-stick pan. Stir-fry the meat for 1½ minutes. Remove.
4. Brown both sides of the bean curd slices with ginger root in the remaining oil. Add the last 7 ingredients; bring to a boil.
5. Add blended cornstarch and meat. Cook until the sauce thickens. Add sesame oil; mix well. Garnish with green onions. A few snow pea pods can be added at the last step. Serve hot.

Makes 4-6 servings.

Calories: 1119	Cholesterol: 144mg	Vit. B2: 0.62mg
Carbohydrates: 33gm	Calcium: 641mg	Vit. A: 704IU
Protein: 84gm	Iron: 13mg	Vit. C: 9mg
Fat: 69gm	Vit. B1: 0.57mg	Fiber: 1gm

蕃茄豆腐

BEAN CURD WITH TOMATOES
(Fan Qie Dou Fu)

Ingredients:

½-1 lb bean curd, sliced (2"x1"x½")
¼ lb ham or ½ lb pork
½ lb Bok Choy or more
½ lb tomatoes or more, cubed
3 T oil
2 green onions or more, shredded
2 slices of ginger root
3 T soy sauce
¼ t pepper
½ t sugar
Salt to taste
1 t sesame oil (optional)

Method:

1. Wash Bok Choy and cut into 1" sections. Separate the white parts from the green parts. Set aside.

2. Cut the ham into thin slices (or slice the pork and mix it with 1 T soy sauce and 2 t cornstarch.)

3. Heat oil in a pan or wok; sauté onions and ginger root. Add meat and stir-fry for 1-2 minutes.

4. Add bean curd, the white parts of the Bok Choy, tomatoes and the last 5 ingredients, bring to a boil.

5. Add the green parts of the Bok Choy and cook over high heat for one minute. Serve hot.

Makes 4-6 servings.

Calories: 1094
Carbohydrates: 30gm
Protein: 44gm
Fat: 91gm
Cholesterol: 112mg
Calcium: 470mg

Iron: 11mg
Vit. B1: 1.2mg
Vit. B2: 0.9mg
Vit. A: 2752IU
Vit. C: 91mg
Fiber: 3gm

MA PO BEAN CURD, SICHUAN STYLE
(Jiao Ma Dou Fu)

Ingredients:

- ½ lb ground pork or beef
- 1 T soy sauce
- 1 t cornstarch
- 1 t sesame oil
- 2 t cornstarch blended with 2 T water
- 1 T oil
- 2 T minced fermented black beans
- 1 T minced garlic
- 1 T minced ginger root
- 1 lb bean crud, diced
- ¼ t pepper
- 2 T soy sauce
- ½ t Sichuan peppercorn powder for seasoning (page 314)
- 1 t hot pepper oil or sauce (page 313)
- 1 t sugar
- ½ C water
- 1 t sesame oil (optional)

Method:

1. Mix the first 3 ingredients together thoroughly.

2. Heat oil in a pan or wok; add meat, black beans, garlic and ginger root. Stir and mix for 2-3 minutes, separating meat while stirring.

3. Add bean curd and mix gently.

4. Add the last 7 ingredients, bring to a boil.

5. Add blended cornstarch and sesame oil; cook and stir until sauce thickens. Serve hot.

Makes 4-6 servings.

Calories:	1067	Iron:	19mg
Carbohydrates:	44gm	Vit. B1:	2.4mg
Protein:	85gm	Vit. B2:	0.8mg
Fat:	64mg	Vit. A:	7IU
Cholesterol:	142mg	Vit. C:	2mg
Calcium:	670mg	Fiber:	1gm

家常豆腐

BRAISED BEAN CURD IN MEAT SAUCE
(Jia Zhang Dou Fu)

Ingredients:

¼ lb ground meat, pork or beef
1 T soy sauce
¼ t onion powder
⅛ t pepper
1 t sherry
1 t cornstarch
1 lb bean curd
1/3 t salt
3 T oil
2 green onions, minced
1 t minced ginger root
1 T minced garlic
1-3 t hot pepper paste (page 312)
2 t cornstarch blended with 1 t water
1 t chicken bouillon dissolved in 1 C of water
1 t sugar

Method:

1. Mix the meat with the next 5 ingredients. Set aside.

2. Cut the bean curd into 1½" x ½" squares, then cut the squares into triangles.

3. Heat oil in a non-stick pan or wok; put the bean curd triangles in the pan. Sprinkle 1/3 t salt evenly over the bean curd.

4. Fry the bean crud until brown. Brown the other side. Remove.

5. Add meat, ginger, garlic and hot pepper oil; stir and mix for 1 minute. Add the last 2 ingredients; bring to a boil.

6. Add cooked bean curd; cook for 2 minutes. Add blended cornstarch and cook until the sauce thickens. Transfer to a serving dish and sprinkle the minced green onions over the bean curd. Serve hot.

Makes 4-6 servings.

Calories: 1024	Cholesterol: 71mg	Vit. B2: 0.43mg
Carbohydrates: 28gm	Calcium: 610mg	Vit. A: 400IU
Protein: 57gm	Iron: 13mg	Vit. C: 7mg
Fat: 79gm	Vit. B1: 1.3mg	Fiber: 1gm

BRAISED FRIED BEAN CURD
(Hui You Dou Fu)

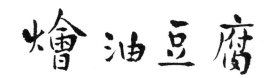

Ingredients:

¼ lb	shelled shrimp, fresh or frozen
⅛ t	salt
¼ t	onion powder
⅛ t	pepper
1 t	cornstarch
	Oil for deep-frying, about 1 cup
1 lb	bean curd cut into 2″x2″x¼″ squares
2	cloves of garlic, sliced
1 t	minced ginger root
1 T	cornstarch blended with 2 T water
1 t	sesame oil
¼ lb	snow pea pods, cleaned
¼ lb	fresh mushrooms, washed and sliced
2 C	water
1 t	chicken bouillon
¼ t	pepper
2 T	soy sauce or more
1 t	sugar

Method:

1. Mix the shrimp with the next 4 ingredients. Set aside.
2. Heat oil; deep-fry the bean curd until golden brown. Remove.
3. Pour off all but 1 T oil. Stir-fry the shrimp for 1 minute. Remove.
4. Sauté ginger root and garlic in the remaining oil. Add fried bean curd and the last 5 ingredients; bring to a boil. Turn to medium heat and cook until the liquid is reduced to 3/4 cup.
5. Add 1 t sesame oil, snow pea pods, mushrooms, and blended cornstarch; cook and stir until the sauce thickens. Add cooked shrimp; mix well. Serve hot.

Makes 4 servings.

Deep-fried bean curd can be purchased from Oriental grocery stores. It freezes well.

Calories: 1055	Cholesterol: 140mg	Vit. B2: 0.9mg
Carbohydrates: 38gm	Calcium: 139mg	Vit. A: 680IU
Protein: 62gm	Iron: 3mg	Vit. C: 21mg
Fat: 73gm	Vit. B1: 0.4mg	Fiber: 2gm

蠔油豆腐　　　OYSTER SAUCE BEAN CURD
　　　　　　　　　(Hao You Dou Fu)

Ingredients:

1 lb	bean curd, cut into ½" dices
½ C	water
1 t	cornstarch, blended with 2 T water
3 T	oil
2-4	cloves of garlic, minced
1 t	or more minced ginger root
1 T	minced ham
1	green onion, minced
¼ t	pepper
3 T	oyster sauce
1 t	hot sauce or more (optional)
1 t	sesame oil (optional)

Method:

1. Heat oil in a pan or wok; sauté garlic and ginger root.

2. Add bean curd and the last 4 ingredients; cook for 1 minute. Stir gently while cooking.

3. Add water and bring to a boil.

4. Add blended cornstarch; mix well. Transfer to a serving dish; garnish with minced green onion and ham. Serve hot.

Makes 4 servings.

Calories: 832		Iron: 12mg	
Carbohydrates: 23gm		Vit. B1: 0.5mg	
Protein: 43gm		Vit. B2: 0.3mg	
Fat: 68gm		Vit. A: 200IU	
Cholesterol: 15mg		Vit. C: 4mg	
Calcium: 630mg		Fiber: 1gm	

FERMENTED BEAN CURD WITH MEAT
(Fu Lu Dun Rou)

Ingredients:

- 2 lb   pork (butt, fresh ham, or shoulder etc.)
- 4   pieces of 1"x½" square fermented bean curd
- 3 T   Hoisin sauce
- 1 T   sherry
- ½ t   pepper
- 1   small onion, chopped
- 4   slices of ginger root
- 3 C   water

Method:

1. Cut the pork into 1½" cubes.
2. Place the fermented bean curd, Hoisin sauce, sherry and pepper in a small bowl and mash into a paste. Mix the paste with the pork. Let stand for 2 hours or more.
3. Put the last 3 ingredients in a medium sauce pan. Add pork; cover and bring to a boil.
4. Reduce to medium heat and cook until the meat becomes tender and the liquid is reduced to ¼ C. Serve hot.

Add more water if it evaporates before the meat becomes tender. If too much liquid remains after the meat is tender, turn heat up and cook until liquid evaporates.

Makes 6 servings.

Calories:	1657	Iron:	28mg
Carbohydrates:	18gm	Vit. B1:	8mg
Protein:	179gm	Vit. B2:	2mg
Fat:	90mg	Vit. A:	22IU
Cholesterol:	566mg	Vit. C:	5mg
Calcium:	272mg	Fiber:	1gm

炸豆腐球

FRIED BEAN CURD BALLS
(Zha Dou Fu Qiu)

Ingredients:

½ lb	ground pork or beef
2	green onions, minced
½ t	minced ginger root
¼ t	pepper
1 t	sherry
½ t	salt
2 T	soy sauce
½ t	chicken bouillon
1 t	sesame oil
6-8	water chestnuts, coarsely minced
1 lb	bean curd
2 T	cornstarch
	Sichuan peppercorn powder for dipping (page 314)
	Oil for deep-frying
	Lettuce leaves (optional)
	Minced green onion or parsley for garnishing

Method:

1. Mix the first 11 ingredients together thoroughly. Add cornstarch and mix well.

2. Heat oil in a pan or wok.

3. Form the bean curd mixture into 1″ balls.

4. Deep-fry the balls until golden brown. Transfer to a lettuce-lined plate. Garnish with minced green onion or parsley. Serve hot with a small dish of Sichuan peppercorn powder for dipping.

Calories: 1302		Iron: 16mg	
Carbohydrates: 34gm		Vit. B1: 2.3mg	
Protein: 79gm		Vit. B2: 0.76mg	
Fat: 96gm		Vit. A: 400mg	
Cholesterol: 141mg		Vit. C: 7mg	
Calcium: 634mg		Fiber: 1gm	

Calculated with 4 T oil for deep-frying.

SICHUAN BEAN CURD
(Chuan Wei Dou Fu)

Ingredients:

- 1 T sherry
- ¾ t salt
- ¼ t onion powder
- ¼ t pepper
- 1 lb bean curd
- ½ C flour
- 1 egg, beaten
- 1 t sesame oil or more
- 3-4 T oil
- 1 C chicken broth (or 1 C water + 1 chicken bouillon cube)
- 1 t sherry
- 2 green onions, minced or 1 T minced garlic
- 1 t minced ginger root
- 1 T hot bean sauce or more
- ½ t sugar
- ¼ t Sichuan peppercorn powder for dipping (page 314)

Method:

1. Cut bean curd into 1½" x 1" x ¼" pieces. Spread the first 4 ingredients evenly on bean curd pieces. Let set for 10 minutes or more.

2. Coat the bean curd pieces with a layer of flour and dip in egg before frying.

3. Heat oil in a non-stick pan or wok; fry bean curd pieces until both sides brown.

4. Add the last 7 ingredients to the bean curd and bring to boil. Turn to low heat and simmer until the cooking juice reduces to ¼ C.

5. Add 1 t sesame oil and mix well. Transfer the bean curd to a serving dish and serve hot.

Calories: 1070	Cholesterol: 275 mg	Vit. B1: 0.82 mg
Carbohydrate: 58 gm	Calcium: 620 mg	Vit. B2: 0.50 mg
Protein: 47 gm	Iron: 12 mg	Vit. C: 5 mg
Fat: 70 gm	Vit. A: 600IU	Fiber: 0.5 mg

麻辣豆腐

Ingredients:

2 T	oil
½ lb	ground pork or beef
1 t	or more hot pepper flakes or cayenne pepper
1 t	finely minced ginger root
1 T	salted black beans, minced (from Oriental grocery store)
1 lb	bean curd, diced
3 T	soy sauce
½ t	brown sugar
1 T	sherry
½ C	minced green onions
½ C	water
1 T	cornstarch blended with 2 T water
1 T	sesame oil
	Salt or soy sauce to taste
½ t	Sichuan peppercorn powder for seasoning (page 314)

Method:

1. Heat oil in a pan or wok; add meat. Stir and toss until color turns and meat particles separate.

2. Add hot pepper flakes, ginger root and salted black beans; stir and mix for 1 minute.

3. Add diced bean curd, soy sauce, brown sugar and sherry; stir carefully for ½ minute.

4. Add green onion and water; mix and bring to a boil. Add blended cornstarch and sesame oil; cook until the sauce thickens. Transfer to a serving dish and sprinkle the Sichuan peppercorn powder over the bean curd and serve hot.

Calories: 1290	Protein: 75gm
Carbohydrates: 22gm	Fat: 99gm

This is a well known Western dish of the Sichuan province. The dish is famous not only for its hot and spicy flavor but also because it causes a tingling and numb sensation to the tongue. In Chinese

"Ma" means numb, the sensation coming from the Sichuan peppercorn powder and "La" means hot, the flavor coming from the hot pepper. Ma and La are the two popular spicy flavors represented in most of the Western dishes.

SWEET SOY MILK WITH FRIED BISCUITS
(Dou Jiang You Tiao)

Ingredients:

2 biscuits (ready-to-make, home-style chilled biscuits in tube)
1 C hot soy milk (recipe on page 318, using Step 5)
1 T sugar or to taste
Oil for deep-frying, about 1 cup

Method:

1. Roll each biscuit into a ½" cylindrical roll.
2. Heat oil in a wok; deep-fry the biscuits until brown.
3. Place the boiled hot soy milk in a soup bowl; add sugar. Cut the fried biscuits into 1" sections.
4. Add the biscuits to the hot soy milk and serve.
Soy milk is sold in some health stores.
Makes 1 serving.

Calories: 296	Cholesterol: 1.5mg	Vit. B2: 0.2mg
Carbohydrates: 42mg	Calcium: 90mg	Vit. A: 100IU
Protein: 12mg	Iron: 3mg	Vit. C: 0
Fat: 10gm	Vit. B1: 0.3mg	Fiber: 0.5gm

Deep-fry oil is not included in this calculation.

In China, fried You Tiao with sweet soy milk is the nationally popular breakfast. The fried biscuit here is a short cut for fried You Tiao. The flavor and texture of fried biscuit and You Tiao are very much alike.

dim sum

Dim Sum is a broad name for many dishes which could be served as breakfast, brunch, lunch, a snack, dessert, appetizer, or hor d'oeuvres. Many of these Dim Sum dishes are nutritious, tasty and balanced meals by themselves.

SPRING ROLLS (EGG ROLLS)
(Zhun Juan)

Ingredients:

¼ lb beef, pork, or chicken breast, shredded or diced raw
      shrimp
{
2 T   soy sauce
1 T   sherry
¼ t   pepper
1 T   ginger root, minced fine
½ t   brown sugar
2 T   cornstarch
}
4 T   oil
1 lb egg roll skins, about 20 pieces (homemade, recipe on page
      343) or ready-made from grocery stores in the produce
      section)
{
1 C   onion, shredded
1 C   shredded celery or bamboo shoots or fresh bean sprouts
½ lb cabbage, or celery cabbage, or Napa, shredded
¼ lb fresh mushrooms, shredded or 4-5 dried mushrooms,
      soaked and shredded
1 oz bean threads, soaked, drained and cut into 1-inch lengths
2 T   soy sauce or to taste
¼ t   salt
1 C   egg shreds (page 197)
}

Sealing:
A mixture of 1 T flour and ½ C water
Oil for deep-frying, about 1-2 cups

Method:

I. Filling:

1. Mix the meat with the next 6 ingredients.

2. Heat 4 T oil in a pan or wok. Add meat and stir-fry until color
turns. Separate meat particles while cooking.

3. Add the last 8 ingredients, mix and cook until the cabbage is
half done. Cool completely before using.

II. Wrapping:

1. With about one pound of Spring Roll skins (wrappers) on a cutting board, trim off one corner.

2. With the trimmed corner opposite you, place a heaping tablespoon of cold filling across the upper part of the wrapper, spreading the filling into a 3½"x1" portion.

3. Fold both uncut ends over the filling.

4. Roll the folded Spring Roll up to within about 3" of the end.

5. Brush the end flap of the wrapper with a thin layer of sealing.

6. Finish rolling, making sure the sealing-brushed end is completely sealed.

III. Deep-Frying:

1. Heat oil in a pan or wok. Fry the folded spring rolls, 2-3 at a time, until golden brown.

2. Serve hot, plain or with dips of your choice. (See below).

Dips:

1. Half soy sauce and half vinegar

2. Plain vinegar

3. Sweet and Sour Sauce:

Bring to a boil a mixture of 4 T catsup, 4 T sugar, 4 T vinegar, 4 T water and 1 t cornstarch. Cool before using.

4. Apricot Sauce or Orange Sauce:

Mash one can of mandarin oranges or apricots (11-12 oz size). Put the mashed fruit and the syrup in a sauce pan; add 2 T vinegar, 2 T sugar and bring to a boil. Add 1 T cornstarch blended with a little water; bring to a boil. Cool before using.

5. Mustard Sauce:

Mix 2 T mustard powder, 2 T cold water, ½ t vinegar and ⅛ t salt into a smooth paste and chill.

6. Plum Sauce:

Soak the following dried, pitted fruits: ½ C plums, ½ C apricots, and ¼ C raisins in 3 C water until softened. Puree the fruits in a blender. Pour the mixture in a sauce pan; add 1 C sugar and ½ C vinegar and bring to a boil. Turn to low heat and simmer until the sauce thickens. Chill.

Makes 20 spring rolls.

Calories: 2320	Carbohydrates: 219gm
Protein: 78gm	Fat: 124gm

Calculated with beef chuck and 4 T oil for deep-frying. The dips are not included.

Approximately 120 calories per spring roll.

红油炒手

HUNG YOU CHAO SHOU
(WONTON SICHUAN STYLE)
(Hung You Hun Dun)

Ingredients:

- ½ lb   ground pork
- ¼ C   bamboo shoots, minced
- 2-3   Chinese dried mushrooms, soaked and minced
- 2-3   green onions, minced
- 1 t   finely minced ginger root
- 1 t   salt
- 1 t   sherry
- ¼ t   pepper
- 1 t   sesame oil
-    Wonton skins
- 2 C   chicken broth, canned or 2 chicken bouillon cubes in 2 C water
-    Minced green onions
-    Minced Sichuan pickle
-    Red hot pepper oil (page 313)
-    Sesame oil

Method:

1. Combine the first 9 ingredients in a bowl; blend well. This mixture will be used as the Wonton filling.

2. Place 1 teaspoon of filling in the center of a Wonton skin and fold. (See instructions on page 344).

3. Boil the chicken broth in a small sauce pan and keep warm while cooking the Wontons. Have 4 small Chinese bowls or soup bowls ready.

4. Fill a medium sauce pan one third full of water. Cover pan and bring to a boil.

5. Drop 20 Wontons into the boiling water. Stir gently with a pair of chopsticks to prevent the Wontons from sticking to each other and to the bottom of the pan. Cover pan and bring to a boil.

6. Add 2 C cold water; cover pan and bring to a boil. Remove lid and cook for ½ minute.

7. With a slotted spoon, transfer the cooked Wontons into 4 Chinese rice bowls. Add 1/3 C chicken broth to each of the bowls. Add a small portion of minced green onions, Sichuan pickle, red oil

and sesame oil to your taste. Serve hot as a snack, for breakfast, or as one of the many courses of a formal dinner or banquet.
(The filling makes 40-50 Wontons.)

Nutritional information for the filling and broth.

Calories: 620   Carbohydrates: 8gm
Protein: 38gm   Fat: 47gm

FRIED WONTON
(Zha Hun Dun)

炸 馄 饨

Ingredients:

Wonton filling (pages 63-64)
Wrapped Wontons (follow the instructions on page 344)
Oil for deep-frying

Method:

Heat oil in a wok and deep-fry the Wontons until golden brown. Serve the fried Wontons with the following dips:

Soy Sauce Vinegar Dip
Mix equal amounts of soy sauce and vinegar together.

Sweet and Sour Sauce
Bring to a boil a mixture of 4 T sugar, 4 T catsup, 4 T vinegar, 4 T water, and 1 t cornstarch blended with 1 T water.

Orange Sauce
Bring to a boil, a mixture of ½ C mandarin oranges in syrup (canned), 4 T sugar, 4 T vinegar, and 1 t cornstarch. Break the orange segments into small pieces while cooking. Cool before using.

Fried Wonton can be prepared in advance and kept frozen. Before serving, reheat in a preheated 350° oven for 5-8 minutes or until they are completely heated through.
Makes 70-80 Wontons.

担々餛飩

DAN DAN WONTON
(Dan Dan Won Don)

Ingredients:

- 2 oz   ground pork
- 1   water chestnut, minced
- 1   green onion, minced
- 1 t   sherry
- ¼ t   salt
- ½ t   minced ginger root
- 16   Wonton skins
- 2 T   sesame paste
- 1 T   oil
- ¼ t   pepper
- 1 T   sesame oil
- 2 T   soy sauce
- 1 T   vinegar
- 2   cloves of garlic, minced
- 2 T   minced Sichuan pickles or Tientsin preserved vegetables
- 2-3 t   hot pepper oil (optional)
- ½ t   Sichuan peppercorn powder
- 2   green onions, minced
- 2   slices of ginger root, minced
- 1 t   sugar
- ⅛ t   MSG (optional)

Method:

1. Mix the first 6 ingredients together as Wonton filling. Use the filling to make 16 Wontons. (Follow directions on page 344).

2. Mix the last 14 ingredients in a small bowl.

3. Put the Wontons in boiling water and bring to a boil. Add 1 C cold water and bring to a boil once more. Transfer the cooked Wontons with a slotted spoon into two soup bowls.

4. Add the sesame paste mixture to the Wontons. Mix before eating.

Makes 2 servings.

Calories: 669	Cholesterol: 81mg	Vit. B2: 0.3mg
Carbohydrates: 48gm	Calcium: 259mg	Vit. A: 723IU
Protein: 21gm	Iron: 5mg	Vit. C: 10mg
Fat: 44gm	Vit. B1: 0.9mg	Fiber: 2gm

SPRING ROLL (EGG ROLL) AND WONTON SKIN
(Zhun Juan Pi)

Ingredients:

- 2 C   flour
- 1   large egg
- ½ C   cold water

Method:

1. Place flour and egg in a mixing bowl; add water and mix until the mixture holds together to form a dough. Transfer the dough to a floured board and knead for 10 minutes.

2. Return the dough to the bowl; cover with a damp towel. Let stand for 1 hour or more.

3. Remove the dough to a lightly floured board. Knead the dough for a few minutes until very smooth.

4. Roll the dough with a rolling pin until very thin. Cut the dough into 6″ squares for Spring Roll skins; 3″, for Wonton skins and steamed meat in noodle cases. Wrap the skins in a plastic bag before using.

Makes about one pound of skins.

Ready-made skins are sold in all supermarkets at the produce section. They can be frozen when wrapped in a well-sealed plastic bag. Thaw (in the bag) before using.

When the skins are stored in the freezer too long, the edges of the skins will be dried and slightly brittle. The skins can be revived. To revive the skins:

Unseal the plastic bag (leave the skins in the bag); place bag with the skins in a larger plastic bag. Put a damp towel in between the two bags and seal. Store the package in the refrigerator for two days or more. The skins will be as good as fresh ones.

Calories: 920   Carbohydrates: 176gm
Protein: 30gm   Fat: 8gm

Wonton Wrapping:

1. Put ½ teaspoon of filling in the center of a Wonton skin (wrapper).

2. Fold the wrapper in half toward you (with the filling in the center).

3. Fold the wrapper in half once more in the same direction.

4. Holding the two corners at the top (leaving the bottom 2 corners free), pull the corners forward. Overlap the corners; moisten and press to seal.

5. Wontons should have the appearance of little nurse's caps.

Quilin, famed as being "second to none in scenery in China" is situated in the southern part of China. It is surrounded by abrupt rock hills rising straight out of the ground.

DUMPLING FILLINGS

Ingredients and methods for fillings:

Choose any one of the following fillings.

I. Meat Filling: 鮮肉水餃

1 lb	ground lean pork butt or ground beef
1	10 oz box of chopped frozen vegetables (spinach, mustard greens, turnip greens etc.) thawed and squeeze-dried
2-4	green onions, minced or 1 onion, chopped
1 T	ginger root, minced fine
3 T	soy sauce
1/3 t	salt
¼ t	pepper
1 T	or more sesame oil
1 T	sherry

Mix all the ingredients in a mixing bowl. The mixture is ready to use as a dumpling filling for boiled dumplings, fried dumplings, or steamed dumplings.

Calories: 980	Cholesterol: 320mg	Vit. B2: 1.5mg
Carbohydrates: 17gm	Calcium: 414mg	Vit. A: 22521IU
Protein: 95gm	Iron: 20mg	Vit. C: 87mg
Fat: 58gm	Vit. B1: 4.3mg	Fiber: 2gm

II. Meat and shrimp filling: 鮮蝦肉餃

½ lb	ground lean pork butt
½ lb	fresh or frozen shelled, raw shrimp, diced
3	dried mushrooms, soaked and minced

1 T	ginger root, minced fine
3 T	soy sauce
¼ t	salt
¼ t	pepper
½	onion, minced fine
1 T	sherry
1-3 t	sesame oil
2 t	cornstarch

Mix all the ingredients together thoroughly in a mixing bowl. Use as dumpling filling for boiled dumplings, fried dumplings, or steamed dumplings.

Calories: 665	Cholesterol: 442mg	Vit. B2: 0.7mg
Carbohydrates: 15gm	Calcium: 219mg	Vit. A: 166mg
Protein: 85gm	Iron: 10mg	Vit. C: 19mg
Fat: 27gm	Vit. B1: 2.1mg	Fiber: 1gm

III. Shrimp filling (Har Gou):　蝦仁餃子

½ lb	fresh or frozen shelled, raw shrimp, diced
¼ lb	ground lean pork butt
½ C	bamboo shoots, coarsely minced
4	dried mushrooms, soaked and minced
¼	onion or more, minced fine
2 T	soy sauce
½ t	salt
¼ t	pepper
1-3 t	sesame oil
1 T	sherry
2 t	cornstarch
⅛ t	MSG (optional)

Mix all the ingredients together thoroughly in a mixing bowl. Use as a filling for boiled dumplings, fried dumplings, or steamed dumplings.

Calories: 515	Cholesterol: 360mg	Vit. B2: 0.6mg
Carbohydrates: 20gm	Calcium: 209mg	Vit. A: 25IU
Protein: 67gm	Iron: 10mg	Vit. C: 6mg
Fat: 17gm	Vit. B1: 1.2mg	Fiber: 1gm

Ingredients:

2½ C   all purpose flour
  1 C   water or more

Method:

1. Mix flour and water in a mixing bowl to form a dough.

2. Knead the dough on a floured board for 5 minutes, or until soft and smooth.

3. Return the dough to mixing bowl; cover with a dampened cloth. Let it stand for 3 hours or more.

4. Remove dough to a floured board; knead again until smooth.

5. Form the dough into a sausage-like cylinder, about 1" in diameter.

6. Cut the cylindrical roll, crosswise into ½" thick pieces.

7. Flatten each piece of the dough with the palm of your hand and roll with a rolling pin into a round wrapper about 2½" in diameter. The center of the wrapper should be thicker than the edges. It is ready to use.

Ready-made wrappers are sold frozen in Oriental grocery stores. Thaw before using.

Calories: 1017	Cholesterol: 0	Vit. B2: 1.4mg
Carbohydrates: 212gm	Calcium: 42mg	Vit. A: 0
Protein: 29gm	Iron: 2mg	Vit. C: 0
Fat: 2gm	Vit. B1: 1.6mg	Fiber: 1gm

Procedure for Wrapping:
(Bao Jiao Zi)

1. Roll dough pieces into 2½" wrappers.

Photographs by Sherl White

2. Place 1 teaspoon of filling in the center of a dumpling wrapper.

3. Fold the wrapper in half across the filling and pinch once in the center.

4. Make 3 or 4 pleats on one side of the center and the other, shaping the dumpling into a 3-sided, crescent shape.

5. Pinch the edges along the pleated side in order to seal tightly.

Tiers of a stacked steamer in a restaurant in the Sichuan province.

BOILED DUMPLINGS
(Shui Jiao)

1. Fill a large sauce pan ¼ full of water; bring to a boil.

2. Drop 20-25 dumplings, one by one, in the boiling water. Stir gently with the back of a wooden spoon to prevent the dumplings from sticking to each other and to the bottom of the pan.

3. Cover the pan and bring to a boil. Add 2/3 C of cold water; cover pan and bring to a boil again. Add 2/3 C of cold water and bring to a boil once more. Add 2/3 C of cold water for the third time. When the water boils again, the dumplings are cooked and ready to eat.

4. Remove the dumplings, with a slotted spoon or a wire sieve, to a serving dish and serve with dips (page 351).

Adding cold water three times to the boiling water is the method for preventing the dumplings from breaking apart by the rapidly boiling water.

FRIED DUMPLINGS (POT STICKERS)
(Quo Tie)

   1. Spread 2 T oil in a non-stick pan or skillet. Arrange enough dumplings in the pan, without overlapping, to cover the bottom of the pan.

   2. Add 2/3 C cold water; cover pan and bring to a boil.

   3. Reduce to medium heat and cook until water evaporates.

   4. Add 1 T oil and fry for a half minute more.

   5. Remove the dumplings by putting a plate over the pan and quickly inverting the pan. Serve hot with dips (page 351).

STEAMED DUMPLINGS
(Zheng Jiao)

   1. Arrange the dumplings neatly on a greased steamer tier.

   2. Cover the steamer and steam over boiling water for 12 minutes.

   3. Remove to a platter and serve with dips.

Dips to serve with the dumplings:

   Half soy sauce and half vinegar with few drops of sesame oil.

   Soy sauce with mashed garlic.

   Hot pepper paste or sauce, (recipe on page 312).

紅 油 水 餃　　　　DUMPLINGS IN RED HOT OIL
　　　　　　　　　　　　　(Hung You Shui Jiao)

Ingredients:
For filling:

1 lb	ground pork or beef
1-1½ lb	celery cabbage or Napa, finely minced or 1 box (10 oz) chopped frozen spinach, thawed and squeezed dry
4	green onions, minced
1 T	finely minced ginger root
3 T	soy sauce
¼ t	salt or to taste
¼ t	pepper
1 T	sesame oil
1 T	sherry

Place all the ingredients in a large mixing bowl; mix well with hands until ingredients are well blended. If your hands are sensitive to salt, wear rubber gloves.

Wrap according to directions on page 349.

Cooking and serving:

1. Have 4 Chinese rice bowls or soup bowls ready.

2. Fill a large sauce pan to one third full of water. Cover pan and bring to a boil.

3. Drop 20 (to make 4 servings) dumplings gently and separately into the boiling water. Stir gently with the back of a wooden spoon to prevent the dumplings from sticking to each other and to the bottom of the pan.

4. Cover pan and bring to a boil. Add 2/3 C cold water, cover and bring to a boil. Add 2/3 C cold water again; cover and bring to a boil once more. This prevents the dumplings from breaking apart in the rapidly boiling water. When the dumplings are done, they will float to the surface.

5. Place 5 cooked dumplings with a small amount of the boiling water in each of the rice bowls. Add seasonings to individual's taste. Serve hot as a snack, Dim Sum, breakfast or one of the many courses of a formal dinner or banquet. Serve with a spoon.

Seasonings: red oil (recipe on page 313), soy sauce, minced green onion, sesame oil etc.

Nutrition information for the filling:
 Calories: 1065　　　　　Carbohydrates: 17gm
 Protein: 75gm　　　　　Fat: 3gm

Nutrition information for the wrapper:
 Calories: 1050　　　　　Carbohydrates: 220gm
 Protein: 30gm　　　　　Fat: 3gm

A side-walk restaurant in Lanzhou tended by a member of the "Hui" tribe, a Chinese minority.

蘿蔔糕

Ingredients:

- 1-3   green onion, minced
- 1 oz   minced old-fashioned ham, about 2 T
- ¼ t   pepper
- ½ t   salt
- 1 t   sesame oil
- ⅛ t   MSG (optional)
- 3 C   flour
- ½ C   shortening, oil or lard
- ¼ C   shortening plus ¼ C hot water
- 2 T   sugar
- ¼ t   salt
- 1 T   sesame seeds or more
- 1   egg, beaten, for brushing
- 1 lb   Chinese radishes
- 1 t   salt
- 2 T   oil

Method:

1. Peel the radishes, then shred finely. Put the radish shreds in a mixing bowl with 1 t salt. Squeeze and mix by hand until the radish shreds wilt, (about 3-5 minutes). Squeeze out the liquid.

2. Mix radish shreds with the first 6 ingredients. This will be the filling of the cake.

3. Mix 1½ C flour with ½ C shortening to form a dough (We will call this dough, "dough A").

4. Mix 1½ C flour, ¼ C shortening, ¼ C hot water, 2 T sugar, and ¼ t salt to form a dough. (We will call this dough, "dough B".) Knead the dough for a few minutes or until smooth; add a few drops of water if the dough is too dry.

5. Roll dough B from Step 4 into a 8"-9" round sheet. Place dough A from Step 3 in the center of the dough B. Wrap dough B around dough A.

6. Roll the dough (combination of A and B) into a 6"x12" sheet. Fold the sheet in thirds, twice, then roll it into a 12"x12" square sheet. Roll the sheet into a cylindrical roll, about 1½" in diameter.

7. Cut the cylindrical roll into 12 equal pieces. Flatten each piece of the dough (not the cut side) with the palm of your hand, then roll it into 5" round wrapper. The center of the wrapper should be thicker than the edges.

8. Divide the filling (Step 2) into 12 portions. Place one portion in the center of the wrapper. Fold the wrapper to cover the filling; press to seal. Turn seam side down and shape into a round, ball-shaped cake. Repeat to make 12 cakes.

9. Brush a layer of egg on top of the cake, then dip it in a dish of sesame seeds so that the cake is covered with a layer of seeds.

10. Spread 2 T oil on a non-stick frying pan and arrange the cakes in the pan. Add 3/4 C of water; cover pan and bring to a boil. Reduce to medium or low heat and cook until the water evaporates and a layer of brown crust forms on the bottom of the cakes. Remove to a serving platter. Serve hot or warm.

The radish cakes can be baked in 350° oven for 40-50 minutes or until light brown. They also can be deep-fried in hot oil until golden brown and served hot or warm. Cold cakes can be reheated in a 300° oven for 10 minutes before serving.

Makes 12 cakes.

Calories: 3033	Iron: 6mg
Carbohydrates: 302gm	Vit. B1: 5mg
Protein: 47gm	Vit. B2: 3mg
Fat: 178gm	Vit. A: 247IU
Cholesterol: 23mg	Vit. C: 146mg
Calcium: 326mg	Fiber: 5gm

PAN-FRIED MEAT PIES
(Xian Pian)

Ingredients:

- ½ lb   ground pork or beef
- 2 T   soy sauce
- ¼ t   salt
- 1 t   minced ginger root
- 1 t   sherry
- ¼ t   pepper
- 1 t   cornstarch
- 1 t   sesame oil
- ¼ lb   leeks or green onions, minced
- 2 C   flour
- 1 C   boiling water
- 2 T   oil
- ½ C   cold water

Method:

1. Mix the first 8 ingredients together. Add minced leeks, mix well. This will be the filling for the pies.

2. Pour boiling water over flour in a mixing bowl. Mix water and flour with a pair of chopsticks or wooden spoon into a dough.

3. Knead the dough on a floured board until smooth (about 5 minutes).

4. Cut the dough into 12 equal pieces. Roll each piece into a circle, 4" in diameter.

5. Divide the filling into 6 equal portions.

6. Place a portion of filling on circle of dough; cover with another circle and pinch edges to seal. Flute or pleat the edges. Repeat to make 6 pies.

7. Heat 1 T oil in a non-stick pan; add 3 pies and ½ C of water; cover and bring to a boil. Reduce to medium heat and cook until liquid dries. Turn over and brown. Serve hot.

Makes 4-6 servings.

Calories: 1568	Cholesterol: 142mg	Vit. B2: 0.7mg
Carbohydrates: 189gm	Calcium: 143mg	Vit. A: 45IU
Protein: 69gm	Iron: 11mg	Vit. C: 19mg
Fat: 56gm	Vit. B1: 2.3mg	Fiber: 2.1mg

CURRIED PASTRIES
(Ka Li Jiao)

加哩餃

Filling:

Ingredients:

1 T	oil
1	medium onion, chopped
1 T	(or more) curry powder blended with 2 T water
¾ lb	ground beef
¼ t	pepper
¾ t	salt
1 T	soy sauce
1 t	sherry
⅛ t	MSG(optional)

Method for filling:

Heat oil in a pan or wok; sauté onion. Add blended curry powder and stir for ½ minute. Add the next 6 ingredients; stir and mix until the beef is done (about 3-5 minutes). Cool.

Wrapper:

Ingredients:

3 C	flour
½ C	oil, lard or butter
¼ C	oil, lard or butter plus ¼ C hot water
2-4 T	sugar
1	egg, beaten (for brushing)

Method for wrapper:

1. Mix 1½ C flour with ½ C oil. Knead well.
2. Mix 1½ C flour with ¼ C oil and ¼ C hot water. Add more water if it is too dry. Knead well.
3. Roll the dough from Step 2 into a 10"x10" square sheet. Spread the dough from Step 1 evenly on the 10"x10" sheet and press.
4. Roll into a cylinder about 1" in diameter.
5. Cut the roll into 25-30 pieces. Roll each piece of dough (not the cut side) into a 2"x2" square.

Method:

Prepare the wrapper and filling as directed. Place 1 t of filling on the center of a square of dough. Fold the square in half, diagonally, to form a triangle. Press the edges tightly to seal. Place on an ungreased cookie sheet and brush the top with a layer of beaten egg. Repeat the process. Bake in a preheated 350° oven for 25-30 minutes; or until golden brown. Serve hot.

Curried pastries freeze well. Reheat in a 300° oven until they are heated through before serving.

Makes 25-30 pastries.

Calories: 3715		Cholesterol: 382mg		Vit. B2: 0.7mg	
Carbohydrates: 286gm		Calcium: 107mg		Vit. A: 274IU	
Protein: 97gm		Iron: 12mg		Vit. C: 6mg	
Fat: 239gm		Vit. B1: 0.5mg		Fiber: 1gm	

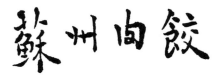

MEAT PASTRIES, SUZHOU STYLE
(Su Zhou Rou Jiao)

Ingredients:

1 lb	ground pork or beef
½	onion, finely minced
2 T	soy sauce
1 t	minced ginger root
1/3 t	salt
1 t	sherry
4	water chestnuts, coarsely minced
⅛ t	pepper
2 t	sesame oil
2 t	cornstarch
2 C	flour
½ C	vegetable oil or lard
½ C	hot water
½ C	sugar
2 T	oil

Method:

1. Mix the first 10 ingredients together thoroughly. this mixture will be used as filling.

2. Mix 1 C flour with ½ C of oil. Knead well.

3. Mix 1 C flour with ½ C sugar; add hot water and knead well.

4. Roll the dough from Step 3 into a 1/6" thick sheet.

5. Spread the dough from Step 2 evenly on the sheet; press. Roll the sheet up into a cylindrical roll, about 1-1½" in diameter.

6. Cut the cylindrical roll into 20-24 equal pieces.

7. Roll each piece of the dough (not the cut side) into a thin, 3"x4" sheet.

8. Put approximately 1 t of filling in the center of a piece of dough, spreading it across the dough lengthwise into a shape about 2"x½"x½".

9. Fold up the two longest sides of the dough to overlap the filling. Turn the pastry, seam-side down. Fold ends down and tuck under. Shape into a 2½"x¾"x2½" rectangular pastry.

10. Heat 2 T oil in a non-stick skillet. Arrange the pastries in the pan. Add ½ C water; cover and bring to a boil. Turn to low heat and cook until water evaporates. Turn to other sides and brown. Remove to a plate (seam side down); serve hot as snack or lunch.

This pastry can be baked. Brush a layer of beaten egg on the top before putting into the oven. Bake 40 minutes at 350° or until the crust turns to light brown.

The pastry also can be deep-fried.

Makes 20-24 pastries.

Calories: 3347	Iron: 16mg
Carbohydrates: 285gm	Vit. B1: 4.2mg
Protein: 110gm	Vit. B2: 1.2mg
Fat: 195gm	Vit. A: 11IU
Cholesterol: 283mg	Vit. C: 4mg
Calcium: 118mg	Fiber: 1gm

HOME-MADE NOODLES
(Mian)

Ingredients:

2 C	flour
¼ t	salt
1	large egg
½ C	cold water

Method:

1. Combine flour, salt and egg in a mixing bowl; add water and mix until the mixture holds together to form a dough. Transfer the dough to a floured board and knead for 10 minutes.

2. Return the dough to the bowl; cover with a damp towel. Let stand for 1 hour or more.

3. Remove the dough to a lightly floured board. Knead the dough for a few minutes until very smooth.

4. Roll the dough into a 1/6″ thin sheet (1/8″ for thiner noodles) Flour the dough from time to time while rolling to prevent stickiness.

5. Fold the rolled-out dough in thirds or fourths and cut into fine strips. Unfold the strips by fluffing up with your fingers. These home-made noodles are now ready to cook.

If you want to make home-made egg noodles, just add 2 more large eggs and eliminate the water. If the dough is too dry, add a little water when kneading.

Pastry makers or machines make perfect Chinese noodles. Makes about one pound of noodles.

Calories: 920   Carbohydrates: 176gm
Protein: 30gm   Fat: 8gm

FRIED NOODLES (CHOW MEIN)
(Niu Rou Chao Mian)

牛肉炒麺

Ingredients:

8 oz	soft (fresh) Chinese egg noodles, home-made (recipe on page 360) or ready made from grocery stores
½ lb	beef flank steak, shredded
¼ t	pepper
½ t	onion or garlic powder
1 t	shredded ginger root or more
1 T	sherry
1½ T	soy sauce
1 T	cornstarch
5 T	oil
½ lb	celery cabbage, shredded or Bok Choy, Napa, spinach etc.
¼ lb	fresh mushrooms, shredded or 3-4 dried mushrooms, soaked and shredded
1-2	carrots, shredded (optional)
2 T	soy sauce or to taste
1	beef bouillon cube (chicken bouillon if using other meats) dissolved in 1½ C water
5 t	cornstarch blended with 2 T water
4	green onions, shredded
1 T	sesame oil

Method:

1. Drop the noodles into 3 qts of rapidly boiling water. Add 1 T salt to the water and cook for 3-5 minutes. Stir with a pair of chopsticks to prevent stickiness. Rinse the cooked noodles under cold water thoroughly. Drain well then mix with 1 T oil. Set aside.

2. Marinate beef with the next 6 ingredients. Set aside.

3. Heat 4 T oil in a non-stick pan or wok; add noodles and fry until brown. Turn over and brown. Remove to a serving platter and keep hot.

4. Add 1 T oil in the same pan, stir-fry meat until color turns. Remove.

5. Put the last 8 ingredients in the pan; stir and cook until the cabbages become tender. Add cooked meat then pour over the fried noodles. Serve hot.

Shredded chicken, pork or shelled fresh or frozen shrimp can be used in this dish. Marinate them in the same way as the beef. This dish would then be called chicken Chow Mein, pork Chow Mein or shrimp Chow Mein, respectively.

Calories: 1920	Iron: 15mg
Carbohydrates: 127gm	Vit. B1: 0.6mg
Protein: 80gm	Vit. B2: 1.4mg
Fat: 121gm	Vit. A: 2043IU
Cholesterol: 410mg	Vit. C: 49mg
Calcium: 247mg	Fiber: 3gm

DAN DAN NOODLES (VENDER'S NOODLES)
(Dan Dan Mian)

Ingredients:

- 2 T   sesame paste, or peanut butter
- 1 T   oil
- ¼ t   pepper
- 1 T   sesame oil
- 2 T   soy sauce
- 1 T   vinegar
- 2   cloves of garlic, minced
- 2 T   minced Sichuan pickle
- 2 t   red oil or more
- ¼ t   Sichuan peppercorn powder
- 2   green onions, minced
- 1 t   finely minced ginger root
- 1 oz   cooked and shredded meat
- 2 oz   thin Chinese noodles
- 1 C   chicken broth, canned or 1 chicken bouillon cube dissolved in 2 C water

Method:

1. Mix the first 12 ingredients in a small bowl; set aside.
2. Boil the chicken broth in a small sauce pan and keep hot.
3. Fill a medium sauce pan half full of water. Cover pan and bring to a boil.
4. Add noodles and stir with a pair of chopsticks to keep noodles separate. Cook the noodles until they are done (about 5 minutes).
5. Transfer the noodles to 3-4 rice bowls with a pair of chopsticks. Add 1/2-1/3 C of chicken broth, the sauce mixture from Step 1, and meat shreds in each bowl. Mix well before eating.

This noodle dish may be served as a snack (Dim Sum), for breakfast, or for one of the many courses at a formal dinner or banquet. Serve with a pair of chopsticks and a spoon.

Calories: 800   Carbohydrates: 192gm
Protein: 96gm   Fat: 504gm

炸醬麵

Ingredients:

½ lb   thin spaghetti or Chinese noodles
½ lb   ground pork
  2 T   soy sauce
  2 t   cornstarch
  1 T   oil
    3   cloves of garlic, minced
  1 C   shredded vegetables of your choice (carrot, cucumber, optional)
  ½ C   Hoisin sauce
    2   thin slices of ginger root, minced
    3   green onions, minced
  ¼ t   pepper
  1 T   sherry
  ½ C   water
        Hot pepper sauce or oil to your taste (optional)

Method:

1. Cook the spaghetti as directions indicate. Rinse and drain; place in a serving dish.

2. Mix the next 3 ingredients together in a small bowl. Set aside.

3. Heat oil in a pan or wok; add pork mixture and garlic. Stir and cook over medium heat until the meat separates and is cooked.

4. Add the last 8 ingredients; stir and cook until the sauce thickens.

5. Pour the sauce over the cooked noodles. Mix before serving. Serve hot.

Makes 4-6 servings.

Calories:	1519	Iron:	18mg
Carbohydrates:	196gm	Vit. B1:	4mg
Protein:	88gm	Vit. B2:	1.4mg
Fat:	39gm	Vit. A:	614IU
Cholesterol:	142mg	Vit. C:	2gm
Calcium:	207mg	Fiber:	2gm

STEAMED MEAT IN NOODLE CASE
(Shao Mai)

烧賣

Ingredients:

½ lb	ground lean pork butt or ¼ lb ground pork and ¼ lb coarsely chopped raw shrimp
¼ C	water chestnuts or bamboo shoots, coarsely minced
¼ C	or more minced onion
3/4 t	salt
1 T	sherry
2 t	ginger root, minced fine
¼ t	pepper
3	dried mushrooms, soaked and minced
1 T	sesame oil
1/8 t	MSG (optional)
2 t	cornstarch
2 T	egg shreds, minced (page 197) (optional)
2	green onions, minced (use the green parts) (optional)
1 oz	minced long-cured dried ham or Canadian ham (optional)
20	pieces of Wonton skin, about ¼ pound (sold in supermarket in produce section)

Method:

1. Mix the first 11 ingredients together thoroughly in a mixing bowl. This mixture will be used as filling.

2. Place 1 heaping teaspoonful of filling on the center of a Wonton skin and moisten the sides with a little water. Gather the sides up to the meat to form a cylindrical shaped noodle case. Press to make sure the skin sticks to the filling. With kitchen scissors trim the corners of the Wonton skin.

3. Flatten the top; garnish with a few pieces of minced ham, onion and egg shreds.

4. Place the noodle cases in an upright position in an oil-brushed tier of a steamer; cover and steam over boiling water for 20 minutes. Serve hot as lunch, a snack, or as a main dish.

Leftover noodle cases can be reheated by steaming for a few minutes. The noodle cases can be frozen after being steamed. Thaw and resteam for a few minutes before serving.

Makes 20 noodles cases.

Calories: 912
Carbohydrates: 55gm
Protein: 71gm
Fat: 43mg
Cholesterol: 294mg
Calcium: 87mg

Iron: 9mg
Vit. B1: 1.2mg
Vit. B2: 0.4mg
Vit. A: 1120IU
Vit. C: 10mg
Fiber: 1gm

Photographs by Sherl White

1. Place heaping teaspoonful of filling in center of Wonton skin.

2. Gather up sides to form cylindrical shape.

3. With scissors trim corners of Wonton skin.

4. Flatten top and press skin to filling.

BASIC FRIED RICE
(Chao Fan)

Ingredients:

3 C	hot cooked rice made from long grain rice (recipe on page 368)
2	eggs, beaten with a pinch of salt
4-5 T	oil
1	onion, chopped
2 T	soy sauce or to taste*
1 C	frozen peas and carrots (about 5 oz) thawed
½-1 C	ham (about 2-4 oz), cut into the size of the frozen carrots, or ½ lb of pork, chicken, or shrimp, diced and mixed with 1 T soy sauce and 1-2 t cornstarch.
½ C	minced celery or more
1/8 t	pepper
3-4	dried mushrooms, soaked and diced, or ¼ lb fresh mushrooms washed and diced (optional)
1 T	sesame oil

Method:

1. Heat 2 T oil in a non-stick pan or wok; scramble eggs. Break the eggs into small pieces and set aside.

2. Add 2 T oil; brown onion. Add hot rice and soy sauce. Stir and cook until soy sauce covers the rice evenly.

3. Add the last 6 ingredients; stir and cook until all the ingredients are heated. Add scrambled eggs and mix well. Serve hot.

If pork, chicken or shrimp is used, stir-fry the meat after the eggs are scrambled. Remove and set aside. Add cooked meat at Step 3 of the "Method." The fried rice will then be called Pork-fried rice, Chicken-fried rice, or Shrimp-fried rice, etc.

Makes 4-6 servings.

*Soy sauce gives the fried rice a brownish color. For white fried rice, omit soy sauce and use 1 t salt (or refer to recipe in *Nutrition and Diet with Chinese Cooking*, pages 222-229).

Calories: 1505	Cholesterol: 514mg	Vit. B2: 1.3 mg
Carbohydrates: 176gm	Calcium: 191mg	Vit. A: 14832IU
Protein: 42gm	Iron: 11mg	Vit. C: 26mg
Fat: 78gm	Vit. B1: 1.5mg	Fiber: 3gm

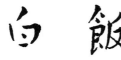 白 飯

Ingredients:

    1 C   medium or long grain rice, enriched
    2 C   water

Method:

1. Place the rice and water in a small sauce pan; cover and bring to a boil.

2. Remove lid; continue boiling over medium-high heat until water has completely evaporated.

3. Cover pan tightly. Reduce heat to lowest setting; simmer the rice for 20 minutes. Turn off heat but do not open lid until time to use the cooked rice.

Do not stir the rice or open the lid while simmering!

If amount of rice is doubled, do not double the amount of water but add enough water to the pan to cover rice about 1".

If you follow the method faithfully, the result will be dry, fluffy rice with no mess and no rice stuck to the pan. This method of cooking rice is only good for small amounts (1-3 cups). When cooking larger amounts, the quantity of water should be readjusted.

Makes 3 cups of cooked rice.

Calories: 670	Iron: 5mg
Carbohydrates: 149gm	Vit. B1: 0.8mg
Protein: 12gm	Vit. B2: 0.06mg
Fat: 1gm	Vit. A: 0
Cholesterol: 0	Vit. C: 0
Calcium: 44mg	Fiber: 1.5gm

SEASONED RICE WITH VEGETABLES
(Cai Fan)

Ingredients:

1	onion, chopped
2	cloves of garlic, sliced
2 T	oil
¼ lb	country-style ham, diced
1 lb	Bok Choy, cut into 1" sections
½ lb	fresh tomatoes, cut into 1" cubes
1 C	long grain rice
1 t	salt
¼ t	pepper
2 C	water

Method:

1. Heat oil in a medium sauce pan; saute onion and garlic. Add ham dices; stir and mix for 1 minute.

2. Add Bok Choy and tomato; stir for 1 minute.

3. Add rice, salt, pepper, and water; mix well. Cover pan; bring the rice to a boil. Uncover and cook until the water is completely evaporated.

4. Cover pan tightly and simmer over the lowest heat for 20 minutes.

Do not uncover pan while rice is simmering.
This rice can be served as a snack, for lunch or as a complete meal.

Makes 4-6 servings.

Calories: 1347	Iron: 9mg
Carbohydrates: 166gm	Vit. B1: 1mg
Protein: 42gm	Vit. B2: 1mg
Fat: 57gm	Vit. A: 2710IU
Cholesterol: 47mg	Vit. C: 125mg
Calcium: 279mg	Fiber: 5gm

ZONG OR TSUNG TZE
(Zong Zi)

Tsung Tze is rice wrapped in fresh leaves of the reed which is then cooked and served hot. It is a special food which is made to commemorate a great ancient statesman and poet, Ch'u Yan 屈原

The story dates back to 295 B.C. when China was divided into feudal states and ruled by a score of rulers. Ch'u Yan was a loyal and faithful minister under the Prince of Huai 懷 of the Chu 楚 State. His loyalty to the Prince never failed. He enjoyed the full confidence of the Prince's sovereignty until he was impeached through the intrigues of rivals. During the impeachment he wrote poems expressing the hope that one day he would regain the confidence of the Prince, but to no avail. Some of his poems became classics in Chinese literature, such as, "Falling into Trouble" 離騷 . Finally, he gave up all hope and plunged into the river of Mi-lo 泊羅, and was never seen again. This took place on the 5th of the 5th moon. The people of Chu loved Ch'u Yan for his fidelity and virtues. They made Tsung Tze and cast it into the river to commemorate him. Ever after, the 5th of the 5th moon has become an annual festival 端午節 . Wrapping and eating Tsung Tze became a tradition which is still celebrated to date.

MEAT ZONG
(Rou Zong)

肉 粽

Ingredients:

1 lb	pork (butt, loin or fresh ham, etc.)
3½ T	soy sauce
2-4	green onions, shredded
¼ t	pepper
2-4	slices of ginger root
½ t	five spice powder
1 T	sherry
¼ t	MSG or more
2 lb	glutinous rice
4 T	soy sauce
½ t	pepper
½ t	onion powder
½-1 lb	dried Zong leaves, reed or bamboo, sold in Oriental grocery stores

Method:

1. Cut the pork into 2"x½"x½" strips; marinate with the next 7 ingredients overnight.

2. Soak the Zong leaves in warm water until softened (about 6 hours or overnight).

3. Soak rice in cold water for 2 hours. Drain. Mix the rice with the next 3 ingredients.

4. Place 2-3 Zong leaves on a flat surface so that they are parallel and overlap about 1 inch.

5. With scissors, trim both ends so that the leaves make a rectangle about 6" wide and 12"-15" long.

6. Fold the long side of the rectangle into three pieces, overlapped in the middle.

7. Fold the bottom edge up about 1".

8. Open the top side. (Now the whole thing becomes an open package.)

9. Place 2-3 T rice in the folded leaf, then 2-3 pieces of pork; cover the pork with 2-3 T more rice.

10. Make the whole a tight package by folding the top over about 1-2 inches.

11. Tie from top to bottom with string in three places, each about 3-4 inches apart, making a neat bundle.

12. Place the wrapped Zong in a large deep sauce pan. Add water until 2/3 full. Cover pan and bring to a boil. Reduce to low heat and simmer for 3-5 hours or until the rice is cooked. Move the top Zongs to the bottom of the pan once during the cooking process.

13. Remove from pan; unwrap and cut the contents into 2-3 pieces. Serve hot. Makes 18-20 Zongs.

Zong leaves can be soaked ahead of time.

Calories: 4060	Cholesterol: 283mg	Vit. B2: 1.5mg
Carbohydrates: 727gm	Calcium: 462mg	Vit. A: 400IU
Protein: 139gm	Iron: 35mg	Vit. C: 6mg
Fat: 52gm	Vit. B1: 4.7mg	Fiber: 3gm

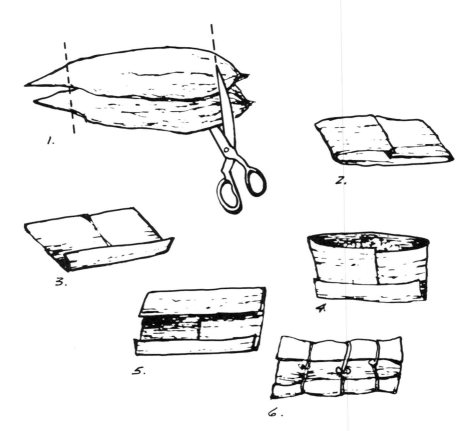

1.

2.

3.

4.

5.

6.

ASSORTED MEAT AND NUT ZONG
(Shi Jin Rou Zong)

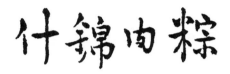

Ingredients:

- 2 lb glutinous rice
- 4 T soy sauce
- ¼ oz dried shrimp, soaked and drained
- 20 dried chestnuts, soaked and drained
- ½ lb old-fashioned, country-style ham, diced
- ¼ C coarsely minced Sichuan pickles
- ½ C soaked and diced dried mushrooms
- 1 onion, diced
- 1 t minced ginger root
- ½ t pepper
- ¼ t MSG
- Zong leaves, dried or fresh

Method:

1. Soak the Zong leaves in cold water overnight or until softened. Soak the rice in cold water for 2 hours. Rinse.
2. Mix the rice with the next 10 ingredients.
3. Follow the meat Zong recipe from Steps 4-8 (page 371).
4. Fill the folded leaf 2/3 full with the rice mixture.
5. Follow the meat Zong recipe from Steps 10-13 (page 371-372). Serve hot.

Zong leaves can be soaked ahead of time.

Calories: 4540
Carbohydrates: 780gm
Protein: 164gm
Fat: 71gm
Cholesterol: 604mg
Calcium: 649mg

Iron: 30mg
Vit. B1: 1mg
Vit. B2: 1.1mg
Vit. A: 22IU
Vit. C: 7mg
Fiber: 5gm

红 豆 粽

Ingredients:

- 1 lb   glutinous rice
- ½ C   Chinese small red beans
- ¼ C   sugar
- ½ lb   dried Zong leaves, reed or bamboo

Method:

1. Soak the Zong leaves in cold water for 6 hours or until they are soften.
2. Soak the beans overnight; rinse and drain.
3. Soak the rice in cold water for 2 hours; rinse and drain.
4. Mix the rice and beans in a bowl.
5. Follow Steps 4-8 of the meat Zong recipe (page 371) to fold the leaves.
6. Fill the leaf pocket 2/3 full with the rice and bean mixture.
7. To cook, follow Steps 10-13 of the Meat Zong recipe. Serve hot with sugar or syrup (page 375).

Makes 12-14 Zongs.

Calories: 2140	Cholesterol: 0	Vit. B2: 0.4 mg
Carbohydrate: 468 gm	Calcium: 265 mg	Vit. A: 20IU
Protein: 47 gm	Iron: 16 mg	Vit. C: 0
Fat: 6 gm	Vit. B1: 0.8 mg	Fiber: 5 gm

豆 沙 甜 粽

Ingredients:

- 2 lb   glutinous rice
- 1   18 oz can sweetened red bean paste, sold in Oriental grocery stores.
  Zong leaves, dried, about ½-1 pound (reed or bamboo)

Method:

1. Soak the Zong leaves in cold water until softened (about 6 hours or overnight).

2. Soak the rice in cold water for two hours; rinse and drain.

3. Follow the Steps 4-8 of the meat Zong recipe (page 371) to fold the leaves.

4. Fill the leaf pocket with 2-3 T rice, 1 T bean paste, then 2-3 T more rice.

5. Follow Steps 10-13 of Meat Zong to cook.

6. Dip the Zong in sugar or syrup (page 375) before eating.
Serve Hot.
Makes 20-24 Zongs.

The nutrition information of the red bean paste is not available, so the calculation of the nutrition information of this recipe can not be done.

ALL PURPOSE SYRUP
(Si Ji Tang Jiang)

四季糖浆水

Ingredients:

- 1 C   sugar
- 1 C   water
- ½ C   honey
- ½   lemon, sliced
- 1   stick cinnamon

Method:

1. Put all the ingredients in a small sauce pan; cook and stir until the sugar dissolves.

2. Boil without stirring until the sauce thickens. Cool before serving.

Calories: 1295	Cholesterol: 0	Vit. B2: 0.8mg
Carbohydrates: 341gm	Calcium: 22mg	Vit. A: 11IU
Protein: 1gm	Iron: 1mg	Vit. C: 30mg
Fat: 0	Vit. B1: 0.2mg	Fiber: 0

红豆蒸糕

RED BEAN STEAMED CAKE
(Hong Dou You Gao)

Ingredients:

1 C	or less, Chinese small red beans or kidney beans
3 C	water
1 C	flour
¾ C	sugar
½ C	oil or lard
2	eggs
½ t	salt
1 t	baking powder
½ T	baking soda
1 t	vanilla

Method:

1. Wash the beans. Place the beans in a medium sauce pan; add water, cover and bring to a boil.

2. Reduce to low heat; cook until the beans are tender and the liquid is reduced to half a cup. (If the beans are tender but too much liquid remains, increase to high heat and cook without covering until liquid evaporates. Add more water if needed.) Cool.

3. Grease a deep heat-proof dish. Set aside.

4. Cream the last 7 ingredients in a mixing bowl. Add cooked beans and flour; mix well.

5. Pour the batter into the greased dish. Set the dish in a boiling steamer and steam for 40-50 minutes.

6. Cut the steamed cake into desired shapes. Serve warm or cold, with or without syrup (page 375).

Green beans (Mung beans) can be used in the same manner. The beans can be reduced to ½ C.

Makes 10 servings.

Calories: 2645		Iron: 15mg	
Carbohydrates: 321gm		Vit. B1: 1mg	
Protein: 62gm		Vit. B2: 0.7mg	
Fat: 127gm		Vit. A: 1213IU	
Cholesterol: 468mg		Vit. C: 0	
Calcium: 256mg		Fiber: 7gm	

RED BEAN NEW YEAR CAKE
(Hong Dou Nian Gao)

Ingredients:

1 C	Chinese small red beans or kidney beans
3 C	water
¾ C	sugar
1 t	vanilla
¼ t	salt
1½ C	glutinous rice powder

Method:

1. Wash the beans. Place the beans in a medium sauce pan. Add water; cover and bring to a boil.

2. Reduce to low heat; cook until the beans are tender and the liquid is reduced to ½ C. (If the beans are tender but too much liquid remains, increase to high heat and cook without covering until the liquid evaporates. Add more water if it is needed).

3. Add sugar and mix well. Cool.

4. Line a 9″ layer cake pan with a piece of plastic wrap. Set aside.

5. Add glutinous rice powder, vanilla, and salt to the cooked beans to form a batter.

6. Pour the batter into the cake pan. Set the pan in a boiling steamer and steam for 1 hour. Cool.

7. Cut the cake into 2″ x 1″ strips. Serve hot by resteaming the cake strips for 5 minutes or fry in a little oil until the cake is soft. Add a little syrup if desired, (page 375).

When doubling or tripling the recipe, this cake can be steamed in the tier of the steamer. Put a damp cheese cloth on the tier of the steamer. Pour the batter over the cheese cloth. Smooth the batter and steam 80-90 minutes.

Makes 4-6 servings.

Calories: 1842		Iron:	16mg
Carbohydrates: 402gm		Vit. B1:	1mg
Protein: 50gm		Vit. B2:	0.4mg
Fat: 4gm		Vit. A:	321IU
Cholesterol: 0		Vit. C:	0
Calcium: 260mg		Fiber:	8gm

蒸　糕

Ingredients:

- 1 C   flour
- 1 t   baking powder
- ¾ t   baking soda
- ½ C   brown or white sugar
- ¾ C   oil
- 2 t   vanilla
- 2   eggs
- ¼ t   salt
- ¼ C   water

Method:

1. Mix the first 3 ingredients in a container.
2. Beat the last 6 ingredients in a mixing bowl.
3. Add flour mixture to the egg mixture and mix well.
4. Grease a deep heat-proof dish and dust with flour. Pour the batter into the dish.
5. Steam the batter in a boiling, covered steamer for 45 minutes. Turn the cake upside down on a platter while it is warm. Cut the cake into pieces before serving. Serve at room temperature with a little syrup if you wish (page 375).

Makes 6-10 servings.

Calories:	2683	Iron:	9mg
Carbohydrates:	248gm	Vit. B1:	0.2mg
Protein:	25gm	Vit. B2:	0.4mg
Fat:	180gm	Vit. A:	1180IU
Cholesterol:	468mg	Vit. C:	0
Calcium:	215mg	Fiber:	0.3gm

**COCONUT AND SESAME
RICE CAKE PATTIES**
(Ye Zi Zi Ma Gao)

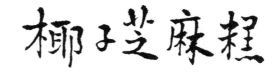

Ingredients:

¼ C   sesame seeds, toasted
¾ C   sweetened flaked coconut
1 C   glutinous rice powder
¼ C   sugar
1/3-½ C   water

Method:

1. Toast the sesame seeds in a 350° oven for 10 mintues. (Or place in a wok and stir over high heat for 1 minute.)

2. Mix the coconut and sesame seeds together in a dish. Set aside.

3. Mix the rice powder and sugar in a bowl. Gradually add 1/3 C of water to the rice powder and mix. If the dough is too dry, add more water until the dough is easy to handle.

4. Fill a medium-sized sauce pan half full of water.

5. Form 1" balls from the dough; drop the balls into the boiling water and bring to a boil. Reduce to medium heat and cook for 2 minutes. Remove.

6. Roll the cooked rice balls in the coconut mixture until covered.

7. Flatten the balls into 2" patties. Serve warm or at room temperature.

Makes about one dozen of rice patties.

Makes 4-6 servings.

Calories: 1222
Carbohydrates: 179gm
Protein: 18gm
Fat: 51gm
Cholesterol: 0
Calcium: 502mg

Iron: 8mg
Vit. B1: 0.5mg
Vit. B2: 0.2mg
Vit. A: 11IU
Vit. C: 0
Fiber: 5gm

反穿皮襖   GLUTINOUS BALLS IN SESAME POWDER
(Fan Chuan Pi Ao)

Ingredients:

 1 ½ C   glutinous rice powder
 2 T   sugar
 ½ C   water
 ½ C   black sesame seeds
 ½ C   powdered sugar

Method:

1. Toast sesame seeds in a 300° oven for 12 minutes. Cool.

2. Mix the toasted sesame seeds with the powdered sugar. Place the mixture in a covered blender, and blend into a fine powder. Transfer to a dish.

3. Mix the rice powder and sugar in a bowl. Add water; mix and knead. If it is too dry, add more water. Knead the dough with hands until smooth.

4. Form ¾" diameter balls from the dough.

5. Fill a medium sauce pan 1/3 full of water and bring to a boil.

6. Add the glutinous rice balls; cover and bring to a boil. Add ½ C of cold water and cook over medium heat until the rice balls float on the surface of the water.

7. Remove the cooked rice balls with a slotted spoon. Cool for a few seconds. Put the cooked rice balls in the sesame powder, two at a time. Shake the dish until a layer of the powder covers them. Repeat for remainder of rice balls. Serve at room temperature immediately.

Makes approximately 1½ dozen ¾" glutinous rice balls.

Calories: 1770		Cholesterol: 0		Vit. B2: 0.3mg	
Carbohydrates: 326gm		Calcium: 981mg		Vit. A: 0	
Protein: 29gm		Iron: 13mg		Vit. C: 0	
Fat: 39gm		Vit. B1: 0.9mg		Fiber: 5gm	

LAUGHING BALLS
(Kai Kao Xiao)

Ingredients:

- 1 C   flour
- ¾ t   baking powder
- 2/3 C   sugar
- ¼ t   salt
- 1 T   oil
- 1 t   vanilla
- 1   egg
- 1-3 T   water or more
-   Oil for deep-frying
- ¼ C   sesame seeds

Method:

1. Put the first 7 ingredients in a mixing bowl. Mix thoroughly to form a dough. If it is too dry, add water a little at a time, until the dough is held together.

2. Form the dough into ¾" balls. Dip in cold water then coat with a thin layer of sesame seeds. Press seeds to make them stick.

3. Heat oil in a pan or wok to 350°. Deep-fry the balls over medium heat until they are golden brown and have cracks (like a laughing mouth). Serve cold.

Makes 4-6 servings.

Calories:	1475	Iron:	6mg
Carbohydrates:	237gm	Vit. B1:	0.49mg
Protein:	25gm	Vit. B2:	0.29mg
Fat:	61gm	Vit. A:	601IU
Cholesterol:	234mg	Vit. C:	0
Calcium:	485mg	Fiber:	3gm

(Calculated with 5 T of oil for deep-frying.)

圆

Ingredients:

For Wrapper:

- 1 C　glutinous rice powder
- ¼ C　cornstarch
- 9-10 T　water

Mix the rice powder and cornstarch in a bowl. Add water gradually to the rice powder to form a dough. (Makes enough wrappers for about 2-3 dozen ¾″ diameter balls).

I. MEAT FILLING:

- ¼ lb　ground pork or beef
- 1 T　sherry
- 1½ T　soy sauce
- ⅛ t　pepper
- ¼ t　minced ginger root
- 1　green onion, minced
- 2　water chestnuts, minced
- 2 T　water (optional)
- ½ t　sugar

Mix all the ingredients together thoroughly. Chill.
Makes 2-3 dozen portions for filling.
Nutrition information of the meat filling and wrapper:

Calories: 827	Cholesterol: 71mg	Vit. B2: 0.4mg
Carbohydrates: 141gm	Calcium: 85mg	Vit. A: 200IU
Protein: 30gm	Iron: 7mg	Vit. C: 3mg
Fat: 12gm	Vit. B1: 1.1mg	Fiber: 0.6gm

II. SESAME SEED FILLING 芝蔴湯圓
(Zi Ma Tang Yuan)

½ C   black sesame seeds, roasted in 300° oven for 12 min. Cool.
½ C   powdered sugar
¼ C   lard

Blend the cold, roasted sesame seeds with the sugar in a covered blender for 1 minute. Transfer to a dish and mix with lard. Makes 2-3 dozen small balls. Chill or keep frozen before using as filling.

III. BEAN PASTE FILLING 豆沙湯圓
(Dou Sa Tang Yuan)

Canned bean paste, sold in Oriental grocery stores

IV. COCONUT AND SESAME SEED FILLING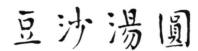

¼ C   Sesame seeds, roasted in 300° oven for 12 minutes. Cool.
½ C   flaked coconut
½ C   powdered sugar
1/3 C   lard

Blend the first 3 ingredients in a covered blender for 1 minute. Transfer to a bowl and mix with lard. Makes 2-3 dozen small balls. Chill or keep frozen before using as filling.

To wrap:

1. Divide the dough into 2-3 dozen portions. Roll each portion into a smooth ball.

2. Press thumb in the dough to make an opening. Use cornstarch to avoid stickiness.

3. Put a chilled ball of filling of your choice in the opening; then carefully close it. Smooth the filled dough balls with the palms of your hands. They are now ready to cook. (Keep the filled balls on a floured tray until used.)

To cook:

1. Boil 2 cups of water in a medium sauce pan. Add the filled balls, 10-12 at a time; bring to a boil. Stir gently with the back of a wooden spoon to prevent the balls from sticking to each other. Cover and bring to a boil.

2. Add ½ C cold water, cover and bring to a boil.

3. Add ½ C cold water once more, cover and bring to a boil.

4. Transfer the cooked balls with a small amount of water to rice bowls or dessert bowls. Serve hot with spoon.

芝麻餅干

SESAME COOKIES
(Zi Ma Pian Gan)

Ingredients:

2 C	flour
2/3 C	(or more) sugar
¼ t	baking powder
¼ t	salt
¾ C	oil
2-3 T	water
1	egg
1 T	sesame oil
½ C	sesame seeds

Method:

1. Mix the first 4 ingredients in a mixing bowl. Add oil, water, egg, and sesame oil; mix well to form a dough.

2. Put the sesame seeds on a plate.

3. Form the cookie dough into 1" balls. Dip the balls in a small dish of cold water, then roll the balls in sesame seeds one by one. Flatten the balls into ¼" patties. Be sure a layer of sesame seeds adheres to both sides of the dough.

4. Place the sesame-seed coated cookies on an ungreased cookie sheet. Bake at 350° preheated oven for 15 minutes.

Makes approximately 2½-3 dozen cookies.

Approximately 112 calories per cookie (for 2½ dozen).

Approximately 93 calories per cookie (for 3 dozen).

Calories: 3489	Cholesterol: 234mg	Vit. B2: 0.44mg
Carbohydrates: 330gm	Calcium: 944mg	Vit. A: 612IU
Protein: 44gm	Iron: 11mg	Vit. C: 0
Fat: 227	Vit. B1: 1mg	Fiber: 5gm

SA JI MA
(Sha Ji Ma)

沙其馬

Ingredients:

1 C	all purpose flour
2	eggs
1 t	vanilla
2-4 T	raisins
2 T	roasted sesame seeds
	Oil for deep-frying
½ C	water
½ C	corn syrup
½ C	sugar
1	1/6" slice of fresh lemon

Method:

1. Mix flour, egg and vanilla into a dough. Knead the dough on a floured board until smooth. Cover with wax paper. Set aside.

2. Put the last 4 ingredients in a small sauce pan; cook and stir over medium heat until the sugar dissolves. Boil without stirring until the sauce thickens. Set aside.

3. Roll the dough ⅛" thin. Cut into 2" wide strips. Dust with flour to prevent sticking while processing. Cut the strips into thin shreds.

4. Heat oil in a pan or wok. Add the shreds and fry until light brown. Put in a large mixing bowl.

5. Pour the syrup over the fried dough. Add raisins and toasted sesame seeds; mix gently. (Make sure every shred is coated with the syrup).

6. Pat mixture into a greased pan. Press lightly then chill in the refrigerator for a few hours. Cut into 2" squares before serving.

Makes 10-12 bars.

Calories: 3107	Cholesterol: 468mg	Vit. B2: 0.3mg
Carbohydrates: 330gm	Calcium: 381mg	Vit. A: 1191IU
Protein: 28gm	Iron: 13mg	Vit. C: 0.3mg
Fat: 192gm	Vit. B1: 0.4mg	Fiber: 2gm

Calculated with 5 T oil

脆麻花

SESAME TWIST
(Cui Ma Hua)

Ingredients:

- 1 C flour
- 1 egg
- 1/3 C sugar
- 3 T sesame seed
- ⅛ t salt
- 2-4 T water
- Oil for deep-frying

Method:

1. Mix the first 5 ingredients in a mixing bowl. Add water gradually, 1 T at a time, until the dough is easy to handle.
2. Knead the dough on a floured board for a few minutes until smooth.
3. On a floured board, roll the dough to a 1/8″ thickness.
4. Cut the dough into 2″x1″ rectangular pieces; cut a slit through the middle, lengthwise, about 1½″ long.
5. Lift up the whole piece of dough and push one end through the slit. Straighten dough into a rectangular shape again.
6. Deep-fry the dough until golden brown. Serve hot or cold.

Makes 4-6 servings.

Calories: 1519	Cholesterol: 234mg	Vit. B2: 0.3mg
Carbohydrates: 157gm	Calcium: 369mg	Vit. A: 598IU
Protein: 23gm	Iron: 5mg	Vit. C: 0
Fat: 90gm	Vit. B1: 0.4mg	Fiber: 2mg

Calculated with 5 T oil for deep-frying.

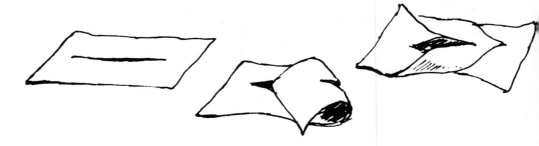

SWEET BEAN PASTE PASTRIES
(Zi Ma Dou Sha Bing)

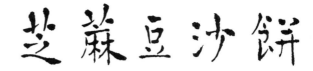

Ingredients:

9 oz	sweetened red bean paste, canned (sold in Oriental stores)
½ C	sesame seeds, regular or black
3 C	flour
¾ C	shortening, oil or lard
¼ C	hot water or more
4-6 T	sugar
¼ t	salt

Method:

1. Follow Steps 3-6 for Radish Cake (page 354) for pastry dough. Note: More sugar is used in Step 4 in this recipe.

2. Cut the cylindrical roll into 20 equal pieces. Roll each piece of the dough (not the cut side) into a 5" round wrapper.

3. Place 1½ T bean paste on the center of the wrapper. Fold the wrapper to cover the bean paste and seal. Turn the folded side down.

4. Flatten the pastry into a ½" thick round cake, about 3" in diameter.

5. Brush a layer of water on top of the pastry, then dip the top in sesame seeds. (A layer of sesame seeds should cover and stick onto the pastry.) Repeat to make 20 pastries.

6. Spread 2 T oil on a non-stick pan or skillet; arrange the pastries in the pan folded side down. Add ½ C water to the pan; cover and bring to a boil.

7. Reduce to low heat and cook until the water evaporates and a layer of light brown crust is formed on the bottom of the pastries.

8. Turn the pastries and brown the sesame seeds (takes only a few seconds).

9. Remove the pastries to a cookie sheet and bake in a preheated oven at 375° for 3-5 minutes. Serve hot.

Makes 20 pastries.

No nutrition information on canned bean paste is available therefore the calculation of the nutrition information of this recipe cannot be done.

 饅 頭

Ingredients:

½ oz	dry yeast (2 packages)
⅓ -½ C	sugar
2 C	warm water
½ t	salt
⅛ -¼ C	oil
5 C	all purpose flour (or ⅔ white and ⅓ whole wheat flour).
1 T	baking powder

Method:

1. Mix yeast and sugar in a small bowl; add ½ C warm water to soften the yeast.

2. Put 1 ½ C warm water in a large mixing bowl. Add yeast mixture and the rest of the ingredients; blend well.

3. Cover the bowl with a damp towel. Let the dough rise until double in bulk (about 1-2 hours, depending upon the temperature).

4. Place the dough on a floured board and knead for 5-8 minutes. Knead additional flour into the dough if it is too sticky.

5. Divide the dough into 4 portions. Form each portion into a bread loaf or round bun.

6. Place a piece of waxed paper under each loaf. Let rise again until double in bulk (about 1 hour).

7. Arrange the bread loaves, with the waxed paper, in tiers of a steamer and steam over boiling water for 15-18 minutes. Serve hot.

The bread slices best when it is cold. Resteam cold bread slices for 3 minutes before serving. Bread slices can be toasted for breakfast or reheated in a microwave oven.

Steamed bread can be kept frozen for months. Place in a plastic bag and seal tightly before freezing.

The bread dough can also be used as wrappers for meat or sweet-bean paste stuffed buns (Pao).

Raisins, cut-up dried fruit, nuts, or cinnamon can be added to the dough for variations. Makes four loaves.

Calories:	2615	Carbohydrates:	509gm
Protein:	63gm	Fat:	32gm

SPUN APPLE OR CANDIED APPLE
(Ba Si Pin Gao)

枝絲蘋果

Ingredients:

  ¼ C   all purpose flour
  2 T   cornstarch
  1   egg
  1 T   or more water
  3   small sized apples
       Oil for deep-frying
       Flour for sprinkling on apple pieces before coating with batter (about 1 T)
  1   large bowl of ice cold water
2-3 T   sesame seeds (black sesame seeds are preferred)
  1 C   sugar
  ¼ C   water
  1 T   oil

Method:

1. Mix the first 4 ingredients in a bowl to form a smooth batter.

2. Peel the apples. Cut each apple into quarters and remove cores.

3. Heat oil for deep-frying in a pan or wok to 375°.

4. Sprinkle a thin layer of flour over the apple pieces. Drop the apples into batter. Deep-fry apple pieces one by one until brown. Transfer fried apples to a dish and keep warm.

5. Heat 1 T fresh oil in a clean wok. (Do not use a nonstick wok). Add water and sugar; stir gently until sugar dissolves.

6. Cook the sugar solution WITHOUT STIRRING until the syrup thickens and turns light brown in color. (To test: dip the tip of a bamboo chopstick into the syrup, then plunge it into cold water. If the syrup hardens, it is ready to use.)

7. Sprinkle the sesame seeds over the syrup. Reduce to low heat; put the fried apples into the syrup. Stir gently but quickly to coat the apples with a layer of syrup.

8. Immediately drop the fried apples in ice cold water one by one. Transfer to a plate when syrup hardens. Serve warm.

Makes 4-6 servings.

Calories: 1833
Carbohydrates: 296gm
Protein: 13gm
Fat: 73gm
Cholesterol: 234mg
Calcium: 275mg

Iron: 5mg
Vit. B1: 0.4mg
Vit. B2: 0.3mg
Vit. A: 744IU
Vit. C: 8mg
Fiber: 4gm

Calculated with 4 T oil

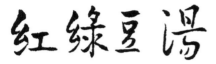

红綠豆湯

DOUBLE BEAN SWEET SOUP
(Hong Lu Dou Tang)

Ingredients:

¾ C   Chinese red beans or kidney beans
½ C   mung beans
1/3 C   large pearl tapioca
1/3 C   (or more) of sugar
5 C   water

Method:

1. Soak the two kinds of beans in cold water for 2 hours. Rinse and drain.

2. Put the soaked beans and tapioca in deep sauce pan; cover and bring to a boil.

3. Reduce to low heat and simmer for 1½-2 hours or until the beans are tender.

4. Add sugar and cook over high heat for 3 minutes. If soup is too thick, add water to make 3-3½ C. Serve hot or cold.

Makes 4-6 servings.

Calories: 1246
Carbohydrates: 261gm
Protein: 49gm
Fat: 3gm
Cholesterol: 0
Calcium: 269mg

Iron: 16mg
Vit. B1: 1mg
Vit. B2: 0.4mg
Vit. A: 521IU
Vit. C: 0
Fiber: 9gm

PINEAPPLE AND ORANGE SWEET SOUP
(Feng Li Ji Zi Geng)

凰梨桔子羹

Ingredients:

- ½ C   tapioca
- 4 C   water
- 1/3 C   sugar (or to taste)
- 1   20 oz can of pineapple tidbits or chunks in heavy syrup
- 1   11 oz can of mandarin orange segments

Method:

1. Put the tapioca and water in a deep sauce pan; cover and bring to a boil.

2. Reduce to low heat and cook for 40 minutes.

3. Add sugar, pineapple, and mandarin oranges and cook over high heat for 3 minutes.

Serve hot or cold.

Add water if too much has evaporated. The total amount of the end product should be 3-3½ C.

Makes 4-6 servings.

Calories: 1254		Iron: 4mg	
Carbohydrates: 320gm		Vit. B1: 0.8mg	
Protein: 6gm		Vit. B2: 0.3mg	
Fat: 1gm		Vit. A: 946IU	
Cholesterol: 0		Vit. C: 200mg	
Calcium: 208mg		Fiber: 4gm	

胡桃椰子糊

COCONUT AND WALNUT SWEET SOUP
(Hu Tao Ye Zi Hu)

Ingredients:

1 C	flaked, sweetened coconut
1 C	walnuts
½-¾ C	sugar
½ t	salt
4 C	water
3 T	cornstarch blended with ½ C water

Method:

1. Blend half of the coconut and walnuts with 2 C of water in a blender for one minute. Pour the blended mixture into a deep sauce pan. Blend the remaining coconut and walnuts with water in the same manner. Pour into the sauce pan.

2. Add sugar and salt and bring to a boil. Turn to medium heat and cook for 5 minutes.

3. Add blended cornstarch and cook until the soup thickens. Serve hot or cold.

Authentically, Chinese people soak the walnuts in boiling water for 5 minutes, then remove the skin. The blanched walnuts are then deep-fried until brown before grinding with the coconut. If this method is followed, the soup tastes more aromatic but the amount of fiber (from the skins of the walnuts) will be reduced.

Makes 4-6 servings.

Calories: 1572	Cholesterol: 0	Vit. B2: 0.2mg
Carbohydrates: 151gm	Calcium: 119mg	Vit. A: 31IU
Protein: 20gm	Iron: 5mg	Vit. C: 2mg
Fat: 108gm	Vit. B1: 0.4mg	Fiber: 5gm

THREE-COLORED BEAN GELATIN
(San Se Dou Ni)

三色豆泥

Ingredients:

- ½ C kidney beans, about 1/5 pound
- 1/3-½ C sugar
- 1 T unflavored gelatin (one envelope)
- 4 C water

- 1¾ C milk
- 1 T unflavored gelatin
- ½ C sugar
- 1 T almond extract

- ½ C green split peas
- 1/3-½ C sugar
- 1 T unflavored gelatin
- 4 C water

Method:

1. Mix sugar and gelatin in a small bowl; set aside.

2. Place the beans and 4 C water in a sauce pan; cover and bring to a boil. Reduce heat and cook until the beans are tender. The total volume of the beans and liquid should be 2 C. Add more water if needed. Cool and blend the beans until smooth. Pour into a sauce pan; add sugar and gelatin mixture and cook until gelatin is melted. Pour into a 11¼"x7½"x1½" tray. Chill in the refrigerator until firm.

2. Mix the ½ C sugar and 1 T gelatin; set aside. Boil 1 C of milk; add sugar and gelatin mixture and stir until gelatin is dissolved. Add ¾ C of cold milk and almond extract. When the liquid is lukewarm, pour over the chilled kidney beans. Chill in the refrigerator until firm.

3. Mix 1/3-½ C sugar with 1 T gelatin and set aside. Wash split peas. Place the peas and 4 C water in a sauce pan; cover and bring to a boil. Reduce heat and cook until the peas are tender and the total volume of the peas and liquid is 2 C. Add more water to make 2 C if necessary. Cool and blend peas in a blender until smooth. Pour the peas in a sauce pan; add sugar and gelatin mixture and cook until gelatin is dissolved. When the pea mixture is lukewarm, pour over the chilled almond gelatin. Chill in the refrigerator until firm.

4. Cut the chilled, three-colored gelatin into 2"x2" squares and garnish with maraschino cherries. Serve cold.

Makes 12-15 pieces.

Calories: 1620	Cholesterol: 42mg	Vit. B2: 1.1mg
Carbohydrates: 300gm	Calcium: 621	Vit. A: 755IU
Protein: 71gm	Iron: 11mg	Vit. C: 0
Fat: 19gm	Vit. B1 1.2mg	Fiber: 5gm

Temple of Heaven, Beijing.

microwave

黄瓜湯

Ingredients:

¼ lb lean pork or chicken breast, thinly sliced
1 T soy sauce
⅛ t onion or garlic powder
⅛ t pepper
1 t minced ginger root
1 t sherry
1 t cornstarch
1-2 green onions, minced
1 t sesame oil
1 cucumber
4 C water
3 chicken bouillon cubes

Method:

1. Mix the first 7 ingredients in a small bowl. Set aside.

2. Peel cucumber and split into halves. Spoon out the seedy portion and cut the cucumber into slices.

3. Place the last 3 ingredients in a 3-quart container suitable for microwave cooking. Cover with plastic wrap and cook in microwave oven on full power for 5-6 minutes.

4. Add meat slices; stir until the meat slices separate. Cover the container and cook on full power for 3 minutes. Garnish with sesame oil and minced onions. Serve hot.

For nutritional value, please see page 60.

MEAT BALL SOUP
(Rou Yuan Tang)

肉丸湯

Ingredients:

- ½ lb   ground beef or pork
- ¼ t   onion or garlic powder
- ⅛ t   pepper
- 1 T   soy sauce
- 1 t   finely minced ginger root
- 1 t   cornstarch
- 2 oz   bean thread
- 5 C   water
- 4 t   chicken or beef bouillon cubes
- ½ lb   celery cabbage, napa or spinach, sliced
- ½ C   sliced bamboo shoots
- ½-1 t   sesame oil
- 1   green onion, minced

Method:

1. Thoroughly mix the first 6 ingredients in a bowl. Form the mixture into ½" balls. Set aside.

2. Soak the bean thread in hot water for 10 minutes. Drain and cut into 2"-3" lengths.

3. Place the last 4 ingredients in a 3-quart container suitable for microwave cooking, cover with plastic wrap and cook in microwave oven on full power for 10 minutes.

4. Drop the meat balls into the cooked liquid, cover and cook on full power for 5 minutes. Garnish with sesame oil and green onion. Serve hot.

For nutritional value, please see page 68.

雪豆牛肉

BEEF WITH SNOW PEA PODS
(Xu Dou Niu Rou)

Ingredients:

1 lb	beef flank steak, sliced in 1″ × 1½″ × ¼″ slices
4 T	oyster sauce or soy sauce
¼ t	pepper
1 t	brown sugar
2-3	green onions, shredded
2 t	finely minced ginger root
1 T	sherry
1 T	sesame oil
2 T	oil
1 T	cornstarch
½ lb	fresh pea pods, washed, cleaned, and dried
½ C	bamboo shoots, sliced
1/3 t	salt
1 T	oil

Method:

1. Mix the first 10 ingredients thoroughly in a 10″ × 10″ × 2″ container suitable for microwave cooking. Cover the container with plastic wrap and cook in microwave oven on full power for 4 minutes. Transfer the meat to a dish.

2. Place the last 4 ingredients in the same container, toss gently so that the seasonings will penetrate the pea pods evenly. Cover the container with plastic wrap and cook in microwave oven on full power for 3 minutes.

3. Add cooked meat to the pea pods; cover and cook on full power for 1 minute. Serve hot.

For nutritional value, please see page 86.

BEEF WITH BROCCOLI
(Niu Rou Chao Jie Hua)

牛肉炒芥花

Ingredients:

¾ lb beef flank steak, sliced into 1½" × 1" × 1/6" slices
3 T oyster sauce
¼ t pepper
1 t brown sugar
¼ t onion or garlic powder
1 T sherry
1 t or more finely minced ginger root
1 t sesame oil
1 T cornstarch
2 T oil
2 stalks of broccoli, cut into 1" pieces
1-2 green onions, shredded
½ t salt
2 T oil

Method:

1. Mix the first 10 ingredients thoroughly in a bowl. Set aside.

2. Gently toss the last 4 ingredients in a 3-quart container suitable for microwave cooking. Cover with plastic wrap and cook in microwave oven on full power for 4 minutes.

3. Spread the meat slices over the broccoli; cover and cook on full power for 3-4 minutes. Serve hot.

For nutritional value, please see page 81.

醬 爆 肉

HOISIN SAUCE PORK WITH NUTS
(Jiang Bao Rou)

Ingredients:

- 1 lb   lean pork, cut into ½" dices
- 4 T   Hoisin sauce
- 1 T   soy sauce
- ¼ t   pepper
- 1 t   or more ginger root
- ¼ t   onion or garlic powder
- 1 T   sherry
- ¼ lb   fresh mushrooms, quartered (optional)
- 1 T   sesame oil
- 3 T   oil
- 1 T   cornstarch
- ½ C   or more nuts of your choice
- ½ C   sliced water chestnuts (optional)
-       Coriander (parsley) for garnishing

Method:

1. Place the first 11 ingredients in a 2-quart container suitable for microwave cooking; mix thoroughly. Cover with plastic wrap and cook in microwave oven on full power for 6 minutes. Stir well.

2. Add nuts, water chestnuts, stir well; cover and cook on full power for 3 minutes. Serve hot.

For nutritional value, please see page 131.

CHICKEN WITH PEAS AND CARROTS
(Wan Dou Ji Ding)

豌豆鷄丁

Ingredients:

- ¾ lb chicken breast, diced
- 4 T soy sauce
- ¼ t pepper
- ¼ t onion or garlic powder
- 1 t sherry
- 1 t sesame oil
- 1 onion, diced
- 1 t finely minced ginger root
- 3 T oil
- 1 T cornstarch
- 1 box (10 oz) frozen peas and carrots, thawed
- 1 T sesame oil
- 1 t cornstarch blended with 1 T water

Method:

1. Mix the first 10 ingredients thoroughly in a 10″ × 10″ × 2″ container suitable for microwave cooking. Cover with plastic wrap and cook in microwave oven on full power for 4 minutes.

2. Add the last 3 ingredients and mix well. Cover with plastic wrap and cook on full power for 2 minutes. Serve hot.

For nutritional value, please see page 193.

豆豉鷄丁

Ingredients:

1 lb	chicken breast, diced
3-4 T	minced fermented black beans
2 T	soy sauce
½ t	onion or garlic powder
1 T	sherry
⅛ t	pepper
1 t	minced ginger root
1	onion chopped
½ t	sugar
4 T	oil
1 T	cornstarch
¼ C	nuts of your choice
½ C	thinly sliced carrot
1	green pepper, diced
1 T	soy sauce
1 t	cornstarch blended with 2 T water

Method:

1. Mix the first 11 ingredients together thoroughly in a 10" × 10" × 2" container suitable for microwave cooking. Cover with plastic wrap and cook in microwave oven on full power for 4 minutes.

2. Add the last 5 ingredients and mix well. Cover with plastic wrap and cook on full power for 4 minutes. Serve hot.

For nutritional value, please see page 184.

BEAN CURD WITH OYSTER SAUCE
(Hao You Dou Fu)

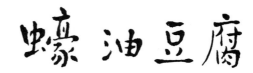

Ingredients:

- 1 lb   bean curd cut into ½" dices
- 3 T   oyster sauce
- ¼ t   pepper
- 1 t   sesame oil
- 3 T   oil
- 2-4   cloves of garlic, minced
- 1 t   or more finely minced ginger root
- 1 t   cornstarch blended with ½ C water
         Minced ham and green onion for garnishing

Method:

1. Place the first 7 ingredients in a 2-quart container suitable for microwave cooking. Toss the bean curd gently, then cover with plastic wrap and cook in microwave oven on full power for 3 minutes.

2. Add the well-blended cornstarch to the bean curd and stir well. Cover and cook on full power for 4 minutes. Garnish with minced ham and green onion. Serve hot.

For nutritional value, please see page 328.

胡桃椰子糊 COCONUT AND WALNUT SWEET SOUP
(Hu Tao Ye Zi Hu)

Ingredients:

1 C	flaked, sweetened coconut
1 C	walnuts
½-1/3 C	sugar
½ t	salt
4 C	water
3 T	cornstarch, blended with ½ C water

Method:

1. Blend half of the coconut and walnuts with 2 C water in a blender for 1 minute; pour the mixture into a 3-quart container suitable for microwave cooking. Blend the remaining coconut, walnuts and water in the same manner and pour into container. Add sugar and salt and mix well.

2. Cook the coconut mixture in microwave oven, uncovered, on full power for 6 minutes. Stir in well-blended cornstarch and cook, uncovered, for 3 minutes on full power.

3. Cover the container with plastic wrap and cook on 50% power (simmer) for 4 minutes. Serve hot or cold, as a dessert or a snack.

For nutritional value, please see page 392.

CARROT CAKE
(Hu Luo Bo Gao)

胡 蘿 蔔 糕

Ingredients:

- 3 eggs
- ½ C oil
- 1 C sugar
- 2 t cinnamon
- 1 T vanilla
- ½ t salt
- 1 C flour
- 1½ t baking soda
- 1 C grated carrots
- 1 C crushed pineapple in its juice

Method:

1. Beat the first 6 ingredients in a mixing bowl until creamy. Add the flour and baking soda; beat until well blended. Fold in grated carrots and crushed pineapple.

2. Line a 3-quart container suitable for microwave cooking with a piece of waxed paper or plastic wrap. Pour the batter into the container and cook in microwave on 75% (roast) power for 18 minutes or until a wooden chopstick comes out clean. Serve cold.

Calories: 2620	Cholesterol: 702 mg	Vit. B2: 0.8 mg
Carbohydrate: 342 gm	Calcium: 146 mg	Vit. A: 7390 IU
Protein: 22 gm	Iron: 8 mg	Vit. C: 21 mg
Fat: 129 gm	Vit. B1: 2.2 mg	Fiber: 1 gm

rice noodles

Notice: The nutritional calculations **for this section only** are calculated on **a per serving basis,** unlike the remainder of the book in which the recipes are calculated for the whole recipe.

Rice noodle dishes are becoming more and more popular in America. All Chinese restaurants serve many kinds of rice noodle dishes. But so far, there have been no good rice noodle recipes available on the market that are low in fat, easy to make, and also nutritious.

Traditionally, Chinese cooks soak dried rice noodles first, then stir-fry them using a large amount of oil in order to make them fluffy and rich in taste. Some restaurants even deep-fry the soaked rice noodles, then add the meat and vegetable mixture to the fried rice noodles. Rice noodles, by nature, have a capacity for soaking up a large quantity of oil. I think we should avoid that.

I took the challenge of writing some rice noodle recipes for this special section. It includes a basic rice noodle dish, spicy and exotic ones, vegetarian rice noodle dishes, soup, and cold-rice noodles (or rice noodle salad). I spent quite a long time, researching and experimenting, in order to create these rice noodle dishes. Using a very small amount of oil, they are easy to make, tasty, nutritious, low in calories and also, no fail.

Rice noodle recipes are varied by changing the different ingredients. You can use these few recipes as a basic technique together with your own imagination and ingenuity to make a host of other rice noodle dishes by simply changing the various meats and vegetables.

In the United States dried rice noodles, also called rice sticks or rice vermicelli, are made from pure rice flour which makes them especially good for people who are allergic to wheat. They come in a variety of sizes, from an angel-hair type to a fettuccini type. They are available at all Oriental grocery stores and many regular supermarkets. And in many larger metropolitan areas, one can even find fresh rice noodles in some Oriental grocery stores.

According to the most recent dietary recommendations made by the USDA, one's daily food intake should consist of a large amount of complex carbohydrates such as rice, bread, cereal, and the pasta group; a fair amount of vegetables and fruit; a lesser amount of meat, poultry, eggs or dried beans; and lastly, a very small amount of fat and sweets. Rice—and rice products such as rice noodles—are particularly suited to supply necessary complex carbohydrates.

The following recipes are samples to get you started. The dishes can be served as a whole meal, snack or appetizer.

RICE NOODLE SOUP
(Mi Fen Tang)

A bowl of rice noodle soup can be served as a whole meal, a snack, or as a soup with a meal. This can be done by manipulating the quantity of rice noodles to be added to the broth. The quantity of rice noodles used in a bowl also can be tailored to a person's appetite.

Nutritionally, a bowl of rice noodle soup can be considered a balanced meal. It contains all the important food groups. The large quantity of liquid contained in the rice noodle soup (in contrast to condensed, thick soup) lowers the total calories, but still gives the feeling of fullness. It is a very tasty diet food in that eating less still fulfills one's appetite.

Ingredients:

¼-½	lb	chicken breast, pork loin, or beef flank steak, shredded; or small raw shrimp
2	t	or more sesame oil
1	T	or more low sodium or regular soy sauce
¼	t	onion or garlic powder
1	t	or more minced or grated fresh ginger root
¼	t	black pepper
2	t	cornstarch
1	T	or more canola, corn or other vegetable oil
2	t	minced or grated fresh ginger root
2		cloves of garlic, minced
2		green onions, shredded
6	C	low sodium or regular chicken or vegetable broth (or beef broth if beef is used), or 6 t of bouillon or soup base dissolved in 6 C of water Soy sauce or salt to taste
½	lb	dried rice noodles
¼	lb	or more Chinese green-leaf vegetable or spinach, cut into 1-inch pieces
¼-½	lb	Napa or celery cabbage, shredded
1	T	or more sesame oil

Continued

Method:

1. Mix meat shreds (or shrimp) with the ingredients enclosed in the bracket.

Heat oil in a nonstick wok on high heat; sauté ginger root and garlic. Add meat shreds (or shrimp) and green onions; stir and turn for 1-2 minutes. Remove to a dish.

2. Place the broth in a deep sauce pan; bring to a boil. Add soy sauce or salt to taste. Add dried rice noodles to the broth and bring to a boil. Add vegetables and bring to a boil. Add cooked meat (or shrimp) and 1 T of sesame oil; stir well.

3. Divide the soup evenly into ten Chinese noodle bowls. Serve hot with a pair of chopsticks and a Chinese soup spoon.

A little vinegar or hot sauce can be added to the noodle soup as you wish.

Makes 8 servings.

Per Serving:

Calories: 127
Carbohydrates: 17 gm
Protein: 6 gm

Fat: 4 gm (Saturated fat: 3%)
Cholesterol: 8 mg
Sodium: 87 mg

Calories from protein: 18%
Calories from carbohydrates: 52%
Calories from fats: 31%

COLD RICE NOODLES
(COLD RICE NOODLE SALAD)
(Lian Ban Mi Fen)

In preparation of this special section, my very good friend, Jacqueline (Jaye) Sharp, designer of this and other books, suggested that a cold-rice noodle dish (or rice noodle salad) be added to this section. For a variety of taste, I have included three different kinds of dressings for this dish. Here it is. Authentically, rice noodles are never prepared and served cold in China, at least I never tried them before. This is a new invention. I hope you will enjoy it.

Ingredients for preparing the rice noodles:

a
⅓	lb	dried rice noodles *	½ lb noodles
2	C	water	chicken broth
1-2	T	sesame oil	
¼	t	black pepper	
¼	t	onion or garlic powder	
1-2	t	finely minced or grated fresh ginger root	
2	T	low sodium or regular soy sauce, or oyster sauce	
1	T	or more Sha-Zha sauce (optional) **	

Salt or soy sauce to taste

* If fettuccini-type noodles are used, increase the amount of water by ½ C.

** Sold in cans or bottles, Sha-Zha sauce is available at Oriental grocery stores. Its English tradename is barbeque sauce. Sha-Zha is a tasty, all purpose flavoring which can be added to many Chinese dishes.

Ingredients for preparing the meat and vegetables:

b
½ -1 C	shredded, cooked chicken breast, pork, beef, lamb or ham *
½ C	seeded and finely shredded cucumber
½ C	or more finely shredded Napa or celery cabbage
1 C	or more finely shredded red bell pepper
2	green onions, finely shredded
1-2 t	finely shredded or grated fresh ginger root
¼ C	finely shredded carrots
½ C	finely shredded fresh spinach or romaine lettuce
½ C	or more fresh mushrooms, shredded

* For vegetarian Cold Rice Noodles, substitute nuts in place of meat. Use your choice of sliced almonds, pine nuts, cashews, walnuts, pecans, or peanuts.

Continued

Method:

1. Prepare the noodles as follows:

Place all the ingredients from bracket "a" in a large, deep sauce pan. Turn on high heat and bring the liquid to a boil.

Add dried rice noodles to the boiling liquid. With a pair of chopsticks or large fork and spoon stir and turn the rice noodles to separate and soften. As soon as the noodles are softened and the liquid is absorbed, cover pan and turn off heat. *

Let the rice noodles remain in the pan for at least 20 minutes. Do not open the lid while waiting.

With a pair of chopsticks or large fork and spoon, fluff the rice noodles after the waiting time. Let cool to room temperature. Do not chill.

2. Prepare the meat of your choice and vegetables from bracket "b". Set aside.

3. In a small bowl, combine all the ingredients of your choice of dressing from pages 415-417. Set aside.

4. Place the ingredients from Steps 1, 2 and 3 in a large mixing bowl. Toss together. Transfer to a large serving bowl or platter and serve at room temperature. This dish can also be served warm; just reheat in a microwave oven.

*If using an electric stove, remove pan from burner after rice noodles are softened and the pan is covered. Electric units retain heat, consequently the noodles would be overcooked.

Makes 10 servings.

Per Serving:

Calories: 85   Fat: 2 gm
Carbohydrates: 14 gm   Cholesterol: 5 mg
Protein: 4 gm   Sodium: 129 mg

Calories from protein: 17%
Calories from carbohydrates: 64%
Calories from fats: 19%

Add the nutritional value of your choice of dressing (pages 415-417) to this dish for total nutritional value.

Dressing I (Soy Sauce and Vinegar)
(Mi Si Zhi)

Ingredients:

2 T	or more vinegar
1 - 2 T	sesame oil
⅓ t	black pepper
2 T	or more low sodium or regular soy sauce
½ t	brown sugar
2 t	or more sherry or cooking wine
1 t	or more Sha-Zha sauce (optional) (see ** on page 413)

Method:

Combine all the ingredients together in a small bowl. Mix well and set aside.

Makes 10 servings.

Per Serving:

Calories: 17
Carbohydrates: 0.8 gm
Protein: 0.2 gm

Fat: 1.4 gm
Cholesterol: 0 mg
Sodium: 120 mg

Calories from protein: 5%
Calories from carbohydrates: 19%
Calories from fats: 76%

落花生醬

Dressing II (Peanut Butter or Sesame Paste)
(Luo Hua Sun Jiang)

Ingredients:

3-4	T	peanut butter or sesame paste (page 315)
3-4	T	vinegar
2-3	T	water
1/2	t	pepper
2-3	T	low sodium or regular soy sauce
2-4		cloves of garlic, minced
1-2	t	finely minced ginger root
1/4	t	chili powder
1/2	t	paprika
1/4	t	or more cayenne (optional)
1	T	honey
1-2	T	sesame oil

Method:

Combine all the ingredients together in a small bowl. Mix well and set aside.

Per Serving:

Calories: 44
Carbohydrates: 3.5 gm
Protein: 1.7 gm

Fat: 3 gm
Cholesterol: 0 mg
Sodium: 140 mg

Calories from protein: 14%
Calories from carbohydrates: 30%
Calories from fats: 57%

416

Dressing III (Hot and Spicy)
(Man Han Zhi)

Ingredients:

- 2 T or more vinegar
- ½ T canola oil
- ¼ t black pepper
- 1 T or more low sodium or regular soy sauce
- 1 T or more Sha-Zha sauce (optional)(see ** on page 413)
- ½ t brown sugar
- 2 t sherry or cooking wine
- 2 or more cloves of garlic, finely minced
- 1 t fresh ginger root, finely minced
- ½ t or more Sichuan peppercorn powder
- ½ t or more hot sauce or Tabasco sauce
- ¼ C or more shredded hot pickled pepper (Del Monte or other brand)
- 1 t or more sesame oil (optional)

Method:

Combine all the ingredients together in a small bowl. Mix well and set aside.

Per Serving:

Calories: 13   Fat: 0.8 gm
Carbohydrates: 1.3 gm   Cholesterol: 0 mg
Protein: 0.3 gm   Sodium: 121 mg
             Calories from protein: 9%
             Calories from carbohydrates: 39%
             Calories from fats: 52%

417

素炒米粉

VEGETARIAN RICE NOODLES
(Su Chao Mi Fen)

Ingredients for preparing the rice noodles:

¹/₂ lb   dried rice noodles *

a {
- 2 C   water
- 2 t   low sodium or regular vegetable bouillon or soup base
- 1 T   low sodium or regular soy sauce
- 2 t   finely minced or grated fresh ginger root
- 2-3   green onions, shredded
- 1-2   cloves garlic, minced or ¹/₃ t garlic powder
- ¹/₄ t   or more black pepper
- 1-2 T   sesame oil

Salt or soy sauce to taste

* If fettuccini-type rice noodles are used, increase the amount of water by ¹/₂ C.

Ingredients for preparing the vegetable mixture:

1 T   or more canola, corn or other vegetable oil

b {
- ¹/₄ -¹/₂ lb   Tofu Gan (dry bean curd)* or extra firm tofu, cut into 1 ¹/₂" x ¹/₈" long shreds
- 2-3   green onions, shredded
- ¹/₄ t   black pepper
- 1 T   low sodium or regular soy sauce
- 2-3 t   minced or grated fresh ginger root
- 2-3   cloves of garlic, minced

c {
- ¹/₄ lb   fresh mushrooms, sliced or ¹/₂ C soaked and shredded Chinese black mushrooms
- ¹/₄ lb   Napa, celery cabbage, or Bok Choy, shredded
- 1   red or green bell pepper, or one half of each, shredded
- 1 C   snow pea pods, washed and stringed, broccoli flowerlets or any green-leaf Chinese vegetable, shredded
- ¹/₂ C   shredded carrots
- ¹/₂ C   vegetable broth
- 1 T   low sodium or regular soy sauce
- 1 t   or more sesame oil

*See page 34

Method:

1. Prepare the rice noodles as follows:

Combine all the ingredients from "a" in a large, deep sauce pan; bring to a boil on high heat. Turn to low heat and stir until the bouillon or soup base is dissolved. Turn back to high heat. Add dried rice noodles to the boiling liquid.

With a pair of chopsticks or large fork and spoon, stir and turn the rice noodles to separate and soften. As soon as the noodles are softened and the liquid is absorbed, cover pan and turn off heat.*

Let the rice noodles remain in the pan without disturbing for at least 20 minutes. Do not open the lid while waiting. With a pair of chopsticks or large fork and spoon, fluff the rice noodles just before using.

If the cooked rice noodles are not to be used right away, they can be reheated in a microwave oven or steamed in a steamer. The cook rice noodles reheat well, so they can be prepared in advance.

2. Prepare the vegetables as follows:

Heat oil in a nonstick wok on high heat. Spread ingredients from "b" evenly in the wok. Cook until the Tofu shreds are brown on one side. Turn to other side and cook until brown. Remove to a dish.

3. Add ingredients from "c" to the wok and stir and cook for 3-4 minutes. Add cooked Tofu shreds; mix well. Pour the vegetable mixture over the hot rice noodles; mix well. Transfer the rice noodle mixture onto a serving platter and serve hot. Or place the hot rice noodles in a large serving bowl first, then pour the vegetable mixture over rice noodles and serve hot.

A little vinegar and hot sauce of your favorite brand can be added to the rice noodles before eating.

* See page 414
Makes 10 servings

Per Serving:

Calories: 135   Fat: 3 gm (Saturated fat: 3%)
Carbohydrates: 23 gm   Cholesterol: 0 mg
Protein: 4 gm   Sodium: 187 mg

Calories from protein: 12%
Calories from carbohydrates: 68%
Calories from fats: 19%

翡 翠 米 粉

BASIL RICE NOODLES
(Fei Cui Mi Fen)

Ingredients:

$\frac{1}{2}$ lb   dried rice noodles
1-2 T   canola, olive or other vegetable oil
$\frac{1}{4}$ - $\frac{1}{2}$ lb   ground chicken or turkey breast
$\frac{1}{2}$ C   chopped onions
$\frac{1}{2}$ t   black pepper
$\frac{1}{3}$ t   low sodium or regular salt
1 C   nonfat sour cream
$\frac{1}{2}$ C   evaporated nonfat milk
$\frac{1}{4}$ C   finely ground fresh basil leaves *
$\frac{1}{2}$ C   chopped walnuts, almond or pecan (optional)

Method:

1. Heat oil in a nonstick wok. Add ingredients enclosed in bracket. Stir and cook until meat particles are loosened. Add sour cream and evaporated milk; stir and bring to a boil. Keep warm.

2. Fill a large, deep sauce pan half full of water. Bring to a boil and add dried rice noodles. Stir and bring to a boil. Continue to cook the rice noodles for 4-5 minutes. Drain and place the rice noodles onto a serving platter.

3. Add ground fresh basil leaves to the cream sauce. Mix well. Immediately pour the sauce on the cooked rice noodles and serve hot.

* Grind the fresh basil leaves just before using them so that the color stays bright and green.

Makes 10 servings

Per Serving:

Calories: 140
Carbohydrates: 24 gm
Protein: 7 gm

Fat: 2 gm (Saturated fat: 1%)
Cholesterol: 7 mg
Sodium: 61 mg

Calories from protein: 19%
Calories from carbohydrates: 70%
Calories from fats: 11%

420

RICE NOODLES, MONGOLIAN STYLE
(Meng Huan Mi Fen)

Ingredients for preparing the rice noodles:

a
{
½ lb	dried rice noodles *	
2 C	chicken, beef or vegetable broth,** low sodium or regular; or 2 t bouillon or soup base in 2 C of water	
1 T	low sodium or regular soy sauce	
1 T	or more Sha-Zha sauce (optional) (see page 413)	
2 t	finely minced or grated fresh ginger root	
2-3	green onions, shredded	
2	or more cloves garlic, minced or ⅓ t garlic powder	
¼ t	or more black pepper	
2 T	sesame oil	

Salt or soy sauce to taste
* If fettuccini-type rice noodles are used increase
the amount of broth by ½ C.
** If beef is used in this dish, use beef broth.

Ingredients for preparing the meat and vegetables:

¼ -½ lb   beef flank steak, chicken breast or pork loin, cut into 1 ½ " x ⅛ " slices

b
{
1 T	or more black bean sauce	
1 T	low sodium or regular soy sauce	
1 T	sherry or cooking wine	
⅓ t	garlic or onion powder	
2 t	or more minced or grated fresh ginger root	
¼ t	black pepper	
1 t	or more sesame oil	
½ t	brown sugar	
2 t	cornstarch	

1-2 T	canola, corn or other vegetable oil	
1 T	or more minced or grated fresh ginger root	
2-6	or more dried hot peppers	
4-6	cloves garlic, minced	
2	green onions, shredded	

Continued

421

$\left\{\begin{array}{ll} ¼ \text{ lb} & \text{Bok Choy or any kind of Chinese green-leaf} \\ & \text{vegetable, sliced} \\ ¼ \text{ lb} & \text{heart of leeks, cut into ½-inch sections or green} \\ & \text{onions, shredded} \\ ½ \text{ C} & \text{or more sliced bamboo shoots} \\ 1 \text{ T} & \text{black bean sauce} \\ ½ \text{ C} & \text{sliced fresh mushrooms or soaked and sliced} \\ & \text{Chinese mushrooms} \\ ½ \text{ C} & \text{thinly sliced carrots} \\ ½ \text{ C} & \text{red bell pepper, shredded} \end{array}\right.$

c

Method:

1. Prepare the rice noodles as follows:

Combine all the ingredients from "a" in a large, deep sauce pan; bring to a boil. Adjust the flavor of the liquid by adding a little salt, or soy sauce to taste.

Add dried rice noodles to the boiling liquid. With a pair of chopsticks or large fork and spoon, stir and turn the rice noodles to separate and soften. As soon as the noodles are softened and the liquid is absorbed, cover pan and turn off heat.*

Let the rice noodles remain in the pan without disturbing for at least 20 minutes. Do not open the lid while waiting. With a pair of chopsticks or large fork and spoon, fluff the rice noodles just before using.

If the cooked rice noodles are not to be used right away, they can be reheated in a microwave oven or steamed in a steamer. The cooked rice noodles reheat well, so they can be prepared in advance.

2. Prepare the meat and vegetables as follows:

Thoroughly mix the meat slices with the ingredients from "b." This step can be done in advance.

Heat the oil in a nonstick wok on high heat. Sauté ginger root until light brown. Add hot peppers and garlic; sauté until fragrant. Add meat and green onions. Stir and cook for 1-2 minutes. Remove to a dish.

3. Add ingredients from "c" to the wok; stir and cook for 3-4 minutes. Return the cooked meat to the wok and mix well. Pour this meat and vegetable mixture over the hot rice noodles; mix well. Transfer the rice noodle mixture onto a large platter and serve hot. Or place the hot rice noodles in a large serving bowl first, then pour the meat and vegetable mixture over the rice noodles and serve hot.

A little vinegar and hot sauce of your favorite brand can be added to the rice noodles before eating.

* See page 414

Makes 10 servings

Per Serving:

Calories: 166   Fat: 4 gm (Saturated Fat: 2%)
Carbohydrates: 26 gm   Cholesterol: 8 mg
Protein: 6 gm   Sodium: 231 mg

                Calories from protein: 15%
                Calories from carbohydrates: 62%
                Calories from fats: 24%

RICE NOODLES WITH ASSORTED
MEAT AND VEGETABLES
(Shen Jin Mi Fen)

Ingredients for preparing the rice noodles:

	½ lb	dried rice noodles *
	2 C	chicken, vegetable, or beef broth, low sodium or regular or 2 t of bouillon or soup base, in 2 C water
	1 ½ T	low sodium or regular soy sauce
	1 T	or more Sha-Zha sauce (optional) (see page 413)
a	2 t	finely minced or grated fresh ginger root
	2-3	green onions, shredded or minced
	1-2	cloves of garlic, minced or ½ t garlic powder
	¼ t	or more black pepper
	1-2 T	sesame oil
		Salt or soy sauce to taste

* If fettuccini-type rice noodles are used,
increase the amount of broth by ½ C.

Continued

Ingredients for preparing the meat and vegetables:

¼ - ½ lb   chicken breast, beef flank steak or pork loin, shredded; or raw shrimp split in half lengthwise

b {
1 T	low sodium or regular soy sauce
1 T	sherry or cooking wine
¼ t	garlic powder
1-2 t	minced or grated fresh ginger root
¼ t	black pepper
2 t	cornstarch

1 T	or more canola, corn or other vegetable oil
2 t	minced or grated fresh ginger root
2	cloves of garlic, minced
1-2	green onions, minced or shredded

c {
½ C	soaked and shredded Chinese mushrooms, wood ears or ½ lb fresh mushrooms, sliced
¼ lb	Napa, Bok Choy or celery cabbage, shredded
1 C	snow pea pods, washed and stringed, broccoli flowerlets or any Chinese green-leaf vegetable, sliced or shredded
½ C	or more, shredded carrots
1	medium green or red bell pepper or one half of each, shredded
1 T	low sodium or regular soy sauce
⅓ C	chicken, vegetable or beef broth
1 t	or more sesame oil

Method:

1. Prepare the rice noodles as follows:
Combine all the ingredients from "a" in a large, deep sauce pan. Turn to high heat and bring the liquid to a boil. Adjust the flavor of the liquid by adding a little salt or soy sauce to your taste.

Add dried rice noodles to the boiling liquid. With a pair of chopsticks or large fork and spoon, stir and turn the rice noodles to separate and soften. As soon as the noodles are softened and the liquid is absorbed, cover pan and turn off heat.*

Let the rice noodles remain in the pan without disturbing for at least 20 minutes. Do not open the lid while waiting. With a pair of chopsticks or large fork and spoon, fluff the rice noodles just before using.

If the cooked rice noodles are not to be used right away, they can be reheated in a microwave oven or steamed in a steamer. The cooked rice noodles reheat well, so they can be prepared in advance.

2. Prepare the meat (or shrimp) and vegetables as follows:

Thoroughly mix the meat (or shrimp) with the ingredients from "b." This step can be done in advance.

Heat 1 T or more of oil in a nonstick wok on high heat. Sauté minced ginger root and garlic until brown. Add meat (or shrimp) and green onions; stir and cook for 1-2 minutes. Remove to a dish.

3. Add ingredients from "c" to the wok. Stir and cook for 3-4 minutes. Add the cooked meat (or shrimp); mix well. Pour this mixture over fluffed, hot rice noodles; mix well. Transfer the rice noodle mixture to a large serving platter and serve hot. Or place the rice noodles in a large serving bowl first, then pour the mixture over the rice noodles and serve hot.

A little vinegar and hot sauce of your favorite brand can be added to the rice noodles before eating.

* See page 414

Makes 10 servings.

Per Serving:

Calories: 154	Fat: 4 gm (Saturated fat: 2%)
Carbohydrates: 24 gm	Cholesterol: 6 mg
Protein: 6 gm	Sodium: 222 mg

Calories from protein: 15%
Calories from carbohydrates: 64%
Calories from fats: 21%

咖喱米粉

SPICY AND HOT CURRIED
RICE NOODLES
(Ka Li Mi Fen)

Ingredients for preparing the rice noodles:

½ lb dried rice noodles*

a
- 2 t   or more minced or grated fresh ginger root
- 1 T   or more minced garlic or ½ t garlic powder
- 1 t   or more cayenne pepper or other hot pepper
- 1-2 T   curry powder
- 2 t   turmeric powder
- ¼ t   or more black pepper
- 1-2 T   sesame oil
- 2 C   chicken or vegetable broth, or 2 t of bouillon or soup base in 2 C of water
- 1 T   or more Sha-Zha sauce (optional) (see page 413)
- 1 ½ T   low sodium or regular soy sauce
- Salt or soy sauce to taste

* If fettuccini-type rice noodles are used, increase the amount of broth by ½ C.

Ingredients for preparing the meat and vegetables:

¼ -½ lb   chicken breast, or pork loin, shredded; or raw shrimp, split in half lengthwise

b
- 1 T   low sodium or regular soy sauce
- 1 T   sherry or cooking wine
- ¼ t   garlic or onion powder
- 1-2 t   minced or grated fresh ginger root
- ¼ t   black pepper
- 2 t   cornstarch
- 1 T   canola, corn or other vegetable oil
- 1-2 t   minced or grated fresh ginger root
- 2   cloves of garlic, minced
- 2-3   green onions, shredded

$$
c \begin{cases}
\text{1/2 C} & \text{soaked and shredded Chinese black mushrooms,} \\
& \text{wood ears or 1/4 lb of fresh mushrooms, sliced} \\
\text{1/4 lb} & \text{Napa, Bok Choy or celery cabbage, shredded} \\
\text{1 C} & \text{broccoli flowerlets, snow pea pods, washed and} \\
& \text{stringed, or other Chinese green-leaf vegetable,} \\
& \text{sliced} \\
\text{1/2 C} & \text{or more shredded carrots} \\
\text{1} & \text{medium green or red bell pepper, or one half of} \\
& \text{each, shredded} \\
\text{1 T} & \text{or more low sodium or regular soy sauce} \\
\text{1/3 C} & \text{chicken or vegetable broth} \\
\text{1 t} & \text{or more sesame oil}
\end{cases}
$$

Method:

1. Prepare the rice noodles as follows:

Place all the ingredients from "a" in a large, deep sauce pan; bring to a boil. Turn to low heat; stir and cook for 2 minutes. Adjust the flavor of the liquid by adding salt or soy sauce to your taste.

Turn back to high heat. Add dried rice noodles to the liquid. With a pair of chopsticks or large fork and spoon, stir and turn the noodles to separate and soften. As soon as the noodles are softened and the liquid is absorbed, cover pan and turn off heat.* Let the rice noodles remain in the pan without disturbing for at least 20 minutes. Do not open the lid while waiting. With a pair of chopsticks or large fork and spoon, fluff the rice noodles just before using.

If the cooked rice noodles are not to be used right away, they can be reheated in a microwave oven or steamed in a steamer. The cooked rice noodles reheat well, so they can be prepared in advance.

2. Prepare the meat (or shrimp) and vegetables as follows:

Thoroughly mix meat (or shrimp) with the ingredients from "b." This step can be done in advance.

Heat oil in a nonstick wok on high heat. Sauté ginger root and garlic until brown. Add meat (or shrimp) and green onions; stir and cook for 1-2 minutes. Remove to a dish.

Continued

427

3. Add ingredients from "c" to the wok; stir and cook for 3-4 minutes. Add cooked meat (or shrimp) and mix well. Pour this mixture over the cooked noodles; mix well. Transfer the rice noodle mixture onto a large serving platter and serve hot. Or place the cooked rice noodles in a large serving bowl first, then pour the meat and vegetable mixture over the hot rice noodles and serve hot.

A little of your favorite vinegar and hot sauce can be added to the rice noodles while eating.

* See page 414

Makes 10 servings.

Per Serving:

Calories: 156	Fat: 4 gm (Saturated fat: 2%)
Carbohydrates: 25 gm	Cholesterol: 7 mg
Protein: 6 gm	Sodium: 226 mg

Calories from protein: 14%
Calories from carbohydrates: 64%
Calories from fats: 22%

海鮮醬末粉

HOISIN SAUCE RICE NOODLES
(Hai Xian Jiang Mi Fen)

Ingredients:

½ lb	dried rice noodles
¼ -½ lb	lean ground pork or beef
1 T	low sodium or regular soy sauce
1 t	or more Sha-Zha sauce (optional) (see page 413)
2 t	finely minced or grated fresh ginger root
2-3	cloves of garlic, minced
½ t	black pepper
½ C	chopped water chestnuts
½ C	Hoisin sauce
¾ C	water
4	green onions, minced
1 T	sesame oil
	Salt or soy sauce to taste

Method:

1. Place all the ingredients from the bracket in a nonstick sauce pan; stir and mix for 3-4 minutes. Loosen the meat particles while stirring. Add water and bring to a boil. Turn to medium heat; cook and stir for 4-5 minutes. Add minced green onions and sesame oil; mix well. Keep warm.

2. Fill a large, deep sauce pan half full of water; bring to a boil. Add dried rice noodles; stir until water boils again. Continue cooking the noodles on high heat for 4-5 more minutes. Drain and place the cooked noodles on a serving platter. Immediately pour the cooked meat sauce on the noodles and serve hot.

Makes 10 servings.

Per Serving:

Calories: 131	Fat: 3 gm (Saturated fat: 1%)
Carbohydrates: 21 gm	Cholesterol: 8 mg
Protein: 5 gm	Sodium: 149 mg

Calories from protein: 15%
Calories from carbohydrates: 65%
Calories from fats: 21%

香菇牛肉米粉　BEEF STROGANOFF RICE NOODLES
(Xiang Gu Niu Rou Mi Fen)

Ingredients:

½ lb	or more lean beef chuck or English roast, cut into ⅔ inch cubes
2	cloves of garlic, crushed
2	thin slices of fresh ginger root
½ C	chopped onion
1 T	or more low sodium or regular soy sauce
¼ t	pepper
¾ C	water
1	can cream of mushroom soup
5 oz	frozen peas and carrots
½ lb	dried rice noodles, fettuccini type
	Salt or soy sauce to taste

Method:

1. Place all ingredients from the bracket in a medium sauce pan. Cover and bring to a boil. Turn to low heat and simmer for 20 minutes. Add cream of mushroom soup; stir and cook until smooth. Add peas and carrots and bring to a boil. Add salt or soy sauce to taste. Remove from heat and keep warm.

2. Fill a large, deep sauce pan half full of water; bring to a boil. Add dried rice noodles; stir and bring to a boil. Continue cooking the rice noodles on high heat for 4-5 minutes. Stir occasionally. Drain and place the cooked rice noodles on a serving platter. Immediately pour the cooked meat sauce over the noodles and serve hot.

Makes 10 servings.

Per Serving:

Calories: 162
Carbohydrates: 22 gm
Protein: 8 gm

Fat: 4 gm (Saturated fat: 5%)
Cholesterol: 19 mg
Sodium: 257 mg

Calories from protein: 20%
Calories from carbohydrates: 56%

RICE NOODLES WITH CREAM OF TOFU
(Bai Yu Mi Fen)

白玉米粉

Ingredients:

½ lb	dried rice noodles
½ T	canola, olive or other vegetable oil
2-3	cloves of garlic, finely minced
¼ C	chopped onion
1 t	or more finely minced fresh ginger root
1 t	pepper
1 T	chicken or vegetable bouillon (low sodium or regular) or soup base dissolved in ¼ C water
1 - 1½ lb	soft or silky tofu
½ C	frozen peas and carrots
2	green onions, minced
1 T	sesame oil
	Salt or soy sauce to taste

Method:

1. Heat oil in a nonstick wok. Sauté garlic, onion, ginger root until fragrant. Add pepper, dissolved bouillon or soup base and tofu. Stir and bring to a boil. Break the tofu while stirring. Add peas and carrots and bring to a boil. Add green onions and sesame oil and mix well. Add salt or soy sauce to taste. Keep warm.

2. Fill a large deep sauce pan half full of water; bring to a boil. Add dried rice noodles; stir and bring to a boil. Continue boiling the noodles for 4-5 minutes. Drain and place onto a serving platter. Immediately pour the tofu sauce on the cooked noodles and serve hot.

Makes 10 servings.

Per Serving:

Calories: 144   Fat: 4 gm (Saturated fat: 3%)
Carbohydrates: 21 gm   Cholesterol: 0 mg
Protein: 6 gm   Sodium: 10 mg
          Calories from protein: 15%
          Calories from carbohydrates: 58%
          Calories from fats: 27%

DAILY DIETARY REQUIREMENTS OF CALORIES, CERTAIN VITAMINS AND MINERALS*

       Calories: 2333
       Protein: 51 gm
       Calcium: 800 mg
       Iron: 12.6 mg
       Vitamin A: 4,500 IU
       Thiamine (Vit. B1):   1.2 mg
       Riboflavin (Vit. B2):   1.4 mg
       Niacin: 15 mg
       Ascorbic acid (Vit. C):   45 mg

For men and women, ages 19-51+, averaged.
Designed for maintenance of good nutrition of practically all healthy persons in the U.S.A. Allowances are intended for persons normally active in a temperate climate.

*Condensed from "Recommended Daily Dietary Allowances," Food and Nutrition Board, National Research Council, Revised 1974.

TABLE OF ABBREVIATIONS AND MEASUREMENTS

Abbreviations

Measurements

Abbreviations	Measurements
t: teaspoon(s)	1 pinch: less than ⅛ teaspoon
T: tablespoon(s)	1 tablespoon: 3 teaspoons
C: cup(s)	8 tablespoons: ½ cup
qt: quart(s)	1 pint: 2 cups
oz: ounce	1 quart: 2 pints
lb: pound(s)	1 quart: 4 cups
min: minute(s)	1 gallon: 4 quarts: 128 ounces
hr: hour(s)	1 fluid ounce: 2 tablespoons: 28.35 grams
in: inch(es)	1 pound: 16 ounces: 453.6 grams
diam: diameter(s)	100 grams: 3½ ounces
doz: dozen(s)	1 kilogram: 2.2 pounds
mg: milligram(s)	1 cup: 8 fluid ounces: ½ pint: 16 tablespoons

VITAMINS and MINERALS

Vitamin/Mineral	Sources	(RDA) for Adults
Vitamin A: Fat soluble; no need to replenish daily	Carrots, green & yellow vegetables yellow fruits, eggs, milk & dairy products, fish liver oil, and liver.	5,000 IU*
Vitamin B-1 (Thiamine) Water soluble. Need to replenish daily.	Most vegetables, whole wheat, oatmeal peanuts, dried yeast, rice husks, milk. legumes.	1.0 to 1.5 mg**
Vitamin B-2 (Riboflavin) Water soluble. Need to replenish daily.	Leafy green vegetables, legumes, yeast, cheese, fish and eggs.	1.2 to 1.7 mg
Vitamin B-6 (Pyridoxine) Water soluble. Need to replenish daily.	Whole grains, brewer's yeast, wheat germ, blackstrap molasses, milk, eggs, beef, liver, kidney,and cabbage	1.8 to 2.2 mg
Vitamin B-12 (Cobalamin) Water soluble.	Beef, pork, liver, kidney, eggs, milk, and cheese.	3 mcg***
Niacin (Vitamin B-3) Water soluble	Lean meat, liver, kidney, white meat of poultry, fish, eggs, roasted peanuts, avocados, dates, figs, and vegetables	13 to 19 mg
Vitamin C Water soluble. Need to replace daily.	Sweet potatoes, potatoes, green leafy vegetables, tomatoes, cauliflower, citrus fruit and berries.	60 mg
Vitamin D Fat soluble	Sunshine, eggs, Vit. D fortified milk, dairy products, fish liver oils, and fish.	
Vitamin E Fat soluble	Eggs, wheat germ, soybeans, vegetable oils Brussels sprouts, broccoli, spinach, whole grains and seeds.	8 to 10 IU
Calcium	Soybeans, tofu, milk, dairy products, sardines salmon, peanuts, walnuts, sunflower seeds, and legumes.	800 to 1,200
Iron	Pork liver, beef kidney and liver, red meat, egg yolks, oysters, nuts, beans, oatmeal, asparagus, dried peaches, and molasses.	10 to 18 mg
Magnesium Necessary for calcium & Vit.C metabolism	Dark green vegetables, nuts, seeds, corn, figs, lemons, grapefruit, and apples	300 to 450 mg
Potassium	Green leafy vegetables, potatoes, tomatoes, citrus fruits, cantaloupe, sunflower seeds, and bananas.	NO RDA
Zinc Essential for protein synthesis.	Steak, lamb, pork, wheat germ, brewer's yeast pumpkin seeds, and eggs.	15 mg

*IU = International units, **mg = milligrams, ***mcg = micrograms
Source: Earl Mindel, *Vitamin Bible*, Warner Books, Inc., N.Y. 1985

References

Bean, L.H.: *Closing the World's Nutritional Gap with Animal or Vegetable Protein*. FAO Bull. 6. 1966

Bogert, L.J., et al: *Nutrition and Physical Fitness*, 8th edition. Saunders Company, 1966

Caliendo, Mary Alice: *Nutrition and the World Food Crisis*. Collier Macmillan Publishers, 1979

FDA Report on *Monosodium Glutamate*, Nov. 17, 1969

Federal Cosmet. Toxical., Vol. 11: *More Meditation on MSG*, Pergamon Press, 1973

Furia, T.E., ed: *Handbook of Food Additives*. Chemical Rubber Company, Cleveland. 1968

Halpern, M.D., Seymour L.: *Quick Reference to Clinical Nutrition*. J.B. Lippincott Co., 1979

Jacobson, M.F.: *Eater's Digest, The Consumer's Factbook of Food Additives*. Anchor Books. 1972

Krause and Mahan: *Food, Nutrition and Diet Therapy*. W.B. Saunders Co. 1979

Lappe, F.M.: *A Diet For A Small Planet*. Ballantine Books, Inc. N.Y. 1971

Lewis, R.D., M.S., Clara M.: *The Basics of Nutrition*. F.A. Davis Co. 1976

Mitchell, H.S., et al: *Nutrition in Health and Disease*, 16th edition. Lippincott Company. 1967

NAS-NRC Food Protection Committee Report: *Safety and Suitability of MSG of Use in Baby Foods*. July, 1970

National Academy of Science: *Recommended Daily Dietary Allowances*. 8th, 1974

National Dairy Council: *A Source Book On Food Practices*. 1971

Piltz, Alber Ph.D.: *How Your Body Uses Food*, National Dairy Council, 1971

Report Of A Joint FAO/WHO: *Protein Requirements*. Rome. 1965

Smith and Circle: *Soybeans: Chemistry and Technology*. Volume 1. Proteins. The Avi Publishing Company, Inc. 1972

Stare, Frederick J.: *Eating for Good Health*. Cornerstone Library, N.Y. 1969

The Year Book of Agriculture: *Protecting Our Food*. 1973

United States Department of Agriculture, Bureau of Human Nutrition and Home Economics: *Composition Of Foods Used In Far Eastern Countries*. Agriculture Handbook No. 34

United States Department of Agriculture, Home and Garden Bulletin: *Nutritive Value Of Foods*. No. 72

United States Department of Agriculture, Agriculture Handbook: *Composition Of Foods, raw, procssed, prepared*. No. 8.

Wolfe, W.J., et al: *Soybeans As A Food Source*. CRC Press, 1970

General Index

A

Abalone
description, preparation, uses, 33
Abalone with Chicken Breast, 273
Additive, food (MSG), see Monosodium
Glutamate
Agar-agar
description, uses, substitutes, 33
Almonds
uses, 33
Chicken with Almonds, 170
Pressed Duck in Almond Sauce, 201
Amino acids, 9-10
Anise, star
description, uses, storage, substitutions,
47
in Five-Spice Powder, 38
ingredient in recipes, 79, 80, 100, 141, 146,
160, 171, 200
Appetizers, 7 (see also, Dim Sum, 335-393)
Bean Pasted Nuts, 306
Barbecued Spareribs, 144
Braised Beef Shank, 80
Braised Mushroom Balls, 293
Braised Pork, Tripe and Liver, 146
Breaded Shrimp Balls, 255
Braised Steamed Gluten, 308
*Chicken Liver with Sichuan Peppercorn
Powder, 195*
Crispy Skin Chicken, 166
Curried Pastries, 357
Deep-fried Fresh String Beans, 282
Fried Wonton, 341
Onion Saturated Chicken, 179
Orange Dry Cooked Beef, 93
"Racing" Shrimp Balls, 256
Red Braised Spareribs, 145
Salted Steamed Duck, 203
Sesame Pork, 115
Shrimp Patties, 254
Smoked Duck, 204
Soy Sauce Boiled Chicken, 171
Spring (Egg) Rolls, 337

(Appetizers continued)
Steamed Dumplings, 351
Steamed Meat in Noodle Case, 365
Apple, 17
Spun Apple or Candied Apple, 389
Apricot
Apricot Sauce, 339
Asparagus
Oyster Sauce Beef with Asparagus, 82
Stir-Fry Asparagus, 285

B

Bamboo shoots
description, uses, storage, substitutions, 33
symbolism, 33-34
Basil
Basil Rice Noodles, 420
Bean curd (To Fu), 317-333
description, uses, storage, 34
as protein source, 34
coagulants (solidifiers), 36, 318
Bean Curd Soup, 61
*Bean Curd with Oyster Sauce (micro-
wave), 405*
ingredient in recipe, 58
dried (To Fu Gan),
description and uses, 34
fermented (To Fu Lu),
description, uses, 34
Fermented Bean Curd with Meat, 329
fried,
description, uses, 34
Braised Fried Bean Curd, 327
Fried Bean Curd Balls, 330
making, 318
solidifiers (coagulants), 36, 318
sticks or sheets,
description, preparation, uses, storage,
34-35
Bean paste
Hot (Sichuan),
description, 35
Hot Bean Sauce (Paste) Fish, 222
*Shrimp with Hot Bean Sauce (Paste),
240*

Romanization of Chinese words used in this book is based on the Pinyin system.

Nutrition and Diet with Chinese Cooking

Christine Y. C. Liu

Nutrition and Diet with Chinese Cooking is Christine Liu's first book on Chinese cooking. First published in 1976, *Nutrition and Diet with Chinese Cooking* is now in its sixth edition, a testament to its continued popularity and success.

A unique contribution to the overcrowded world of cookbooks, *Nutrition and Diet with Chinese Cooking* was among the very first to offer valuable nutritional calculations for each recipe. In compiling the recipes, the author has successfully adapted traditional Chinese cooking, food preparation, and ingredients to the American kitchen. For those new to Chinese cooking, this is an excellent introduction. For more experienced cooks, the book remains a standard, to be used again and again.

The meticulous research and careful development of recipes is typical of Christine Liu's methods. There are many 'pluses' contained in this volume. Among them: Important discussions which address MSG; Is Chinese food nutritious? And Menu Suggestions with a breakdown of calories and nutrients for every recipe.

Contains 340 pages; black and white line drawings and woodcut illustrations. Paperback, $17.95

ORDER FORM

Christine Liu
P. O. Box 1332
Ann Arbor, Michigan 48106

Please send _____ copies of *Nutrition and Diet with Chinese Cooking* at $17.95 per copy (plus $3.50 for postage and handling). Payment should be enclosed with order.

Name _____

Address _____

City _____ State _____ Zip _____

Enclosed is _____ check or money order. Autographed copy ❏

Nutritional Cooking with Tofu

Christine Y. C. Liu

Tofu (or bean curd) has long been recognized as a "miracle food." A product of the ever versatile soybean, tofu is a rich source of high quality protein and calcium and is also low in calories and sodium.

In this, her third Chinese cookbook, Christine Liu successfully 'demystifies' tofu and demonstrates in her step-by-step instructions how to prepare wholesome, nutritious, and tasty tofu dishes. Try the delicious *Mushroom Tofu Soup;* the exotic *Tofu with Fish in Earthenware Pot;* or *Cha Shao Tofu Stuffed Steamed Buns,* Christine's interpretation of the traditional Chinese dish. Recipe categories include: Soup, Main Dish, with a small portion of meat; Vegetarian Main Dishes; A Meal Itself; and Desserts and Snacks.

The introduction includes an enlightening discussion about the history and nutritional qualities of tofu. Every cook, neophyte or experienced, will benefit from "Tips for Keeping and Using Tofu." And for the truly adventuresome, there are detailed and illustrated instructions on "Making Tofu."

Over 100 recipes; black and white photographs; nutritional calculations for each recipe. Paperback, $15.50.

ORDER FORM

Christine Liu
P. O. Box 1332
Ann Arbor, Michigan 48106

Please send _____ copies of *Nutritional Cooking with Tofu* at $15.50 per copy (plus $3.50 for postage and handling). Payment should be enclosed with order.

Name _____

Address _____

City _____ State _____ Zip _____

Enclosed is _____ check or money order. Autographed copy ❑

449

ORDER FORM

Christine Liu
P. O. Box 1332
Ann Arbor, Michigan 48106

Please send _____ copies of *More Nutritional Chinese Cooking* at $27.95 per copy (plus $3.50 for postage and handling). Payment should be enclosed with order.

Name _____

Address _____

City _____ State _____ Zip _____

Enclosed is _____ check or money order. Autographed copy ❏

ORDER FORM

Christine Liu
P. O. Box 1332
Ann Arbor, Michigan 48106

Please send _____ copies of *More Nutritional Chinese Cooking* at $27.95 per copy (plus $3.50 for postage and handling). Payment should be enclosed with order.

Name _____

Address _____

City _____ State _____ Zip _____

Enclosed is _____ check or money order. Autographed copy ❏

ORDER FORM

Christine Liu
P. O. Box 1332
Ann Arbor, Michigan 48106

Please send _____ copies of *More Nutritional Chinese Cooking* at $27.95 per copy (plus $3.50 for postage and handling). Payment should be enclosed with order.

Name _____

Address _____

City _____ State _____ Zip _____

Enclosed is _____ check or money order. Autographed copy ❏
